To Be Frank...

TO BE FRANK...

The authorised biography of

FRANK THORNTON

Brian Slade

fantom
publishing

First published in 2024 by Fantom Publishing, an imprint of Fantom Films
www.fantompublishing.co.uk

A catalogue record for this book is available from the British Library.

Hardback edition ISBN: 978-1-78196-393-7

Typeset by Phil Reynolds Media Services, Leamington Spa
Printed and bound by CPI Group (UK) Ltd, Croydon, CR0 4YY
Jacket design by Stuart Manning

Contents

Acknowledgements

I FIRST MET FRANK THORNTON'S DAUGHTER JANE in the winter of 2019 at a memorial service for the late Dame June Whitfield, one of Frank's many friends across the business. As we chatted, Jane talked about the archive that Frank had left, gathered over a career spanning more than seventy years. I was somewhat surprised to hear that although he had been told by many of his friends that he should publish his story, Frank – in what I have since discovered as typical modesty – had always declined. He wrote very well and had plenty of stories to tell, but he simply felt that nobody would be interested in him. He was a character actor and didn't see himself as a star, nor did he ever consider stardom to be something he should aspire to. Appropriate billing was important to him, but stardom and adulation was not. I would discover that this modesty was more reflective of him as a person than his career achievements, which included helping provide the laughter for almost any successful comedian in the history of British television, in addition to his own vast acting career.

Modesty and humility were doubtless a part of his reluctance, but one of the most frequent words used to describe Frank, both in interviews for this book and in reviews of his work, is lugubrious. It seems a harsh word: Collins dictionary defines it as 'excessively mournful'. Frank was a serious man and certainly needed the occasional shove in the right direction from his beloved wife of sixty-seven years, Beryl. But his lugubriousness manifested itself in the most lovable of ways, personified perhaps by how both he and his family, along with fans and critics, took to his portrayal of Eeyore in two stage musical adaptations of the stories of Winnie the Pooh. Perhaps that lugubriousness denied us his autobiography.

After several subsequent conversations, Jane agreed to let me delve into the archive that included Frank's journals and keepsakes to see what he had left, and upon so doing Jane and her three boys were kind enough to give me the go-ahead to bring Frank's career to print.

Frank was a private man, shying away from publicity and celebrity. But he once joked that it would take around sixteen hundred removal lorries to get him out of his home if he were to retire to the country, such was the archive he built up over the years. I hope to have repaid Jane and the boys' trust by striking the right balance between detailing Frank's story and respecting his privacy. For that faith I can only thank Jane, Jonathan, Andrew and David. It's been an honour to learn more about Frank, and of course Beryl; after speaking to family friend Gyles Brandreth, it became clear that I would be hearing as many references to 'Frank and Beryl' as I would to Frank Thornton!

There are many other friends and colleagues of Frank's who gave up their time to answer emails, discuss things on the telephone, have a video call or meet for a lunch. Researching during pandemic years was not always easy, so I am grateful to each and every person who made the time to assist me. Not everything made the cut and alas some people were for the best of intentions unable to assist, but I am grateful to all who took the trouble to be in touch, along with their agents where appropriate. I offer my sincere gratitude to Suzy Aitchison, Robin Askwith, David Aukin, Pam Bannister, Terry Bartlam, Richard Bentine, Gyles Brandreth, Morris Bright MBE, Brandon Brock, Nigel Burwood, Julian Clary, John Cleese, Ray Cooney OBE, Beckie Croft, David Daly, Lesley Duff, Noel Edmonds, Tim Elms, Graeme Garden, Mike Grady, Joanne Heywood, David McGillivray, Mary McNulty, Anya Noakes, Jeff Nunner, John O'Farrell, Lloyd Peters, Gemma Ross, Robert Ross, Catherine Russell, Mandy Shepherd, Melanie Shepherd, Kathy Sheldon, Madeline Smith, Alan Titchmarsh MBE, Graham Turner and Nicola Waddington.

My additional thanks to Dexter O'Neill at Fantom Publishing for giving Frank's story a home.

On a personal note, I would like to thank my own family and friends for putting up once again with relentless updates of my progress over the research time.

Last, but certainly not least, to Frank Thornton himself. For many people, Frank's face and voice were instantly recognisable throughout the golden age of television and radio. For some years, they didn't always manage to put a name to both, at least not until a certain Captain Peacock arrived with his handkerchief appropriately plumed and his red carnation perfectly pinned, but they knew it was familiar and they knew it meant quality. If Frank was in something, it had to be worth watching. His journal began at the very beginning of his professional career: 1ˢᵗ April, 1940. Many of his words are included on these pages, and I cannot help but feel honoured to have discovered through those words what it was like To Be Frank…

Brian Slade, 2024

Foreword

FRANK THORNTON WAS SOMETHING OF AN ENIGMA: a man who became known to millions as a television comedy actor in such memorable series as *Hancock's Half Hour*, *Last of the Summer Wine* and *Are You Being Served?* but whose roots were firmly established in Shakespeare. As part of the company presided over by one of Britain's most renowned classical actors of the first half of the twentieth century, Sir Donald Wolfit, Frank learned his art – and his craft – in the halcyon days of 'weekly rep', going on to work on stage and film alongside not only the greatest dramatic actors of his time but also the greatest names in comedy, Tony Hancock and Spike Milligan among them.

Frank was married to the redoubtable Beryl, whom he met in Wolfit's company, and my wife and I got to know both of them rather late in life. As a result Alison and I were invited to the Twelfth Night dinner they gave every year at their home in Barnes, south-west London. We would sit around a lavishly decorated table in the company of their daughter Jane and such august names as Sir Donald Sinden, the wildlife artist David Shepherd and his wife Avril, and Lord and Lady Rix – Brian and Elspet. The conversations that ensued were founded on anecdotes which could so easily have been nothing more than actors droning on about 'the good old days'. They never did. They recalled experiences, yes, but the repartee and reportage were always seasoned with a twinkle in the eye and encouragement of those of us of lesser years: my wife and I along with Gyles and Michèle Brandreth. Such company can either intimidate or encourage one to raise one's game. I like to think it was always the latter. Surrounded by walls on which barely a square inch was left uncovered by paintings – mainly of wildlife, David Shepherd's offerings among them – the air would ring with laughter until the early hours.

Frank would listen attentively before chipping in with a well-placed and well-timed *bon mot*, invariably delivered in that familiar deadpan style that became his stock-in-trade. But he was never intimidating; even though, on the evening that he sat in the audience of a one-man show I was presenting at Chichester Festival Theatre, his very presence made me more anxious to impress than ever before. I need not have worried. "You'll need a drink, dear boy!" he greeted me with after the performance. A remark which would have been accurate whatever he had thought of my performance. The knowing wink led me to believe that I had not done too badly.

To be in Frank and Beryl's company was always uplifting, whether the conversation was about the theatre or gardening (Beryl's interest outside the thespian world), and the memories of our meetings continue to make me smile.

I'm delighted that Frank's unique talents have at last been recognised by Brian Slade and that his sterling contribution to stage and television has at last been documented. I think you'll be surprised at the breadth and variety of his experiences. I certainly am, and I'm glad that I can still hear the sonorous tones of his greeting at the door of his house: 'Dear boy! Come in!'

Alan Titchmarsh MBE, 2024

Prologue
The Fellow to Shoot For

'FRANK, OLD BOY, YOU WON'T DO ANY GOOD until you're forty. You see, you're not very pretty, you're not very ugly or very fat or very thin. You're nothing definite yet.'

As pep talks go to a young actor trying to make his way in the post-war theatre era, these words from renowned farceur Robertson Hare may not have seemed particularly encouraging. However, Hare was almost spot on with his assessment of the chances of success for his impatient young protégé, Frank Thornton. Frank was just shy of forty years old when he got his first significant television break in *It's A Square World* under the tutelage of Michael Bentine, who would be arguably the biggest influence on Frank's television career.

At the time Hare was despatching his pearl of wisdom Frank had been in the business for twenty years, interrupted briefly by a stint in the Royal Air Force. He had performed Shakespeare with two of the greatest to tread that particular path in Donald Wolfit and John Gielgud. He had even worked for the GPO and supported his family through harder times by earning money taking *Spotlight* photographs for other actors already well established, such as Clive Dunn, Peter Jones and Hattie Jacques. What

Robertson Hare would not have foreseen, however, was the worldwide success that Frank would gain from a situation comedy that cemented his place in television history arriving when he was fifty-one years old. Nor indeed that despite his late arrival in the fame stakes, Frank's final screen role would be when in his nineties after an acting career that overlapped eight decades.

Frank Thornton was humble about his talents as an actor and shied away from stardom and yet he became one of the most recognisable performers on television, radio, film and stage. His instantly identifiable voice, fine diction and that disapproving glare gave him the ability to play (as he called them) smell-under-the-nose characters, resulting in the opportunity to work with the finest names in theatre and comedy. But despite his success, any suggestion that he could become a star in his own right he would invariably dismiss. In countless interviews at the height of his fame he always deflected any questions that suggested he could have achieved success as a headline act or a leading man.

Equally, despite his fame from two of the most popular British comedy series of all time, *Are You Being Served?* and *Last of the Summer Wine*, and his comedy CV reading like a who's who of television's finest, he could get frustrated that he was dismissed consistently by drama departments, being almost permanently associated with that harshly judged collective title, light entertainment.

In 1940 Frank Thornton Ball, to give him his full name, began keeping a scrapbook documenting his theatrical career, having given up on a desk job in insurance. It included many thoughts and opinions written by hand and has proven an invaluable source for much of the information in this book. Within the first few pages he included two additional sheets inserted in later years that neatly showcase the man and his career along with his thoughts on how actors who achieve fame in comedy are viewed differently to others. The first of these he kept in his wallet and was a cutting containing some lines from one of Frank's favourites, Groucho Marx's autobiography, *Groucho and Me*:

> When funny men play a serious role it always gives me a lingering pain to see the critics hysterically throw their hats in the air, dance in the street and overwhelm the comic with assorted kudos. Why this should evoke such

astonishment and enthusiasm in the eyes of the critics has always baffled me. There is hardly a comedian alive who isn't capable of doing a first-rate job in a dramatic role. But there are mighty few dramatic actors who can essay a comic role with any distinction… compared to being funny, dramatic acting is like a two-week vacation in the country.

To convince you this isn't just a notion exclusively my own, here are the words of S. N. Behrman, one of our better playwrights: 'Any playwright who has been up against the agony of casting plays will tell you that the actor who can play comedy is the fellow to shoot for. The comic intuition gets to the heart of a human situation with the precision and velocity unattainable in any other way. A great comic actor will do it for you with an inflection of voice as adroit as the flick of the wrist in a virtuoso fencer.'

Nevertheless, the critics are always surprised.

Frank had humility in abundance about his own abilities, but was confident in his talents, especially in his younger days as he eagerly awaited his big opportunity to prove his worth. He also firmly believed in Groucho's message: that a trained actor pulling off comedy was a much scarcer talent to find than the other way around. Perhaps it was for this reason that Frank found himself cast opposite some of the greatest talents in comedy, bringing his serious look and intimidatingly authoritative voice to films, sketches and shows of Frankie Howerd, Tommy Cooper, Ken Dodd, Norman Wisdom, Morecambe and Wise, The Goodies, The Goons in their various solo careers, The Two Ronnies, Dick Emery, Benny Hill and Tony Hancock. Then, as tastes changed and a new guard in comedy came to the fore, he remained in demand for his gravitas opposite the likes of Kenny Everett, Kelly Monteith and Julian Clary.

For all his comedic successes, Frank was a trained dramatic actor of the stage. While his co-stars like John Inman and Mollie Sugden headed off for summer seasons and pantomimes between series of *Are You Being Served?*, Frank would head back to the stage for different reasons, be it Shakespeare, Pinter or Stoppard. But there was no dismissing of the achievements of his colleagues or disdain for the characters that brought him his greatest fame.

The additional sheet within his scrapbook that demonstrates the measure of the man is dated towards the end of the 1980s, a letter within which Frank wrote a note to his family regarding his journals. He played down his skills once again and on reviewing his scrapbooks had subsequently bemoaned the tone of his younger self, who had recorded being particularly critical of some of the players in the early days of his career. He remarked, 'I was quite insufferably arrogant and priggish on occasions with obviously a high opinion of my own abilities in contrast to those of my colleagues. Time has proved me to be wrong on both counts…'

Frank Thornton was in many ways the classic example of the quintessential old English gentleman. He knew how things should be done and the appropriate way to behave and would happily take people to task if their standards fell short of such expectations, but he had far too much humility to allow himself to bask in the glow of the light that shone on the many talents he worked with. I hope that the book that you are about to read allows Frank to have a much-deserved posthumous light shone on his own glorious career.

1

A Long Way to Tipperary

A S THE WINTER TEMPERATURES DROP and the winds begin to bite, most people in early January are resigning themselves to the end of the festivities. Twelfth Night is upon them, and the Christmas decorations are coming down, fearful as many superstitious folks are of upsetting the corresponding gods. The holidays are over, and the offices and workplaces await... but not everywhere.

At 27 Westmoreland Road, Barnes, south-west London, Beryl Thornton (nee Evans) is hard at work. An enjoyable family Christmas has been had with her husband, cherished daughter and three grand-sons. They have enjoyed their New Year's Eve visit to great friends, painter Michael Noakes and wife Vivien, and now the focus has shifted to what has become a traditional event – the Thorntons' Twelfth Night party.

The Thorntons have become well known for the gloriously lavish Victorian welcome they offer their guests. Afternoon tea is exactly that – brewed tea leaves, scones and cakes on a cake stand. For those fortunate enough to be invited for dinner, the full treatment is offered – wine glasses appropriate for each course, silverware placed to perfection. It is safe to say that when one is invited to the home of Frank and Beryl Thornton, the reception will be an exceptionally warm one.

Twelfth Night is no exception. What awaits the lucky recipients of an invite is a veritable winter wonderland. The Thorntons' home at any time is an homage to the life they have led and the passions that they share. Walls are adorned with mementos of a lengthy career in television and the theatre, such as original Michael Bentine sketches; but not exclusively so – Frank was too humble for that. Decoration and the evening's guest list are not typical of a theatrical couple. Frank adored the golden age of comedy, with books of Groucho and Harpo Marx, Laurel and Hardy and Buster Keaton sharing the bookshelves with those that critiqued his own work in television. But the entertainment profession did not hold exclusivity on the walls of the Thornton home. Frank and Beryl had plenty of interests away from acting and comedy. Originals of David Shepherd, wildlife painter of significant renown, were scattered plentifully on the walls, dwarfing the number of items of theatrical memorabilia and reflecting Frank's love of the animal kingdom; indeed, the Thorntons were great supporters of the David Shepherd Wildlife Foundation. At this time of year, the wall decorations took a back seat to the festive adornments. Barely a blank piece of wall existed as Beryl left hardly an undecorated space to be seen.

The doorbell would ring and the first guests would arrive. Enter Gyles Brandreth and his wife Michèle. Gyles seemed to know everybody in showbusiness and beyond. He and Frank had become acquaintances when Frank wrote to congratulate Gyles on his biography of John Gielgud, *An Actor's Life*. It was then that they realised Gyles was a neighbour of the Thorntons in Barnes and the pair became a welcome addition to their gathering, with stories aplenty on anybody and everybody.

As the evening moved on and the couples divided, Frank would share some of his limerick collection with Gyles. Beryl was not a fan of what one might consider to be lowbrow humour; but for all his love of the classics and his theatrical training, Frank could still be reduced to tears with a good five-line stanza and he even managed to recite one in an episode of his most famous career success, *Are You Being Served?*:

On the chest of a barmaid from Sale
Was tattooed all the prices of ale
Whilst on her behind
For the sake of the blind
Was precisely the same, but in Braille.

Next to arrive, the Shepherds. David Shepherd's wildlife images are to this day a joy to behold, and the Foundation under the stewardship of his daughters continues its good work around the world. Frank admired Shepherd and the subjects of his life's work. His love of animals could be traced back to an early appearance in one of his many commercials with a cluster of elephants for Slumberland Beds. In the less enlightened times when chimpanzees pushing pianos advertised tea, the five elephants had been painted white for the advert, filmed at Pinewood Studios. After the overly amorous bull and one potential mate had been removed, Frank was surrounded by three African elephants, and he simply considered them to be 'charming friendly young things' and bemoaned the stupidity of anybody who could consider being cruel to such beautiful creatures. For a great many years, when touring Australia, Canada and America, Frank and Beryl would be as at home birdwatching as they would with the enforced social circles their theatrical trips might require.

As much as Frank and Beryl were not a standard showbusiness couple, some guests were icons of their chosen profession. Enter the Sindens, Sir Donald and his wife Diana, and Lord and Lady Rix, famous farceur Brian and his wife Elspet. Through his clouds of smoke one could see Donald exchanging theatrical anecdotes aplenty with Brian, leaving the normally chatty David Shepherd at a loss for words. On occasion, Richard Briers would be among the guests and, as the wine flowed, Donald, Frank and Richard would take on the challenge of outdoing one another with their preferred theatrical warm-up exercises – Frank's favourite is often fondly used by Gyles Brandreth: 'Hip bath, hip bath, lavatory, lavatory, bidet, bidet, douche!'

Alan Titchmarsh and his wife Alison would become good friends of the Thorntons. The Titchmarshes enjoyed many a Twelfth Night event, standing somewhat wide-eyed at the array of characters before them. Alan recalled: 'Frank, in that glorious deadpan way he had, would chip in with his own stories of those early theatrical days when he and Beryl first met in Sir Donald Wolfit's company – Wolfit being an especially rich source of material for all concerned. I managed to chip in on this one since, as an apprentice gardener pushing my bike to work through Ilkley station, I had watched Wolfit strutting his stuff on the station platform when filming *Room at the Top* with Laurence Harvey. "Are you in the cast?" asked one of the film crew. I wished I'd had the nerve to say yes, but as a shy fifteen-year-old I simply shook my head and was shown the door – of the station.'

Beryl in particular was very active in the world of horticulture and so was naturally drawn to the Titchmarsh couple. She regularly headed off to the Chelsea Flower Show with Pam Bannister, wife of *Are You Being Served?* star Trevor, and she was a frequent winner in various local flower competitions. Being involved in their local community activities was a very important element of life for the Thorntons.

In the early hours of the morning, Frank and Beryl would bid a fond farewell from the doorstep to their guests as they departed into the cold night, well fed and watered – sometimes more wine than water – and royally entertained. 'People talk about houses having atmospheres,' Frank would later recall after decades ensconced at Westmoreland Road. 'I'm not much of a believer in the supernatural or anything like that, but it's extraordinary the number of people who have come here and said: "This house has a very happy atmosphere."'

Frank and Beryl were well-educated, well-spoken people, although Frank considered himself a philistine in comparison to his good lady wife. They were always turned out in pristine fashion, but they carried no showbusiness airs and graces and were one of the great showbusiness marriage successes. They were to all intents and purposes a double act. 'She's Welsh and quarrelsome, I'm English and pedantic,' Frank would later joke. 'We met in 1941 in Donald Wolfit's Shakespeare Company and we married in 1945 and I don't think we've stopped arguing since.'

Those joyous Twelfth Night events were evocative of those that might have been enjoyed several generations previously. The Ball and Thornton families were both very large, Frank having six uncles on his father's side alone.

There was nothing artificial about these gatherings, no television to accompany or distract them… just a collection of people enjoying one another's company. This was the world that Frank and Beryl created and cultivated during their sixty-seven-year marriage. Theirs was a partnership in every sense, Beryl often being the driving force in convincing Frank to take a part or attend an event.

'She pushed him when he lacked confidence,' recalled their only daughter, Jane, of the relationship dynamic. 'She could play-read for him and say, "That's good," or, "No, don't touch that." She was there behind him and that's the way it worked. My mother got out of the relationship what she was happy to have and he got his career – and they had a jolly good time of it. Doing the dinner parties was part of the bigger picture; she was very creative with that.'

The Thornton name was actually Frank's mother's maiden name but given to both him and his older brother John as a middle name. Their father was William Ernest Ball, their mother Rosina Mary Thornton, but their sister Margery was given the Rosina middle name to continue her own maternal connection.

The earliest known connection to the performing arts in the Thornton family history came from Frank's maternal grandfather, Joseph. Joseph was born in Yorkshire but moved down to the capital and plied his trade as Assistant Vicar Choral within the imposing surroundings of St Paul's Cathedral. He also began organising performances, with family documents including a one-sheet announcement for 'A Grand Evening Ballad Concert' shortly before Christmas 1884.

Joseph's son, Frank's uncle, Herbert Fletcher Thornton, inherited his father's musical talents. His first venture into the industry came when he was taken under the wing of Moore & Moore, an established London-based company who had been making pianos and American organs since 1838. Joseph signed his approval for his young son to be taken on as an apprentice at their Bishopsgate base, 'to learn the art of tuning and to serve him after in the manner of an apprentice from this date faithfully and obediently from this date until the mid-summer 1895'. In keeping with his new industry, 'H. F. Thornton (from Moore & Moore)' set about establishing a reputation as a tuner and repairer, and was swiftly earning high praise for his standards of workmanship.

Herbert diligently learned and honed his craft, completing his apprenticeship in 1895, Henry Moore being 'glad to have the opportunity of expressing our satisfaction with his conduct during the term'. High praise for the officialdom of turn-of-the-century England.

With his apprenticeship complete, Herbert set about the performance side of the music industry alongside his piano-tuning business and was amongst five hundred and fifty-one people across the nation to vie for one of only seventeen free scholarships available at the Royal College of Music. The hopefuls were assessed over a three-day period in February 1896; Herbert successfully came through the examination process on the French horn.

The scholarship was an opportunity that he grasped eagerly and over the next three years he was frequently involved in public performances. After an appearance at a chamber concert in December of 1898, the *Musical Times* was decidedly impressed with young Herbert's performance as part of an interpretation of Brahms's Trio for Pianoforte: 'Herbert Thornton bids fair to become an excellent performer upon the most human amongst orchestral instruments.'

Herbert's younger brother Harold wasn't far behind, also gaining entry to the Royal College of Music, and five years after his brother his own musical talents were acknowledged as admirable in an adaptation of a concerto in C by George Dyson.

In total, there were six older brothers to Frank's mother Rosina, and while archives and family documents make it clear that there were musical talents, none gave any hint of any theatrical leanings that Frank would attain in acting, with the possible exception of Sydney Thornton. The fourth of Joseph's sons, Sydney ended up settling in Africa where he surprisingly became known for after-dinner speaking. In 1944 after Sydney's death, friends had published a small book titled *The Sayings of Syd* in aid of the British Legion, and the foreword contained passages that would not have seemed amiss years later to describe his nephew:

> He himself would never lay claim to any great gift of oratory but, though his speeches were light and airy, they were more admirably adapted to the occasion than many more pretentious utterances.

Under cover of his wit and humour the inherent honesty and sincerity of the man himself was only partially hidden. Like his life, his speeches and writings were imbued with a kindly, humorous outlook, a wisdom which is more than knowledge and a wide sympathy with others.

He set a high standard for after-dinner speeches and, though he had a masculine relish for a clever Rabelaisian story, he was an outstanding example of the truth he often preached that to be funny it is not necessary to be vulgar.

The talents of the Ball family were less creative, perhaps explaining why Frank's father didn't feel comfortable with his young son's preferred career choice. William was a bank manager at the local Midland Bank, having an eye for the fiscal that always stayed with Frank. That wasn't to say that William was devoid of any creativity: while being a very practical man, he was also an expert photographer, particularly of landscapes, and a fine pianist.

William was a church organist and choirmaster at St James's Church, Church of Scotland in Dulwich for many years until he retired from duties there in 1938. Some forty years later, when William Ball passed away, Frank referenced his musical talents, which were put to use in the church purely for income purposes as opposed to any Christian faith:

> My father, who was still driving his car, albeit a mite erratically, at the age of ninety finally departed this life four days after his ninety-fourth birthday without pain and in the peaceful untroubled atheism that saw nothing beyond the oblivion of death. During the many years when he was a church organist of great musical ability and adventuresomeness the constant repetition of the Christian message, far from wearing away his resistance, only hardened his belief that they'd got it all wrong and he'd got it all right.

Frank's early education began at Sydenham Hill School before he moved on to Alleyn's, whose notable alumni include Julian Glover, Leslie Howard and Ray Cooney OBE, for whom Frank would work many times in his career.

Formal education it is safe to say was not Frank's strongest point. He was undoubtedly a very intelligent man, but in his school years he was focused on other things. He was quick to realise that laughter may be the optimum way to keep classmates on side: 'When I was a boy, I found people laughing at me when I was trying to be serious and that hurt rather. So, I decided that if they were going to laugh I'd capitalise on it.'

In early February 1929 the theatrical publication *The Era* announced the opening of the Capitol Cinema in Forest Hill, south-east London. A glorious building of a bygone era it was, like so many cinemas of its time, a dazzling spectacle, with a domed roof, oak panelling and a wonderful contrasting array of blue, gold and ivory fittings. It opened with the MGM silent picture *Man, Woman and Sin*, but would very soon be equipped with the necessary system to allow talkies and people would queue around the block to see the latest films.

Among those hopefuls was a young Frank Ball, who would become a regular visitor to the Capitol. As fog descended on the region, he dutifully waited in line to see the latest offering from the screen idols that made his imagination run wild – Buster Keaton, Harold Lloyd, Laurel and Hardy and the Marx Brothers. He would rush to the front row of the auditorium and look up in wonder at the greats before him, imagining himself on that screen one day. He burst from the cinema brimming with ideas as he merrily wandered home oblivious to the conditions around him. He impersonated Stan and Ollie on his way home, stopping only at schoolfriend Peter Hull's house to enlighten him: 'Peter, you must see this film – the fat one and the thin one,' he implored. The acting bug had bitten. An already distracted pupil had made up his mind where his future focus would be, and it wasn't with education or banking – it was acting.

Frank's adulation for the stars of the silver screen in that era never faded, although he did struggle to balance Chaplin the star with Chaplin the political speaker years later. Of Keaton, his only reflection would be that while Chaplin had owned his films, Keaton had not been wise when moving to MGM, losing creative control, artistic independence, and financial success. Of his movies, Frank was never in doubt as to his talents. Years later, he remembered, 'Rediscovering him with *The General* at the Academy [cinema on Oxford Street] all those years ago was a revelation. One needed to make no concessions for the age of the film or any of the others that followed. Bright, crisp, very funny, marvellously satirical, and totally unsentimental. The man was brilliant in all departments of film making, artistic and technical. He remains my God!'

It is no surprise then that among Frank's collection of movie-star biographies, the Marx Brothers and Laurel and Hardy share their place with all manner of Keaton publications. Frank would also have humbly dismissed, but been privately proud of, a 1974 review that suggested his performance as Sir Andrew Aguecheek in *Twelfth Night* had echoes of Buster Keaton and Stan Laurel. He would also appear on stage in 1992 in a tribute to Flanagan and Allen alongside Ray C. Davis, earning praise for 'his pouchy blue eyes suggesting decades of expertise cheering up grumpy audiences in improbable little theatres'. How those early imitations would pay off!

Aside from skipping down the road doing Laurel and Hardy routines, Frank set about doing comic turns with his brother John when his large family gathered for Christmas. With parents, aunts, uncles and cousins assembled along with sister Margery, the pair would present rewritten versions of Noël Coward and the Western Brothers tunes with their own lyrics, making a verse for each of their attending family members. One typical example was named 'Keeping Up the Old Tradition (with apologies to the Western Brothers)', the Western Brothers having released their effort as a B-side to a track entitled 'We're Frightfully BBC', a title that would have been somewhat appropriate for Frank to use given the years of service he would give the corporation. Of particular interest in the Thornton brothers' version is the reference to their parents:

INTRODUCTION:
Let us now praise men, you've heard the poet say
So in the example of the bard we've made our own array
Of those who in a smaller sphere have made themselves a name
So listen here, you hounds, while we present our hall of fame

(W. E. BALL)
Now first of all there's William Ball, the handsomest of men
Keeping up the old tradition
He's first class with the camera and handy with the pen
Keeping up the old tradition
He'll sit and write for hours and hours when he's in the mood
He'll stay up in his desk room for half the night without his food
And he hopes one day to get a snap of some girl in the 'nood'
Keeping up the old tradition

And also as a gardener his praises must be sung
He's fond of ponds and rockeries, with bush trees overhung
And he goes out very early with a spade collecting dung
Keeping up the old tradition ('Oh, piles of it!')

(MRS W. E. BALL)
Next to him there is our Rosie, a sweet old girl is she
She was the first effort of the Thornton family tree
She suffers from her heart at times – the doctors say it's true
And when it starts to throb, she sits and makes her rug of blue
But it seems to happen mostly when there's lots of work to do.

(VERSE)
You've heard of Alexander and also Hercules
Of Hector Powe and Harry Roy and such great men as these
But have you heard about yourselves, the funny things you do?
You haven't? Well, we'll give you some – They're great, I'm telling you

(THE WRITERS)
And lastly, there's the writers of this frightfully clever song
We hope you have enjoyed it, and we trust it's not too long
We've sweated morning, noon and night to get it done on time
We've had the very devil's job to make the last words rhyme
But we think the finished article is very much sublime
Keeping up the old tradition...

Mum and Dad and the boys themselves weren't the only subjects of scrutiny within John and Frank's efforts. Sister Margery and a number of aunts, uncles and cousins were given the same treatment, but the jolly jibes give an interesting insight to the characters and pastimes that occupied the most influential of the Thornton/Ball family, along with the characteristics present in William that would be reflected in Frank's adult life.

As young Frank began to lose himself in his artistic dreams, so he started to lose interest in his educational aspirations and indeed the career choices that would ordinarily follow a conventional education. He was now allowing thoughts of stage or screen stardom to fully occupy his mind. When he had started at Alleyn's he had been described as 'an intelligent boy with a pleasant sense of humour, clever and well read'.

However, as the 1930s progressed he began to get noted for other things, being noted as 'dreamy' and 'inclined to pose'.

In 1935 Frank obtained matriculation and achieved the rank of corporal in Alleyn's Officer Training Corps, but his most notable achievement was continuing the musical talents of his family by joining the school orchestra. He found himself on violoncello in the December 1935 production of the Greek tragedy *Alcestis*. Frank had become an accomplished musician; but there were eleven credited characters, fifteen citizens, eight dancers and ten minor roles: forty-four people doing what Frank wanted to be doing – entertaining people on stage. He once recalled in an interview his frustration at being in the orchestra for other school shows such as *The Mikado* and *The Yeomen of the Guard*: 'I used to sit in the pit going bomp-bomp while the others on stage reaped the glory.'

Aside from his distraction from his academic studies, Frank also had no aspirations for physical success (the closest he came to any sporting achievement was a successful run in a snooker competition, the Green Room Club tournament in 1973, surprising himself with a run that saw him eliminate the defending champion) and his masters were frustrated. Playing the cello, it seems, was not considered a manly enough occupation for his only notable success at school and Frank recalled his housemaster commenting that 'it is time he showed some good hard wood!'

In his final year at Alleyn's Frank was noted for improving, but he was subsequently held back as one of a clutch of schoolboys believed to have no chance of passing the Higher School exam of summer 1937.

Frank's father was very clear in his opinions: acting was all well and good, but it would offer no security and therefore potentially no income. An office job offered both, and that is where Frank's future should lie.

Unperturbed, Frank knew that the financial world and desk jobs were not for him. After leaving Alleyn's School, Frank ventured into office work in the form of a clerk job at Guardian Insurance in the city, earning the princely sum of £70 a year. But his heart was most definitely not in it.

Although against acting as a chosen profession, Frank's father was not domineering enough to forbid his son from pursuing his dreams; but if he were to do so, it would need to be alongside his day job. As a bank manager, William was likely to have been comfortable enough financially to have been able to pay for drama school, especially given that the Ball family had also been comparatively well off. It is more likely that this was the compromise: Frank could pursue acting, but not to the exclusion of a steady income.

Frank's stay in the insurance world was always going to be a brief one. It was a grudging acceptance that the acting profession did not provide a steady income and would come with no guarantee of work. What the insurance industry could not provide was one ounce of interest for a teenager whose love of all things theatrical called him to the stage. The final straw came when the person sitting at the desk next to him left to become an actor. 'Good heavens, if he can do it, I can do it,' surmised Frank and he set about training for an acting career.

Research found one outlet for Frank: studying drama at the London School of Dramatic Art. It was the only acting school in London that offered the option of evening classes and so Frank would commit to his day job in the city before heading to the West End to learn the craft that he so desired on a scholarship.

It could have proven a hasty move. Just as for so many people, war would have an immediate impact on Frank's career aspirations. The London School of Dramatic Art was evacuated to Witney in Oxfordshire and at that point Frank decided to go with them; and, even though still a student, he was able to join the local repertory company. Rep was something that appealed to Frank throughout his career, and he bemoaned that as repertory began to disappear, too many people were emerging from universities with grandiose ideas of how things should be done in theatre without having had the level of groundwork that a season or two in repertory theatre could provide.

In the 1930s, repertory theatre was the learning ground for aspiring performers, and in Frank's case the recipient of his talents was the Witney Repertory Players under the guidance of Miss Gertrude Pickersgill – Picky as her players came to know her. She had been well established in the theatre long before the First World War and was the author of a book on miming. Although the Witney Rep offered Frank his first break into a theatrical career, nothing could have been further from the glamour of the West End.

Witney Rep was battling the early stages of the Second World War and so their venues and audiences were at the mercy of outside forces. Establishing a subscription programme in 1939 in order to combat the financial challenges of using unlicensed halls, by January 1940 Miss Pickersgill had found a venue for her group. What she referred to as a 'Little Theatre' was actually little more than a loft to the rear of a high street business in Witney, but it was home to the fledgling group of players who were all members of the London School of Dramatic Art, Frank included.

Frank was still completing his study time with the school and so collected a number of small parts in the new company's initial productions: *Sixteen*, *London Wall* and *Jane Eyre*. Even as a teenage amateur he was already receiving personal praise in the local press, particularly for the three roles he juggled in *Jane Eyre*. But the challenges faced by the company were reflective of those that the theatre industry as a whole would face in the wartime years to come. Frank appeared in forty-seven performances of a forty-nine-night run. Of the missing two, one was down to having no audience, the other down to damage to the Little Theatre.

With his scholarship progressing well, it was time for Frank to lay to rest his job in insurance and turn professional – on, of all days, April Fools' Day – as he headed for his first professional tour: a fit-up company starting their time in Tipperary.

2

An Invasion Begins

I N 1940 FRANK THORNTON BALL WOULD EMBARK on his professional acting career and in so doing began keeping a record of his progress. Under his full name of Frank Thornton Ball, albeit ditching the Ball for his acting career, Frank's scrapbook cover page recorded his career move thus:

OF LITTLE OR NO INTEREST

Being a record of the attempts of the above-mentioned individual to justify his invasion of the theatrical profession after deciding that his sojourn in the insurance world was not lucrative enough to compensate for the boredom thereof.

(Sounds good, anyhow) 1940.

Unperturbed by the challenges of his performances with the Witney Repertory Company, Frank turned professional on 1st April 1940, boarding a ferry with his new colleagues in the Yorke-Clopet Company bound for Southern Ireland and a tour of three plays around the theatres of provincial Ireland. The headline piece was Terrence Rattigan's *French*

Without Tears, supported by productions of *White Cargo* and *The Sport of Kings*. Frank's first professional role was that of Brian Curtis, with Eugene Leahy leading the company, starting out at the Confraternity Hall in Thurles, County Tipperary. It earned him £2.50 a week and thanks to minimal cost of digs and the fact that he neither drank nor smoked, he was delighted to be pocketing twenty-five bob a week.

Manager of the Yorke-Clopet Company was Philip Yorke, who Frank described as having 'no use for dramatic schools, producers and organisation'. He remembered Yorke as 'a pleasant eccentric with red hair, pale blue eyes behind spectacles, a brown trilby, a sports jacket and grey flannels in cycle clips'.

In a further example of the challenges of wartime productions, Yorke could often be seen cycling to the train stations with knapsack, gas mask case (minus gas mask), rolled umbrella and chair all stacked to the rear of his bicycle. The company themselves had as much work to do offstage as on, making lighting battens and curtain mechanisms, selling tickets and programmes and on occasion loading and unloading their scenery and belongings onto railway freight carriages and pushing them themselves, Frank remembering that, 'Some Irish stations being deficient in shunting engines, we had to understudy.'

The tour received widespread praise, Frank noting that Yorke 'played the leads with panache unchecked by much consideration for textual accuracy'. Frank's first professional tour concluded its successful run on 19th May, returning from Killarney to the mainland where blackouts and the hovering threat of an armed forces call-up awaited.

His initial return almost saw Frank's film debut as a soldier in the Will Fyffe film *Neutral Port*, but as became a disturbingly frequent occurrence and perhaps an inevitable by-product of playing smaller roles, his appearance was not seen by the cinema audience as it remained on the cutting-room floor.

Young actors earning their stripes frequently found themselves taking up the task of assistant stage manager, and for Frank that meant joining the Harry Hanson Court Players at the Palace Theatre in Reading in June of 1940. He was getting frustrated at his lack of involvement, voicing disapproval at 'a combination of frantic rush and monotonous inactivity coupled with a feeling of envy towards the people on the stage getting all the fun'. He enjoyed life with the company itself, but business for the season was dropping, something he considered was primarily down to the fall of France.

Despite the poor takings, Hanson's company battled on with a lengthy tour of *Smilin' Through* where once again Frank would take a minor role in the lower echelons of the play. Spending so much of his time observing rather than acting, he was beginning to understand the nuances of his profession and wasn't afraid to note the good and the bad of the performers higher up the bill, at one point pondering, 'I wonder what people would say about these remarks from a nineteen-year-old ASM with but six months' experience, though two of them in the good school of Irish fit-ups.'

Amongst Frank's comments on the performances was a critique of the accents used by Betty England. He advised that she should 'watch her speech which tends towards Mayfair on the stage and a flat "A" off the stage as well as the good old glottal schock, especially where a perfectly good "R" is provided by the previous word'. Frank would throughout his career have a desire for the Queen's English to be enunciated in an appropriate manner. It was not a class thing – he well understood the colourful mixture of dialects across the land and became hugely adept at mimicking them all. However, the destruction of the spoken word was something he always bemoaned, in later years addressing the American interpretation: 'My wife and I watched the *Jurassic Park* sequel. It was opened and closed by Richard Attenborough. In the couple of hours between those two scenes the dialogue of the American actors was only marginally more intelligible than the dinosaurs.'

Frank's comments about Betty England's speech patterns were attributable to youthful exuberance and his frustrations born of still waiting in the wings. He had a minor part in *Smilin' Through* and the show was received to good reviews, but his own involvement was too small for his liking: 'I should be grateful that I was complimented by all and sundry on my performance in understudy rehearsals of Kenneth and Jeremiah, but that only made it more galling when I had to sit in my little corner for the shows… such are the toils of the tyro.'

Despite his frustrations, things were starting to change. Frank's talents were gradually being recognised, and when his old drama teacher and Witney Rep leader Gertrude Pickersgill advertised for an actor to join the Witney Repertory Company as Major Petkoff in *Arms and the Man*, he was delighted to rejoin his old company. The press were delighted too, with the *Witney Gazette* commenting: 'Frank Thornton, making a welcome return and giving his best performance as yet in our theatre, draws an authentic picture of the Major proud of his rank and his library.' It was praise that young Frank was delighted to receive, and the brief run was a welcome one. His progress was noted somewhat playfully, recognising 'quite a pleasant week, including a gloat over people doing what I cursed at nine months ago'.

The upturn in fortunes now brought Frank Thornton into a whole new sphere of acting. Following a brief but successful performance in *The Scarlet Pimpernel* in Dundee, in February of 1941, less than a year into his professional career and despite the fact that he had agreed to eventually return to *Smilin' Through*, he was now joining the Donald Wolfit company in a production of *The Merry Wives of Windsor*. This was Shakespeare, the kind of play Frank had always aspired to appear in; and not only that, but he was also now under the tutelage of the last of a dying breed: Donald Wolfit, described by his official biographer Ronald Harwood as one of the very last of the old-style actor-managers. It was a whole new level of acting experience for young Frank.

Wolfit had been on a personal crusade to bring Shakespeare to theatregoers while the country was under the constant bombardment of the Germans. He had combined his own Home Guard duties with immersing himself in every aspect of his company's production. Shortly before Frank joined his troupe, Wolfit noted in his accounts, 'Dressing room destroyed. Co. dressed on stage. No water. No heat. Stalls only used. Coffee and sandwiches served in Stalls Bar.'

Earlier in 1940, Wolfit had made what he conceded had been a crazy offer of ten pounds per week rental for the Strand Theatre in the West End, which had lost its existing production, *Aren't Men Beasts!* and was now standing in darkness. In return for the offer, surprisingly accepted, he would run a selection called Lunchtime Shakespeare to only the stalls section of the theatre. Wolfit's Advance Players Association kept costs to a minimum, which included the acting talent, who received three guineas a week, including the stars of *The Merry Wives of Windsor*, Irene and Violet Vanbrugh.

The more the elements and the Germans conspired against him, the more galvanised Wolfit became. The only way he knew he could contribute to the war effort was in the theatre, keeping them open with Shakespeare's finest. In Harwood's biography of Wolfit, he noted, 'If enemy bombers were approaching, Mary Pitcher, dressed as an Elizabethan page, announced cheerfully: "The warning has just gone. We shall proceed. Would those that wish to leave do so as quietly as possible."'

Frank's debut role in the company was that of Fenton, an amorous juvenile character which allowed him to 'impress some people with the knobbly nature of my knees and Jessica Morton, the stage manager, with the abject misery that my performance was apparently infused with'. It was a significant breakthrough to join Wolfit, but even this didn't satisfy Frank's ambition and perhaps more importantly, it didn't satisfy the bank balance:

> D.W. wants to go to Bournemouth on 3/3/41 and then Cheltenham but with the uncertainty of his plans, their intermittent nature and small remuneration I fear I shall be financially compelled to leave Wolfit and Co to Hanson's Co notwithstanding my preference for Shakespeare.

It wasn't Frank penny-pinching or angling for higher pay. Wolfit and finances were well known by now as being non-negotiable. Wolfit was continually appealing for funds to support his company, despite regularly ploughing much of his own money into the coffers.

Despite the feeling that he may be forced to look elsewhere, Frank stayed with Wolfit as the tour plans came together and continued around the West Country through the spring of 1941. Still only twenty years old, Frank was captivated by the performances of the lead actors:

> Wolfit was marvellous as Falstaff, and the Vanbrughs as the Wives, and pleasant – very pleasant to work with. Both very charming with no side that might go with women of their position.

His admiration of the Vanbrugh sisters, both in the twilight of their careers, was only reinforced when Irene fell during a blackout in Bath and was hospitalised only to return swiftly to complete the tour, her fractured arm not detracting from her spirit or performance.

It was a happy initial taste of a more significant company for Frank, lauded by the *Chronicle and Herald* who commented, 'How splendidly Frank Thornton, as Fenton, interprets the stately measure of Shakespeare's blank verse.' Frank had obligations, however, to fulfil a promise he had made to continue with *Smilin' Through* with the Hanson company; but when Wolfit offered him the opportunity to join him in his own production of *The Scarlet Pimpernel* he jumped at the chance, a decision Frank made with regret as it soured his relationship with Harry Hanson, for whom he never worked again.

The Scarlet Pimpernel experience was not as enjoyable for Frank as his previous time with Wolfit had been. He had seen how Wolfit the manager operated, oozing theatre from every pore, meticulous in his knowledge of every aspect of company production. But as Wolfit the actor, Frank was less certain that this was the way forward for his career at that time.

The role Frank was brought in for was one that could arguably be said to have been him to a tee: Lord Anthony Dewhurst, a perfect English gentleman. But at this stage Frank found him boring to play, taking more joy seemingly from doubling as a French yokel who manages to tease a few laughs from the audience in Act Four.

In addition to *The Scarlet Pimpernel*, Frank had signed with Wolfit to continue in both *Hamlet* and *Richard III*, breaking only for a brief time in Southport with the Sheffield Repertory Company. Financially he would have again been better off staying in Southport, but he felt duty bound to fulfil his obligations with Wolfit and he returned to the company in the autumn of 1941 for the Shakespeare tour.

Frank took the role of Laertes in *Hamlet* and Sir William Catesby in *Richard III*, but only the former play generated significant box-office returns. As *Richard III* failed to find an audience, *The Merchant of Venice* was swiftly added to the company's repertoire in order to generate more income. But by this time, Frank was finding Wolfit's actor side to be somewhat detrimental to his own ambitions.

Wolfit was an enigma. To some he was deemed an egotistical character who surrounded himself with support players who either lacked the drive or the talent to try and outshine the star, who was very much Wolfit. Others saw Wolfit in a more forgiving light, as a man who knew that the audiences wanted that star quality presence and all he wanted was to be the principal man to deliver it. Either way it was certainly not his style to allow other cast members to dictate the direction of the plays being performed.

The *Gloucestershire Echo* commented on the excessive pace from the company when performing *Hamlet*. It was a comment not lost on Frank, who felt that while the company were expected to go through their lines at pace, Wolfit himself spent excessive amounts of time delivering his own performance.

It was all part of the complex nature of Wolfit. He demanded pace at rehearsals and in performances and was a fearsome opponent to any actors who dared to challenge him. Yet away from the theatre, he showed loyalty and sacrifice to his players, keeping them employed when offers elsewhere were not forthcoming, taking minimal or even no wage when takings were poor and loyally holding on to players during wartime. At twenty-one years old, Frank had neither the optimism to believe he could justify questioning his manager on his theatrical demands, nor had he become acquainted with Wolfit well enough to experience the kinder side to the man, something he would learn in later life.

By 1942 the company had gone through *A Midsummer Night's Dream* and moved on to *Volpone*. Musical director Rosabel Watson received a note from a friend delighted to hear the news that Frank would be playing the part of Mosca: 'I'm so glad Frank Thornton will play Mosca. He is a nice intelligent actor and has no silly mannerisms so obviously has enough brains to know what the words he speaks actually mean.' But by now Frank's patience was being tested by Wolfit's domineering stage presence:

> The rest of the cast, particularly those new to their parts – including myself with Mosca, a very large chunk of the play, were just sufficiently good to support D. W. competently but not capable of outshining him – which is of course the way to be an actor-manager... In spite of this terrific handicap I

managed to put in a performance which seemed to please, in various degrees, most of the critics that came to the show.

Mosca was almost certainly Frank's most significant and best received performance thus far in his career, but it was also his most frustrating. Wolfit was known for budgeting very little when it came to sets, costumes and publicity; equally so, he was known for ensuring that he was the star. Ronald Harwood, whose Wolfit biography was written to honour a request in Wolfit's will, wrote of the air of fear around productions:

> A light or an actor out of position, and Wolfit would hiss a reprimand from behind his beard. A throne wrongly angled would produce a terrifying glare at the prompt corner, a surreptitious moving of the offending piece of furniture (and sometimes even of an offending actor) with his upstage knee.
>
> Above all, inside the theatre, Wolfit created an atmosphere of terror which any dictator would have envied. In later years, ex-war heroes, men who had braved the Nazi onslaught in North Africa or France, former prisoners-of-war, men who had suffered torture at the hands of the Japanese, would dart into dressing rooms or cower in the shadows rather than meet him in the corridor after a scene that had not gone to his liking. It was not a threat of dismissal that produced fear; it was the very intensity of Wolfit's personality when enraged.

While Harwood's comments on Wolfit's personality seem extreme, Frank was finding the practical elements of his performances to be accurate. Wolfit would position scenery that involved him centre stage, even if the principal dialogue was with another character whose portrayer was forced to deliver their lines downstage. Mosca was one such character, with the bulk of the dialogue in the first scene.

Frank's opinion was that Wolfit's style of acting as the front and centre of everything was not the way to bring in the public. The theatre was also unheated, so he took action on behalf of the cast to implore Wolfit to provide money for long johns in order that the supporting players were not freezing to death on stage. Audiences would huddle together in their jackets and coats, Wolfit would return to his dressing room where he had installed a heater, but the cast were forced to endure the somewhat arctic conditions until Frank took the star to task.

With Frank gaining the confidence needed to blossom from out of Wolfit's shadow, he took the decision that to be seen on stage he had to move on. He reluctantly conceded on 12th March 1942 that he needed to find himself another job.

Opportunity did not take long to knock on Frank's door. Twelve days after he had recorded his need to leave the Wolfit company, *Spotlight* telephoned asking him to start rehearsing immediately for the part of Sandy in *Hay Fever* in an upcoming tour. Then almost immediately, and somewhat ironically after his recently completed run with Wolfit, came a call asking Frank to join John Gielgud's production of *Macbeth*. 'Amusing?' was the simple additional note Frank made in his journal.

Gielgud himself had been running a wartime offensive in support of the British theatre, albeit in a somewhat different manner to Wolfit. By the time he came to trying a production of *Macbeth* he was having problems with casting. Conscription was taking more and more able-bodied young men off to war, leaving Gielgud scrambling for talent and relying somewhat on Equity's list of those unfit for military duty.

Frank may have found a new home for his Shakespearean talents, but he was largely restricted to minor parts. But he found the whole experience a total contrast to the one he had experienced under Wolfit:

> On seeing John Gielgud I found him infinitely more approachable and un-Godlike than Wolfit. In fact, a charming, ordinary (in the best sense) sort of man. As a producer, he is overflowing with ideas and not a week goes by on tour without a rehearsal, and not a rehearsal goes by without a dozen little changes somewhere in the play: and sometimes they aren't so little. It is perhaps a little wearying to do the same scene twenty times over in quick succession, but it serves to keep the company on their toes and the production fresh if it does nothing else – but it does usually.

Frank was mesmerised by Gielgud's *Macbeth*, the sort of performance that sent shivers down his spine because he was just so good. Some thirty-two years later, even though he had never played the lead role himself, Frank found himself appearing in the play again and being capable of reciting the full text of leading actor Nicol Williamson, so entranced had he been by Gielgud's *Macbeth*.

Gielgud was certainly a less temperamental soul with a gentler demeanour than Wolfit and with fewer demands for the limelight. Performing as Angus after existing actor Terence Alexander was called into the Tank Corps, Frank recalled that, 'Mr Gielgud reprimanded me at rehearsal for playing the scene as a rather nervous, self-conscious young actor playing to the star. "That's how Donald Wolfit has taught you to act – I don't want it."'

The conflict Frank felt between his loyalty to Wolfit and his enjoyment of his new freedom under Gielgud was never further evident than when he sent a telegram to the Wolfit company wishing them well upon the opening of their next show, *The Romance of David Garrick*, in which for the first time in his career, a part had been written specifically for Frank by new British writer Constance Cox. The irony was not lost on Frank that this part, that of the Honourable Edward Farren, was written for him, but he insisted he had no regrets about his decision to join up with Gielgud. There appeared genuine hurt, however, in Wolfit's response, where he questioned the wisdom of Frank's decision. 'I thought you said you didn't want any more costume and less Shakespeare. I think you have made a mistake frankly to go from a London season of Laertes, Mosca and Bassanio to small parts.'

Despite his departure from Wolfit's company, and his criticism of Wolfit's onstage craft at that point in his fledgling career, Frank found a permanent connection with the Shakespearean legend. As time went by, Frank began to value the appeal of the actor-director star power. They remained firm friends for the remainder of Wolfit's life and continued that friendship with Wolfit's daughter, Margaret, frequently attending events raising funds under the Wolfit name or simply paying tribute to his legend.

Years later, Frank would be more circumspect about Wolfit's approach to acting, remembering, 'If Donald had a lack, he lacked a certain self-criticism, but that wasn't necessarily a bad thing because it meant he could be great – like all great actors he could be ten times better than we were or sometimes ten times worse!'

'The bedrock of their theatrical lives was being part of the Donald Wolfit company,' recalled Frank's friend and neighbour, Gyles Brandreth. 'Sir Donald Wolfit was a key figure in their lives and I think they got to know him in a way that others didn't. I remember they went to stay with Sir Donald and Lady Wolfit, Rosalind Iden, and they couldn't believe it: these were low players as it were, and Sir Donald brought them breakfast in bed, eggcups, eggs that he had boiled with, on top of the eggs, egg cosies that he, the great Donald Wolfit, had knitted. They fundamentally saw themselves as members of the Donald Wolfit company for the rest of their lives.'

That occasion saw the gentler side of Wolfit come to the fore, hosting Frank and Beryl as Beryl convalesced after a serious illness. His reputation did not always allow his gentler side to be shown, but actor Brian Sanders was one to defend his former employer. He had experienced this kinder side himself, years later recalling that as three of Wolfit's company were under eighteen, one of which was Sanders, Wolfit funded three hundred pounds to the authorities of his own money to permit them to travel, changing Sanders' career path. It was a side Frank recalled as well: 'He didn't pay much, but then he didn't take much. There were weeks where he didn't even draw his own salary.'

Wolfit was equally kind to Frank about the state of his career. Frank had bemoaned to Donald that his career had not brought the success he had hoped. 'When you were my age, you were already a star. I'm just a failure,' he was reported to have told him. Wolfit responded encouragingly: 'No, you're a success. You're still in the business. Think back to all the people who were in my company with you. Who else is still here?'

Getting a grounding in Shakespeare and securing the most significant theatrical entry on his CV that he would ever use – he referred to both Wolfit and Gielgud in his *Spotlight* summary for the entirety of his career – were not the only thing working with Wolfit brought Frank; he also found the most important person he would ever meet.

Aspiring actress Beryl Evans had spoken to Donald Wolfit in an effort to get a break into the business. To her delight, the impresario, intimidating but often kind to young acting talent, agreed to take her on as a student for a tour of Wolfit's company in autumn of 1940. It was hardly what one would call a big break and certainly not a lucrative offer. The emphasis was very much on a studentship, with Beryl receiving no salary, being expected to reimburse the company for any travel tickets supplied for her, and with duties that ranged from being prepared to take walk-on parts in productions to costume and stage management work. Wolfit expected her to conform to all the established rules of the theatre, but as chairman of the Advanced Players Association he welcomed her to the company and sincerely hoped that her stay 'would prove a profitable start to your career'. As it turned out, Beryl's acting career was comparatively short-lived, but she would profit from meeting the love of her life.

Beryl had first crossed paths with Frank briefly when working in *The Scarlet Pimpernel*, chatting at the stage door about the clothes she was wearing, a particularly fetching royal blue corduroy trouser suit. They would get to know one another better, however, when Beryl was playing an elf in Wolfit's production of *A Midsummer Night's Dream* with Frank playing Lysander. Outfits were again the topic of conversation. Beryl on this occasion was wearing a tunic and was required at one point to sit on her knees on the floor of the stage. Frank was in the stalls during a rehearsal and couldn't help but notice that the outfit suggested that Beryl was wearing nothing underneath. Ever the gentleman, he swiftly pointed out that she might prefer a less revealing outfit, after which she made hasty alterations to her undergarments.

Frank's own acting talents had attracted Beryl's attention for all the wrong reasons. She had seen his interpretation of Bassanio in *The Merchant of Venice*. Renowned theatre critic James Agate had reviewed the show extensively and yet mentioned only the characters rather than the performers, something which irked Frank because it transpired that Agate wrote the review without actually attending the performance. Frank did concede, however, that 'considering my own opinion of Bassanio, it may be as well that he did not come'. After seeing a production of *Merchant of Venice* while training in the RAF, Frank wrote home to Beryl of a dreadful ham in the part: 'Bassanio was much worse than me – need any more be said?' The critique of his work from Beryl was somewhat more succinct: 'She thought I was the worst Bassanio she had ever seen.'

Where Frank had to combine his acting studies with a paid desk job when learning his craft at drama school in order to pay his way, Beryl had fewer challenges. While she had no formalised training, Beryl's maternal grandparents had been somewhat more affluent. Hailing from north Wales, Beryl's grandparents were Porthmadog ship people, which funded their comparatively well-off lifestyle. Her grandmother retained receipts from the finest clothing and material stores. Undoubtedly this was passed down through the generations to Beryl, who of course loved to host social gatherings with standards, and one of the most frequent comments on her during research was that she was always elegantly turned out. Her father's family had a very different career, hailing from workers in the slate quarries.

After its pre-London tour, the opening night of Gielgud's *Macbeth* at the Piccadilly Theatre in July 1942 saw audiences back to pre-war levels. With a selection of bow-tied celebrities enjoying front-row seats, Frank recalled how 'everybody from Macbeth to the Third Murderer had thousands of unctuous friends congratulating them'; although he himself hastily made his getaway, in one of the first indications that widespread adulation was not a priority for him.

When the reviews for *Macbeth* came in, Frank had even less reason to doubt his career choice. The *Telegraph* claimed that the much-anticipated production had one of the strongest casts ever seen on one stage. But of course, there was a certain amount of truth in what Wolfit had told him about his career move. While he had revelled in the more enjoyable atmosphere Gielgud encouraged, Frank knew that even the most extensive reviews would not actually get so far down the billing as to review his interpretation of Angus. But it mattered not. He reflected, 'I shall always remember *Macbeth* as the show in which I played a small part in the centre of the stage... and John Gielgud as one of the nicest producers I've ever worked for.'

Frank played in *Macbeth* for all one hundred and nine London performances, having appeared in seventy-three on tour; and thoroughly enjoyed his altogether different experience, right down to the more elaborate costumes and make-up, something Wolfit was notoriously reluctant to spend money on, which Frank said made him look like any one of his maternal grandfathers, a costive goat or Jesus Christ!

Of course, Gielgud's initial challenges in recruiting actors for *Macbeth* were not a challenge isolated to him. The dreaded call-up was always just one communication away for those eligible and, while being prepared to do his duty, Frank was all too aware of the realities such a summons would bring. Towards the end of the *Macbeth* run he recalled the final performance of Alan Badel, noting that he left 'with the air of a soul condemned to the everlasting bonfire'. He himself had only been promoted to the role of Angus due to a call-up; and upon the end of *Macbeth* he was almost immediately brought in to replace another departing soon-to-be soldier within the cast of the H. M. Tennent production of Daphne du Maurier's *Rebecca*.

While working with Gielgud, Frank had one eye on how next he would earn a wage. Minor roles would not keep him fed and watered for long, and so he took Gielgud's recommendation that he contact his brother Val to see if there were any opportunities in BBC drama on the radio. The response was sadly negative, with drama auditions having seemingly been suspended indefinitely. Despite the news, his persistence in contacting a variety of people at Broadcasting House resulted in him getting some consistent work on *London Calling Europe*, part of the information and propaganda efforts during the years of conflict.

Frank was delighted to have made it into what he referred to as 'the marble and red tape portals' of the BBC and made his first appearance with broadcasters Alan Wheatley and Elizabeth Cowell, the latter having been one of the very first announcers for the corporation.

Frank's diction was perfect for such work, recording such grandiose titles as 'Stalin's Russia', 'The Shadow of 1918' and 'Polish Navy Day', appearing many times from late 1942 through to the summer of 1943. He was further recommended for additional broadcasting work in October 1943; but, as so often during wartime, his fate was in other hands.

After the two weeks on *Rebecca*, Frank had been preparing for rehearsals for a one-week run in *Housemaster* at the Richmond Theatre when he received the letter he had been dreading, headed OHMS. Sure enough, it contained a command to attend a selection board assessment on 24th November 1942 at Euston House for flying with the Royal Air Force. He accepted a request from H. M. Tennent to do three lines and three understudies, which while not particularly enthralling would keep him in the city to the last minute. Ironically, Frank's final role before his assessment came the previous night in *Flare Path*, Terrence Rattigan's highly charged and hugely successful play about RAF airmen and their sweethearts as they faced potential death in bombing raids. Frank's role was a minor part as Corporal Wiggy Jones, a perpetually cheerful airman; but he was decidedly not cheerful at the prospect of taking up a military position.

The following day Frank headed off at 8.30am, armed with a letter from H. M. Tennent requesting the presence of F. T. Ball at the Apollo Theatre by 5.30pm if possible so that he could appear in that evening's performance of *Flare Path*. This gained him the red pencil comment of 'priority' so instead of waiting in crowds for up to several days as many were forced to, he went through the process on day one, managing to return by 6.15 in time for his evening's walk-on.

'The selection board schemozzle consisted of a variety of maths, general knowledge and aptitude tests,' remembered Frank, 'most of them that a five-year-old child could do with his eyes shut and his hands tied behind his back, frequent requests from corporals for complimentary seats to *Flare Path* and man-to-man chats with Wing Commanders (on what effect) on the theatre and such like. I was eventually accepted for flying duties even when I said I couldn't swim and didn't like cricket. I imagine I shall be a navigator as something in my sight barred me from a pilot's job.' Frank would later joke that he chose flying duties because fliers had sheets on their beds while the rest only had blankets.

Frank was subsequently told that despite his acceptance, owing to training facilities being shut he would, in common with the rest of the intake, be put on deferred service for eight months. And so that day he left the assessment board as No. 1811967, AC2, Ball, F. T. and returned to his role in *Flare Path* for the foreseeable future, although his confidence was somewhat shaken.

He was asked to stand in for Leslie Dwyer, who would of course gain television notoriety decades later as grouchy Punch and Judy man Mr Partridge in *Hi-de-Hi!* and Frank considered only his first short-notice performance as Sergeant Dusty Miller of merit, with a subsequent five performances deteriorating in quality as he became more and more conscious of his position as a stopgap. Just a few weeks later he had a similarly urgent need to understudy, this time for George Cole, where he was equally frustrated by his initial performance, a harsh self-criticism given that he had less than twenty-four hours' notice and no rehearsals with props or principals. Writer Terrence Rattigan was happy enough, but the unsettling clock was ticking for F. T. Ball.

That Frank returned to Rattigan's *Flare Path* was a somewhat ironic step. He applied to be considered for the cast of *Journey Together*, an RAF film about the importance of navigators within the team of a bomber crew, something Frank would be trained on in the very near future. Years later when corresponding with the Imperial War Museum, he wrote:

> I was told there was no question of my being released for a film because I was untrained air crew. The fact that I then had to kick my heels at Heaton Park for fourteen weeks before then going to No 1 A.O.S. Malton, Ontario was a mite frustrating, particularly as I knew of two other ex-actor untrained air crew who got into the picture. They, however, had taken the precaution of becoming stars before joining the RAF. I believe one of them was posted to ACRC – normally a three-week entry process – and never left it, which was mightily convenient for excursions to stage or studio during the day and back in barracks (commandeered blocks of luxury flats) before 'Lights Out'.

The irony of course was in the fact that one of the writers of *Journey Together*, which eventually starred Richard Attenborough and Jack Watling, was one Terence Rattigan.

The clock also seemed to be ticking for Frank and Beryl. As he toured while Beryl remained in London with Wolfit's company, their relationship hit the rocks. Years later during Frank's appearance as the subject of *This is Your Life*, he recalled how he had briefly broken off their relationship. With the razor-sharp timing that comes from what was then fifty-three years of marriage, she swiftly interjected, '*You* broke it off?' Letters between the pair in the spring of 1943 do indeed suggest that Beryl had at some level decided things were not working. Frank wrote on a number of occasions to see where they stood, asking if she was still happy to meet or whether she was looking for a complete break. Whatever the reason for the bump in the road, they patched up their differences as Frank awaited his final call to leave with the RAF.

On the 14th and 21st September 1943, Frank took the part of Flight Lieutenant Teddy Graham in *Flare Path*, an experience he admitted was pleasant but a trifle frightening. Less than a week later he confirmed:

On Monday, 27th September '43 the stage saw my back for some time to come. From ten months of well-fitting RAF uniform (Corporal, Sergeant and Flight Lieutenant) I passed to Christ knows how many months of ill-fitting RAF uniform (AC2) and remain stewing in the personal frustration of Democracy's Fight for Freedom. In regarding the ulcerated condition of many young actors' stomachs, I can but retain as my motto whilst serving my King and Country, 'Per duodenal ad Thespis'.

With that brave stab of reflective Latin, Frank headed off to St John's Wood and eventually to Torquay for training before heading to the Despatch Centre in February of 1944.

While he and his new collection of friends waited at the RAF Air Crew Despatch Centre at Heaton, Manchester, with waits of a few weeks not uncommon, the cadets were assigned a variety of tasks. They were given a booklet upon arrival with a welcoming message from their commanding officer, including the warning that, 'Each Cadet who succeeds in his training at the earliest possible moment will shorten the war, and each Cadet who falls by the wayside lengthens the war.' The same booklet contained a section referring to Heaton Park Station Radio, with a suggestion that anybody with broadcasting experience or entertainment talents of any kind should leave their details in the cafeteria's Station Radio box, with the assurance of a speedy reply.

F. T. Ball was not going to let that opportunity pass and so he responded and was assigned to the broadcasting unit. Frank later clarified this as 'a fancy name for a small hut with a microphone in it, from which station announcements were sent out over the Tannoy and light music from the BBC played in the middle of the day to help lunch go down and, believe me, it needed all the help it could get'.

Alongside Frank was Leading Aircraftsman J. Herrod, who Frank described as 'an ebullient character who radiated optimism'. Despite admitting that he himself was a somewhat dour young man at the time, Frank struck up a lifelong friendship with his radio hut colleague, who would become better known after the war as comedian Johnny Ladd. He emigrated to Australia and became one of the country's favourite funny men on stage.

Frank set sail on the RMS *Andes* from Liverpool on 20th May 1944 on a seven-day voyage bound for Nova Scotia and then travelling eventually to Ontario. A number of his travelling companions fell victim to seasickness owing to the availability of an array of comparative luxuries in the form of chocolate, sweets, tinned fruit and condensed milk! Frank himself had no issues though and was more than ready to indulge in the free coffee and doughnuts awaiting them at the quayside upon docking.

From the port they travelled by train through stunning countryside of thickly populated woods, punctuated by the occasional small village with no platforms at their station and no guard rails at their crossings – no more than a sign, a red light and a bell to warn potential rail walkers of oncoming peril.

After his lengthy journey, Frank finally arrived in Moncton, from where he wrote home to Beryl:

> Moncton is not exactly a whirl of gaiety. Apart from the houses, there is about one main street for shopping containing innumerable barbers, a drug store incorporating soda fountains (or should I say, chemists incorporating milk bars). There is some rationing – sugar, butter, tea and coffee and petrol; chocolate is in somewhat short supply compared with pre-war standards, but it's still a long way from the state of affairs at home. So far, I haven't had much opportunity to get around and see things, but I think things might be quite interesting.

Despite the quaintness of his new home, Frank could not help already pining for his life in England:

> I might be able to send a small present or three from this land of (comparative) plenty, but I wish I could take you into one of these drug stores or our camp canteen and indulge in doughnuts and a bottle of milk, topped by an ice cream cornet of lavish proportions.

A common theme in his letters to home was the despair of missing his beloved and working out how he could make his meagre income cover presents for her.

The brighter side of his new location was that Frank saw an opportunity to get to New York and sample the shows there on Broadway that he had read so much about in his copies of *Theatre Arts*. Finances were stretched as he lived solely on his RAF wages, his savings at home being inaccessible. And then there was the small matter of his obligations to the war effort. If these factors outside of his control were to deny him his trip to the Big Apple, he had to console himself with letters from home as he yearned for the simplicity of meeting Beryl somewhere in Euston for a cup of tea.

Frank's training was going exceedingly well, despite a distinct lack of desire or enjoyment on his part. His flying time started in July of 1944 as he went into the skies as second and then first navigator to a number of pilots in an Avro Anson Mark IV, a British-made plane powered by engines installed in Canada. He recorded his flight details and times in his logbook, on the cover of the first of which he had fearfully written the line, 'This is indeed a bloody business.'

Frank's first two flights lasted just short of six hours between them. His initial interest quickly waned, but he was particularly wary of the impact of failure should he not excel. He wrote home:

> They haven't yet decided that I'm no good for aircrew, but I don't think it will take them very long. I went for my first flight yesterday. At first it was quite interesting, but later on I got heartily bored, went to sleep, woke up – not sick but thoroughly fed up with flying as a pastime. Cooped up in a small box a mile or two up doing arithmetic is an occupation for which I feel so unsuited that I don't know what will happen about it. But should I fail the course, I don't know where they will send me. It might be England, but it will just as likely not.

By September Frank had started night flying. He found the visuals more interesting than the routine daytime flights, seeing an elegant tranquillity in the lit towns below. His concerns about failing the course were by now largely unfounded. He topped the scores in his seventh week exams, despite conceding that he had barely done any work for them. His photographic memory that impressed his colleagues was proving useful. By week fourteen, he was still coming out tops, but his success only served to frustrate him further, guiltily reflecting, 'It's really very discouraging to spend my time bemoaning my divorce from the stage and my utter unsuitability for this existence and then to be treated as the bright boy of the class.'

Frank's appetite for the theatre was finally fed when he eventually made it to Manhattan in the winter of 1944, having been delayed until the completion of his training, combined with a lack of finance and an outbreak of infantile paralysis in the city. He had kept his eye on theatre whenever it came close enough to him in Canada, but found the weaker productions only made him pine for home more. After a particularly poor production of *The Merchant of Venice*, he bemoaned, 'I spent a most miserable evening (by myself) after almost weeping with nostalgia just as the curtain was going up.'

Frank had completed his training on 30th November, coming second on his course before being commissioned on 1st December. The resultant days of leave allowed him to head for the bright lights of Broadway, where he spent a week at the Soldiers and Sailors Club on Lexington Avenue. He needn't have worried too much about the financial implications as he came to realise that it was possible to get into most shows for free courtesy of his uniform and American hospitality making it almost impossible to spend money.

What he saw there – essentially every play worth seeing in the space of seven days – was a welcome respite, letting him back into the world in which he felt most comfortable. It was such a success that he even pondered attempting to get onto a Canadian tour at the end of the war if they ever transferred to Broadway.

'New York is, to say the least of it, interesting,' he enthused in his next letter home. 'Streets crammed with highly coloured taxis driven by homicidal maniacs, some rather tall buildings and miles of neon lighting and flashing signs. Combined with the shop windows, which are full of everything but cigarettes (bad shortage) this creates an incredibly prewar atmosphere.'

In all, Frank made his money stretch further than he expected, taking in two symphony concerts, an ice show, a broadcast and thirteen theatrical shows, highlighting Margaret Sullavan in *The Voice of the Turtle* as a particular delight, along with the original Broadway production of *Oklahoma!* at the St James Theatre. After his joyous week in Manhattan, he returned to a White Christmas in Moncton, exhilarated by his experience and now desperate to return home to recover his career.

During his stay in North America, the temptations of the flesh were the same for Frank as for any young serviceman miles away from home. His eye was caught, but his head was not turned by the locals that he would meet at a station dance or some such event. They would keep his attention for barely five minutes, but his true love was back at home looking for work after leaving the services of Donald Wolfit.

As Frank prepared to return to Great Britain in early 1945, he became firmly of the opinion that Beryl Evans was the woman he wanted to marry. He recalled on his *This is Your Life* in 1998: 'For some reason or another we got on the boat to come back and we anchored in the Clyde on a very cold January day and I suddenly had the idea – I think I'd like to marry this girl.'

Upon return to Britain Frank wasn't able to return to civilian life immediately, having been a comparatively late call-up to the forces. His immediate future lay at the No. 4 Observer Advanced Flying Unit at RAF West Freugh near Stranraer, but with his nine days of leave granted he returned to London to tie the knot with Beryl.

Frank and Beryl married on 5th June 1945 at the Emmanuel Church at The Grove, West Wickham, where former fellow Wolfit company pal Richard Lyndhurst, uncle of Nicholas Lyndhurst, acted as best man.

For most of his remaining working days with the RAF, Frank was stationed at Stormy Down in Glamorganshire which sadly meant he could not be released when Beryl gave birth to their only child, Jane, in March 1946. Frank spent that evening behind the projector, keeping him away from home and indeed from any updates.

Beryl was less concerned about Frank's absence than she was the fact that there was a production of *Jane Eyre* on BBC Radio that evening, so she needed to be done by 6pm – and she was, Jane arriving just in time for Beryl to hear the show.

Frank's enforced absence from the birth and the inability to see his new daughter in the immediate few days afterwards due to Frank's other operators being on leave gave rise to immense frustration for him as he wrote home to Beryl:

It seems to put you on a rather different level to me, as one of the people who have never done anything big or had any really shattering experience... I seem to feel that you are a woman now and I am still a youth. Writing is so damnably inadequate – it's the medium for cold, dispassionate conveyance of fact – and I just want to be with you and say whatever comes into my head and listen to whatever comes into yours or just be silent – which will really be sufficient.

Parenting wasn't something that came particularly easily to Frank and Beryl. They weren't naturally demonstrative people, coming from an age when affection had to take its place within the manners of a bygone era. School and the successful raising of a child were as much about learning discipline as they were about education. It's no great surprise that while a gentle man, Frank's adoration of Jane wasn't always demonstrated. Actress Madeline Smith, who became great friends with the Thorntons, remembered that 'he absolutely adored Jane, he was always talking about her'; but it wasn't always evident in his own direct contact with his daughter. One can only imagine the scowls that made Captain Peacock so famous aimed in the direction of a child. Years later, a more reflective Frank apologised to Jane for being too tough on her during her childhood.

Jane herself very quickly determined that the stage was not for her. She endured a certain amount of teasing at school, given the frequency with which Frank was seen on television, particularly commercials. But Frank was not so much of a disciplinarian as to enforce his career choice on his daughter. He knew too well that the theatre, much like any industry at that time, presented significant challenges for women. Nonetheless he was very happy with her choice to move into stage management over being 'out front'. He was particularly proud the first time people referred to him as Jane Thornton's father as opposed to referring to Jane as Frank Thornton's daughter.

Once back in London on leave, Frank found himself walking past Berman's, a theatrical costumier in Irving Street. An airman coming towards him raised his arm in salute, Frank wearing his officer's uniform. After returning the salute, Frank realised to his surprise that the airman was none other than Johnny Ladd, with whom he had shared the microphone in the Broadcasting Unit in his despatch centre days. The pair got chatting and Ladd revealed that he had tried to return to performing by getting a posting in Ralph Reader's RAF Gang Shows, but he had been unsuccessful. Having previously worked in an accountant's office, he was commissioned to work as an accounts clerk.

The chance encounter however gave Frank the idea of applying too. He was accepted, but as a commissioned officer he was not allowed to perform, so it was an administrative role that awaited him. He was posted to the RAF Entertainment Unit, Air Ministry (Gang Shows), ten days after the birth of his daughter. Ladd subsequently had reason to be grateful to Frank as in his new role he was able to convince Johnny's commanding officer to release him for the Gang Shows, in which he stayed until his demob and which proved a pivotal turning point in his own career.

There were a variety of roles assigned to Frank as he waited patiently for his final release from the RAF. His main set-up was in offices at Victoria where a troop of stage hopefuls would pass before his eyes. His staff at various points consisted of future stars John Forbes-Robertson, Robert Moreton, Peter Sellers and a certain Tony Hancock. 'It wasn't much like an office with that sort of staff,' he once recounted. 'We used to play poker under the counter when the Wing Commander wasn't around.'

Hancock and Sellers also used to pretend that they knew everyone in show business when customers would come to collect costumes. Certainly, a tricky bunch to keep an eye on. Frank also recalled that as they were auditioning for people to go to such far-flung places as Japan, 'there was another airman hanging around the place ready to play the piano – by name Derek Scott'. Scott would actually perform a double act with Hancock as well as Terry-Thomas before having an illustrious career in film and theatre musical direction.

Frank remembered when contributing to the book *Fifty Years of Hancock's Half Hour*: 'I had to go round and watch all the shows, meeting all the participants. I remember seeing this one show and a man walked on playing this dismal character; he did this number which ended "I've 'ad it" and I thought: This man is good, he's going somewhere.'

Despite going on to be a huge fan of The Goons, Frank was slightly less convinced of the direction Peter Sellers would take. 'Pa said Peter

Sellers wasn't a very good actor, but he was a very good mimic,' remembered Jane Thornton

Hancock was clearly an interesting character to Frank and one whose career he followed with interest. He once reminisced:

> I shall always remember a party Johnny [Ladd] gave one evening. While Kenneth Williams was holding forth alarmingly in one room, the house-proud Mr Ladd was in another, on his hands and knees with a dustpan and brush sweeping up behind Tony Hancock, who had arrived with a brown paper bag of prawns, from which he was stuffing his face and scattering the shells on the floor.

Frank and Hancock would of course become reacquainted memorably at the height of Tony's career.

Frank's own performing was limited at this point to *Double Bedlam*, a BBC Light Programme comedy thriller starring Naunton Wayne and Basil Radford. Something he would have to get used to in the coming years at the BBC, Frank was cast as the minor authority figure of Sergeant Byng, but it was work if nothing else. It helped supplement his military pay as he waited for his final release as Flying Officer at No. 1 PDC Warton, Lancs on 5th March 1947. Time for the Ball to be dropped once more and for actor Frank Thornton to recommence his career.

3

Blaze of Glory

WITH FRANK FINALLY FREE TO BEGIN ACTING AGAIN, he was effectively starting from scratch. As impressive as it was to have the names of Wolfit and Gielgud attached to his acting CV, with so many ex-servicemen seeking employment on the stage it meant that he was competing with a deluge of acting hopefuls looking for work, many of whom had been able to gain a few years' head start on him. Frank's inability to go straight back on stage meant he had fallen down the order somewhat. This was demonstrated by a letter exchange he had with Dorothy Slack, Assistant Administrator at the Cambridge Arts Theatre Trust.

Taking an assumed name of Thornton Glossop, Frank wrote requesting an interview to discuss the possibilities of a career, highlighting significant amateur theatrical experience. It was a request of sincerity, albeit with tongue firmly in cheek as he described himself as a member of the Chipping Sodbury Operatic and Dramatic Society (CSODS), a fictitious organisation whose work, Frank proudly proclaimed, had been given an honourable recognition by being affiliated to the National Farmers' Union.

The earnest response clearly didn't recognise the undertones of playfulness, but it did highlight the challenges Frank was now facing. Slack replied:

> I do feel that I should try to dissuade you from attempting to take up a stage career at this moment. The profession, like so many others, has become overcrowded, and so many of our young men are coming back from the forces now and are finding it extremely difficult to get started again.

The echoing of Frank's father's concerns over the fragile nature of an acting career were also touched upon as Slack concluded:

> The stage is a terribly uncertain and very unsatisfactory career for anyone unless they have private means or an uncontrollable urge towards the theatre as a career. There are so many other ways of earning a living, and at the same time there are amateur associations from which you could get a tremendous amount of satisfaction and enjoyment without having to put up with the heartbreaks and disappointments which are inseparable from a stage career.

While Frank didn't necessarily have the requisite private means, he did have the uncontrollable urge.

The response didn't tell Frank anything he didn't already know, although he couldn't resist sending another letter in which he advised that he had 'already taken your sage advice and returned to muck-spreading and once-weekly rehearsals in the village halls of dear old Chipping S'. But the light-hearted exchange did reflect the challenges Frank was facing.

He sent a barrage of notes to the BBC in an attempt to get more consistent paid work. His initial exchanges with Heather Dean within the Drama Booking department were sincere as he pleaded, 'As my time in the RAF can now be measured in days, could you grant me the opportunity of meeting you in your office one morning as I should like to re-establish the contacts I had before joining the RAF in 1943.'

The response was a respectful suggestion that a direct approach to producers would be more appropriate and potentially be more fruitful, but it proved not to be the case. Indeed, among the many 'thank you, but we have limited opportunities at this time, but we will keep you in mind should anything come up' replies was one that simply suggested he should approach the Drama Booking department, back where he started!

So it was that while he attempted to break into the corridors of power of the BBC, Southsea saw Frank Thornton finally return to the stage – or more precisely, the South Parade Pier where he would begin a twelve-week repertory stint for Barry O'Brien and Bernard Delfont, mixing *The Gleam*, *Lovers' Leap* and *Love in a Mist*. He somewhat sarcastically noted of his return on 14th April 1947, 'My theatrical career opens in a blaze of glory on the jetty at Southsea.'

The rep season was an unobtrusive but well-received selection, but nothing meaty enough for Frank to get his teeth into, nor substantial enough to bring home much in the way of income. There was more significant work just around the corner: a long run in a musical, starting at the Davis Theatre in Croydon, though it very nearly signalled a swift end to Frank's career.

The Dancing Years, an Ivor Novello piece following the life of a Jewish composer in the early twentieth century, would begin a tour on 25th August 1947. Frank's role was that of Franzel, opposite Nicolette Roeg. But despite the lengthy tour that offered an income and security for his fledgling family, all was not well for Frank Thornton and his career would soon be under threat.

The show itself had a successful but troubled time. Mollie Moselle, assistant stage manager at the Empire, Sunderland when the play reached there in early 1949, went missing. Seemingly heartbroken over a letter from a spurning lover, she left the digs she was staying at and was never seen again. Her disappearance remained unsolved and to this day rumours abound that her ghost haunts the theatre (along with that of Sid James, who passed away on stage in 1976). Moselle's unexplained disappearance was even the subject of a Thames Television documentary in 1992.

Frank's own unrelated dramas had happened a few months before-hand, in October 1948. Frank was taken to one side at the end of a week of performances at the Coventry Hippodrome. Barry Sinclair, the lead performer as Rudi Kleber, suggested that Frank take a week out of the show to get himself together. Despite having been with the production for a full year, Frank's performances were getting increasingly unsettled by a developing stammer, something that he had never struggled with before. This was his first musical play, but Frank could only attribute his speech problems to being inexperienced as a romantic juvenile lead.

Despite both the play and Frank himself having had largely positive reviews, he returned home on the night sleeper train, mulling over his unwelcome difficulties and struggling to convince himself that his career wasn't already over.

The time off didn't work. He returned to the role when the play reached the Granada, Tooting after the requested sabbatical, but his comeback lasted only three nights – 'Wednesday night's performance finishing me off' – and he left the show on 27th October 1948, seemingly finished as an actor.

Frank turned in desperation to his GP, Dr Leslie Golding, who in turn recommended that Frank see a speech therapist gaining a fine reputation at that time by the name of Dr Leopold Stein.

Dr Stein, or Simon as he was more familiarly known by those closest to him, was born in Vienna but, when the Nazis reached Austria, he obtained enough support to convince the Immigration Department that his research into speech defects and therapy would be a valuable addition to the field for any psychological clinic in Britain. As such, the Home Office concurred and allowed him to settle in London where he would go on to head up speech therapy research at the Tavistock Clinic and also become the adviser in speech therapy to the War Office.

At the time of Frank's career-threatening speech defect, Dr Stein was becoming an eminent, if somewhat provocative expert in the field; in an obituary for Dr Stein in 1969, Joan H. van Thal, herself a pioneer in speech therapy, noted that 'controversy was the breath of life to him and from the first he stimulated British speech therapists into trying to think clearly'.

While Frank's issues became unsustainable and he despaired as to the chances of his career surviving, Dr Stein was taking part in the hugely successful International Speech Conference in London.

Dr Stein's speech outlined his approach to stammering, which was essentially that 'the development of the individual is a brief recapitulation of the evolution of the race', and it was a belief that would form the basis of his 1949 book entitled *The Infancy of Speech and the Speech of Infancy*.

Since Frank's return to acting after his RAF duties, success had been limited as he effectively rejoined the industry several years behind those free to work immediately at the end of hostilities. Dr Stein believed that stammers were invariably induced by a breakdown between thought and utterance, and the reasons for this disassociation could remain unconscious in the mind for a considerable length of time, while attempts to effectively self-diagnose and treat the issue once it became apparent were inevitably doomed to failure.

'This blind-alley situation recurs at intervals, entailing a number of characteristic stages, and ultimately leads to complete discouragement and resignation,' wrote Stein in *The Lancet*. That was certainly borne out by Frank's own feelings at the time as he noted that 'I departed ignominiously, never to act again, I thought.'

Dr Stein had a number of approaches, effectively encouraging the victim of the stammer to return to the more basic form of childhood babbling in an effort to evolve speech once again. In writing at the time of the way to treat stammering, Stein appropriately compared the stammerer's experience to that of an actor:

> The normal speaker constantly behaves like an actor whose performance is in all its details dictated by the 'scene of action'. The stammerer finds himself in the same theatre of life, but the scenery is different, in that spooky objects belonging to the background (past) are frequently shifted to the proscenium where they harass the speaker by incessant pranks. In conclusion, it must be admitted that how stammering comes to be 'chosen' is still unknown.

Stein also noted that options such as Barry Sinclair's suggestion that Frank should 'sort himself out', in a break from the show, while well-meaning, would actually do more harm than good.

One of Stein's theories was that a stammer signified a regression to an earlier stage of development, a yearning to go back to a more secure stage of life with an affectionate maternal relationship. Certainly Frank, being significantly younger than his two siblings, was deemed to be the favourite of the three, and Frank's earlier jolly songs do suggest that his mother was a jovial lady with a warm, but sadly, weak heart.

Stein's summation is intriguing:

Everything should be done to get the patient away from the perfectionism which hides his fear and, at the same time, endeavour to give him insight into the causes of the inner battle created by clinging to the beloved mother on the one hand and striving for independence on the other.

For all of his career Frank strived for perfection in his work, and inevitably came across as a confident man who knew a good actor from a bad one and had strong opinions on every aspect of stage and screen work. And yet, as we will discover, he consistently downplayed his talents and achievements, kept clear of stardom and was seen as shy in some ways despite his perceived 'loveable curmudgeon' demeanour at times.

Perhaps it was the time of his life that was affecting his speech, returning to British shores to marriage and parenthood and a career that had been stunted by nearly five years of stagnation due to his RAF service. Either way, Frank needed to rid himself of his new stammer and get back to acting.

Stein subjected Frank to a sovereign mixture of psychological lectures ('giving me a good talking to' in Frank's words!) and what Frank saw as technical tricks in an attempt to rescue him from his slump, designed to get him over speech hurdles as they arrived. With *The Dancing Years* having finished in Frank's absence, luck would furnish his path back to the stage with the perfect opportunity.

Frank's treatment allowed him to successfully audition for a walking understudy to the juvenile and character juvenile in *One Wild Oat* at the Garrick Theatre in early 1949. It gave him a wage – a much needed twelve pounds a week (he did after all have a three-year-old child to support) – but his 'role' was minor enough to carry no responsibility to an audience. It was the perfect opportunity to recover some confidence while not losing an income, and he was rewarded for his resilience when the show went on tour in early 1950, gaining the juvenile part of Gregory Throstle – ironically, a minor character with a stammer.

Frank's stammer never reappeared, and he maintained a lasting gratitude to both Dr Stein and his GP Dr Golding for navigating what was without doubt the trickiest time of his career.

At the same time as Frank was easing his way back into stage work, his attempts to find a way into the BBC finally appeared to come to fruition.

In February 1949 he was granted an audition for the BBC's Drama department, with a similar opportunity a month later for the Features department. He headed off on 15th February for a late afternoon audition that had the potential to be the big break with the corporation that he had been waiting for.

Frank performed three pieces: one from a Noël Coward play, one from *Richard III* and the other as Mr Manningham from Patrick Hamilton's *Gaslight*, a thriller that was a popular theatre production around the time and had received two movie interpretations to great success. Alas, that success was not to be repeated for Frank. His Coward was dismissed with the suggestion that he had not much sense of comedy – a strange critique for a drama audition – while his Manningham was unconvincingly remarked upon as 'quite good, deepish – harshness shows'. His American accent was dismissed as 'not much good' and this left merely narration as his only potential success as he was described as 'useful for straight narration'.

The dismissal of his Coward attempt was cemented by a second report which suggested that Frank had 'no sense of light comedy', a comment that history can now mock given the incredible success he would achieve at the BBC in the subsequent sixty years.

If that audition failed to wow the corporation talent hunters, worse was to come at the Features one. Offering nothing more complimentary than Frank having a pleasant, deepish voice and good diction, it concluded with a blunt 'Sounds sinister – No.' It would take only days for the Features Organiser to inform Frank that he would not be among those chosen for a second audition.

Despite the setback, in 1950 Frank took a first tentative step into live television, compèring *The Centre Show*, a programme put on for the forces at the Nuffield Centre, a recreational facility for servicemen and women. *The Centre Show* had first appeared in 1943 when the Centre was located in the bomb-damaged remains of the Café de Paris, before it moved to Charing Cross in 1946. The Nuffield Centre itself was a bit of everything: cafeteria, barber's, tailor's, with a twice-weekly variety show. While these periodic hosting duties did not propel Frank to instant stardom, they were nonetheless valuable tools. Benny Hill, with whom

Frank would work many times during his early television days, credited the same compèring duties as having led to him getting his very first television series.

The Centre Show was essentially a variety talent show. Amongst those getting their break on Frank's first show as compère were Leslie Wilson, a comic magician from Esher, Dennis Robertson, a comedy mime, and Marie Reidy, a soprano singing folk songs while playing the harp. Another was Hugh Lloyd, whose future partnership with Terry Scott would provide Frank with a pivotal career opportunity in the form of *Hugh and I*, produced by David Croft and co-starring one Mollie Sugden. Years later Lloyd would recall how Frank was already offering words of encouragement to the young hopefuls: '*The Centre Show* was a sort of stand-up comedy show. It was a first for most of us and there were lots of nerves. But I think it was Frank who gave me some wonderful advice for television: to imagine I was performing to one person. It's stood me in good stead ever since.'

In one of his subsequent shows, Frank would introduce Dick Emery, another friend who would appear many times alongside Frank in his own show years later. Reviews were quite kind, with the only question mark seeming to be how the talent on show was not getting subsequent exposure, given the artists' quality. It was also recorded in front of a live audience, Frank noting that it was the only TV show with a studio audience at that time.

With twelve guineas' pay and only providing two days of work a month, *The Centre Show* was hardly likely to keep food on the table, so Frank set about trying to make best use of the empty days in his diary. He began by once again looking for work at the BBC. Another audition met with a more positive reception than his previous efforts, perhaps because he had now been seen on television. This time, remarks were that he 'has a deep speaking voice, well suited to the mic, a good appearance, sympathetic personality and is altogether a dependable performer. Should prove a useful acquisition for TV purposes.' Quite the prophecy!

Off the back of his latest attempt, Frank managed to secure his first on-screen dramatic role on television, appearing in *The Secret Sharer*, a George F. Kerr adaptation from Joseph Conrad's original short story. He was only an unnamed sailor and was bizarrely referred to in the press as 'an old hand at television'. Factually incorrect, but perhaps indicative of how familiar Frank's face would be to television audiences for the next sixty years!

Despite being keen to break through to any form of acting, Frank was wary, as doubtless many were at the time, of the impact television might have on other mediums. Frank's daughter Jane recalled finding an unopened letter on the subject: 'It had come back to him from America as undeliverable; obviously, he hadn't opened it. He was talking to this man saying how he didn't trust television and television was going to take away from the theatre. He wasn't sure about it at all.'

A review of a play in which Frank was appearing at the time, *The Chiltern Hundreds*, made a more succinct comment on Frank's apparent 'old hand' situation, despite being still only thirty years old. *The Chronicle* suggested, 'Frank Thornton has often been doomed to play parts that are too old for him,' as he portrayed an absent-minded aristocrat in William Douglas Home's play.

In 1952 Frank had been given the role of Vanescu in another Ivor Novello musical, *King's Rhapsody*, setting him up nicely for a long tour. However, the part of Nikki, played by Novello in the original production, saw Jack Buchanan brought in to depose original choice John Palmer. Palmer himself took over as Vanescu, leaving Frank as an understudy: the perils of not yet being a box-office name. Unfortunately for him, Buchanan stayed with the show for thirteen weeks.

After briefly regaining his role for a couple of venues, Frank was again at the mercy of Buchanan's return when the production split into northern and southern tours. It meant sixteen further weeks of being relegated to the sidelines, leaving Frank having played just sixteen weeks in a forty-five-week tour. Reviews such as the *Portsmouth Evening News* reporting that, 'Frank Thornton's Prime Minister was a brilliant piece of acting,' while doubtless welcome, were no match for a full tour and corresponding remuneration and exposure.

It was time for another round of reminders to the powers at the BBC. There was some minimal success initially, collecting a role as Miguel D'Alvarez in *My Dear Petitioner*, but nothing to get him the income or security that he needed. Parts in stage shows came and went as Frank settled into what appeared destined to be a career as a solid supporting character actor.

Later in 1952 he landed a role in *Wild Horses*, which ran at the Aldwych after a five-week tour. It was a Ben Travers farce starring Robertson Hare and Ralph Lynn, two hugely successful farceurs who knew their business very well. When Lynn injured his back during the tour, David Stoll took over, promoting Frank up the cast. With a more significant role, Hare noticed Frank's performance and it was here that he gave Frank advice about his potential future career and his belief that he wouldn't achieve success until he was forty years old – still another nine years away at this point!

With those words of 'encouragement' still ringing in his ears, Frank had a family to feed and rent to pay, and the income from his continuing hosting duties on *The Centre Show* and his stage shows were not going to be enough to cover his expenses. He had already tried his hand as a door-to-door salesman but decided that selling encyclopaedias was not for him. He wasn't averse to the toil involved, but in his mind a successful sale represented convincing someone to buy something they neither needed nor wanted. Deception wasn't something that sat well with him and, as such, he quit after his first day.

Beryl, meanwhile, may have ended her stage career, but she didn't give up work entirely, spending ten years as a receptionist with the Royal Photographic Society at Princes Gate, the building fated to be part of the Iranian Embassy siege in 1980. Frank even got involved, giving a monologue entitled 'Hiawatha's Photographing' in early 1954. But he needed an income.

He had known from the word go that those early days would be a financial struggle. In 1947 he had taken Beryl skiing in Switzerland as he knew that without an established income, further holidays would be unlikely for many years. For his skiing attire, he simply removed the markings from his RAF overalls and used those. His gloomy fiscal prediction was justified, going another seventeen years before a break away. Now, with a sideline in sales not an option, he turned to a family talent in order to raise additional money.

Photography had long been a talent of Frank's, with his father before him being an expert landscape photographer. It was a talent to which Frank tried turning his attention, to see if he had inherited his father's skills. He was getting ample opportunity with the touring of the various productions he was involved with, so he traded in his small folding camera for a Reflex-Korelle in the hope of making the most of the areas of natural beauty he was able to take in upon his travels.

Frank's assessment of his photographic skills was not entirely glowing, which led him to write an article for *Amateur Photographer* in 1951. In some ways it was very reflective of how he would come to view his acting career.

His theory was that without a modicum of natural talent that could be honed and worked upon, there was really no point pursuing a particular path; 'Find your metier, and then stick to it,' was the phrase he used in his article.

He had returned from one particular tour with a hundred and forty-four negatives and of them, he found that only two were of any particular interest; and even then, one of them had been Beryl's idea. 'The results are a series of correctly exposed negatives which show with admirable clarity what was in front of the camera at the time. And that is all that can be said in their favour.' The only product of merit in Frank's view was a photograph of a branch of catkins taken at the shores of Loch Lomond.

Having largely disappointed himself at his success rate with landscape photography, Frank was subsequently approached by an acquaintance who had recently bought a new evening gown and wanted to have some photographs, choosing Frank primarily because he simply appeared to have the best equipment for the job.

Frank did have a relative who had dabbled in portrait photography but had found his own success in landscape photography exhibitions: 'He steers clear of portraiture as his sitters are seldom enthusiastic over the results whereas trees and mountains can't voice any complaints.'

The Thornton family were now living in an old Victorian flat in Nevern Road, Kensington. The flat was across two floors, including a butler's pantry with its own porcelain sink, running water and a large window. Wary of his ability to help, Frank promptly made adjustments to the family home's dining room: buying some photofloods, creating reflectors out of cardboard and aluminium paint, and proceeding to assemble this home-made collection around a stepladder and some chairs. His subject was happy with the results, as indeed was the photographer.

Encouraged by this success, Frank set about making some more permanent adjustments to the flat. The dining room continued to double up as a studio while the butler's pantry became a dark room. He took on more professional equipment as the makeshift cardboard reflectors on the stepladder gave way to appropriate spotlights, diffusers and filters. He would soon start to receive enquiries from a number of budding performers keen to boost their profile with quality *Spotlight* photographs:

> I meet a lot of people of all types, from the aged 'character gentleman' down to the ingenue fresh from drama school, all optimism and eyelashes. There are not so many egomaniacs in the theatre as some people imagine, but even the most modest of the breed have some idea how to sit or stand, are reasonably used to being stared at under studio lighting and, if required, know how to apply make-up. Lastly, they are generally willing to be photographed. At some time or other they all need up-to-date pictures for front-of-house display or for papering the walls of casting directors' offices.

Among the results were pieces for well-known future stars including Hattie Jacques, Peter Jones and Clive Dunn; and theatre programmes from that era can be found to contain Frank's photography within their pages.

As he became more successful, he had to sacrifice his Reflex-Korelle for the appropriate accessories to support this line of photography. It was a bigger success than landscape photography and provided a valuable side income as the search for that breakthrough role continued. His piece in *Amateur Photographer* concluded with the suggestion that any budding novices 'try everything once, in order to find out where their interest and ability lie; to view with suspicion the precept, "If at first you don't succeed, try, try again," but prefer rather, "If at first you don't show a glimmer of success, try something else." In other words, find your metier and stick to it.'

Frank's acting metier was still to be decided. Heading towards the mid-1950s, he was still struggling for paid work. Duplicated letters to the BBC were largely fruitless and increasingly frustrated: 'Unless an empty theatre falls from the skies, one more juvenile character actor will be at liberty on 6th September,' he wrote in 1954. He also made contact with one Ernest Maxin, future producer of *The Morecambe and Wise Show* in its prime. In it, he appealed to Maxin to find time to see a comedy routine that he was trying at the Players. Frank had a trio of solo pieces that he tried during his week there, including 'Artemus Ward', a monologue of an American traveller and lecturer that he had adapted from the original by Charles Farrar Browne. He introduced himself thus:

> I must apologise to you folks. I'm more used to speaking in a field. M'name's Artemus Ward, the great impresario and travelling showman. My amazing exhibition of lifelike waxworks and savage wild beasts is world famous throughout the United States.
>
> I'm very glad for your sakes that Mr Gee-mell here has given me the opportunity of telling you folks about the illustrated lecture I'm a-giving shortly in this town. This lecture of mine is copiously illustrated with breath-taking panoramic pictures beautifully painted in oils. I don't paint myself – though perhaps if I was a middle-aged single lady I should, yet I have a passion for pictures, and I've always been more or less mixed up with Art. I remember once a distinguished sculpist wanted to sculp me. But I said 'No!' I saw through the designing man. My model once in his hands, he would have flooded the market with my bust; everybody'd want one of course – and wherever I went I'd meet the educated classes with my bust in their hands, taking it home for their families. This would be more than my modesty could stand – and I should have to return to America where my creditors are.

The bulk of the lecture discussed the merits or drawbacks of having multiple wives as the Mormons within the lectures were referenced as having. It concluded with:

> Well folks, I've given you a rough idea what's in store for you when you come along in your thousands to my illustrated lecture which is to be given at the Egyptian Hall, Bond Street. And remember, though you cannot expect to come in without paying, you may pay without coming in. And I can't say fairer than that. So goodnight, good luck and here's spitting in your eye.

Frank actually had three pieces that he performed at the Players, the other two being entitled 'Hiawatha's Photographing', the same piece he used at the Royal Photographic Society, and 'The Englishman Abroad', the latter an adaptation from one of his most valued acting pals, Peter Jones. However, it is his Artemus Ward piece that is the most intriguing. There is of course the bizarre nature of the Ward character, coming across almost as an American incarnation of the Mr Moulterd type from the *Are You Being Served?* follow-up *Grace and Favour*. But the more curious parallel is that with the Ward character's creator.

Charles Farrar Browne performed in the mid-nineteenth century as arguably America's first stand-up comedian and was said to be a favourite of Abraham Lincoln. But the parallel comes with his actual character. Ward was said to be an extreme opposite to his creator. T. W. Robertson, co-executor for Browne after his death at the age of just thirty-two, wrote, 'Charles Browne was the least like a showman of any man I have encountered.'

Alas for Frank perhaps the material and his adaptation were too old-fashioned to encourage further work along those lines and his search for more substantial work continued. He did manage to obtain an audition at the BBC with his one-man act in 1955, but the verdict, while positive about the quality, decreed that 'this type of material is highly specialised and might be difficult to place in variety. But with his good appearance, amusing ideas and highly polished style and delivery this should prove well suited for "Old Time" variety programme and possibly compère with the character developed.' Certainly, more encouraging feedback than previous auditions, but no wage at the end of it. Hopes that subsequent income would come in the form of his next play *The Distant Kill* were swiftly dashed, but Frank's talents for the technical element of theatre and television were obvious from his recollections:

The producer, Pierre Rousse, a very charming man, frankly appeared to have more experience of the film studio and directed every small scene as if to be seen by a camera six feet away and when finally polished and the shot was in the can and needed no further attention – thus allowing for the next two pages to be dealt with. We rehearsed for a week and a half before the third act was even read.

The first night ran three hours, and the following morning some of this was removed, as was the producer. From then until the end of the run, rewriting and rehearsal came daily, the rehearsals being as a rule, remarkably drawn-out affairs under the presence of Miss [Wanna] Paul during which the maximum talk produced the minimum effect. There was in fact only one open battle – between two of the three stars – and great credit is due to all artists for a very restrained and demure behaviour, only the occasional murmur of mutiny being heard such as the suggestion that we would all be better off sitting in the pictures.

After a few minor television roles, Frank forlornly noted that his year ended with a temporary role at the GPO, 'at the facing tables of the Western District Office at Wimpole Street. Quite a game! For instance, on Dec 21st, 1,000,594 letters passed through the franking machines!' Alas for Frank, none of them contained the offer yet of a breakthrough role.

The world of film came calling in 1954. Frank had been appearing in a stage version of *Liberty Bill* under the direction of Lionel Harris, with a brief tour planned before opening at the Strand Theatre. Things did not pan out as intended, despite the show boasting once again Frank's old farceur friends Robertson Hare and Ralph Lynn.

The opening night in Blackpool was cancelled and the tour stretched from its initial three weeks to six in order to get things right, but at the end of the tour its Strand opening was pulled to allow for major rewriting. The *Oxford Mail* described the show as 'one of the most unfunny farces which has been let loose on the public for some time'.

Liberty Bill would be reworked and rebranded as *The Party Spirit*, but the two months of unexpected downtime allowed Frank to take on his first decent part in a film, that of Inspector Finch in *Radio Cab Murders* for Vernon Sewell. It wasn't a part to set the world on fire, but things were finally starting to turn.

The Party Spirit had a troubled journey to opening. In its original incarnation it had begun touring in February of 1954. Even as late as September that year the troubles continued as the opening, now at the Piccadilly Theatre, was delayed for two weeks as impresario Cecil Landau, who had a production of *Cockles and Champagne* running at the venue, promptly tried suing the Piccadilly Theatre and lost. 'A most interesting two-and-a-half days spent in court under Mr Justice Sachs,' remembered Frank.

Unlike it had been in its original guise, *The Party Spirit* was far better received as Frank recalled:

The first night reception of *The Party Spirit* was excellent – in fact it was probably the best reception the play had at any time. This reception from an audience of that character should perhaps have worried us that the play was not entirely the cup of tea of the ordinary farce-goer. General opinion seems to be that it falls between farce and satirical comedy. This, combined with having not the most suitable theatre in London, the Piccadilly being rather barn-like and off the map, brought us off after only four months' run.

Close though it did, Frank did substitute one evening for Lynn in the lead role of Leonard Bilker, and when the show wrapped up its West End run it was moved to Windsor where he took the role on a permanent basis. Things were definitely on the up, but the course of a budding actor rarely goes up in a straight line.

By 1955 Frank was getting regular work on stage, screen and radio, even if the exposure on film was still comparatively minor. However, after a few days of filming for *Stock Car* for Wolf Rilla, he went down with rheumatic fever. In his recollections to friend Gyles Brandreth he remembered attempting an audition for the part of Lucky in *Waiting for Godot* for Peter Hall:

I was thirty-four and in bed with a mild attack of rheumatic fever when a script arrived with the request that I read it and then audition for Lucky. After a few pages I took my temperature to reassure myself that I wasn't delirious and wandering. It was 98.7°F: I was in full possession of my faculties, so I read on. When I eventually reached Lucky's monologue I was tempted to take it again. One of the handicaps of this rather simple-minded actor is to be totally incapable of speaking a line if I don't know what it means and here was a whole page of total incomprehensibility. I struggled to the end of the play and handed it to my wife to read. When she pronounced it wonderful stuff and very funny I began to think I really was delirious.

Unemployed and with a bank balance unworthy of the name I had no alternative but to limp off to the New Theatre on my walking stick and present myself for the slaughter. On stage I muttered some lame excuse about being a trifle confused about the exact style required and launched into the speech. It was like standing in a bog, slowly sinking, wondering how long it would take the mud to close over your head.

Mercifully, Mr Hall stopped me, 'Thank you, Mr Thornton, but the orchestra of your voice is not quite what we're looking for.' I hadn't the courage to say, 'What do you want, dear? More flutes?' I just shrunk off.

Some years later Timothy Bateson told me that when they held the auditions he had already been cast. I could have stayed in bed!

Frank's career trajectory was still in the ascendancy when he took a call from Dick Linklater, the Arts Council Assistant Director of Drama. He was encouraged to meet with Frank Dunlop to discuss a part in Peter Ustinov's upcoming tour of a play about the French Revolution, *The Empty Chair*. He liked what he read and took the part of Mouche, the spy with a soul. It was Frank's first fit-up tour since his Yorke-Clopet days but played to a considerably stronger reception as it toured Wales for five weeks to packed houses. When it broke records at the Playhouse, Oxford, Frank earned glowing praise in the local press: 'Special praise, however, should go to Frank Thornton for his gently humorous portrayal of Mouche, the omnipresent spy who served as a kind of chorus to the terror,' with the *Manchester Guardian* calling his performance 'beautifully measured and modulated'.

The gushing reviews of Frank's performance were not always reflected more generally in the press reaction to the show itself; and, away from *The Empty Chair*, Frank began looking beyond.

The bread-and-butter minor television roles were trickling through, but after a brief stint at the Lyceum in *The Whole Truth*, he prepared for what turned out to be a very public battle of wills in a play at the Edinburgh Festival, *The Hidden King*.

Jonathan Griffin's play was getting its world premiere at the Assembly Hall of the Church of Scotland and was the major production of the festival. Griffin described it in his programme notes as 'an adventure story in a Renaissance setting and meant to be enjoyed straightforwardly as that'. It turned out to be anything but.

Frank himself held four parts in a remarkable four-hour production, leading critics to bemoan how anything so long could be deemed as straightforward. His own characters were comparatively minor, but perhaps indicative of the key complaint in the press, exemplified by the *Evening Despatch* who bemoaned that 'while a play lasting about four hours long is not necessarily too long, what is particularly irksome about *The Hidden King* is the feeling that so much time is being wasted on so many words from so many characters.'

What followed on from a general mauling at the hands of the press then turned into a very public spat. The author, producers and cast members of the play met press representatives at the Press Bureau to discuss the criticism. Stephen Mitchell, who along with the Edinburgh Festival Society presented the production, was unrepentant of the play's length and scathing of the press approach:

> I think critics have a responsibility to Edinburgh and the Festival in what they write and the way they write it. I have read the notices with care. Some have been written with care, and others with no care at all. I think some of the critics, as soon as they realised they were getting a long strange work, decided early in the proceedings to throw up their hands and attack it.

From there things simply became more argumentative, the *Express* drama critic John Barber hitting back at what he saw as a disingenuous response from the Festival Arts Director Robert Ponsonby to his summation that a more experienced director than Christopher West was needed. Barber had been particularly cutting, asking and answering his own questions: 'Can it be made into a good play? Never. Can it be made less stupefyingly dull? Yes. CUT IT.'

Frank, like many actors, was never fond of critics. In his days with the Wolfit company he had particular issues with several, including James Agate. When Agate criticised Wolfit's *Merchant of Venice*, Frank acknowledged that his performance as Bassanio was not of great quality, but in noting that Agate had written a lengthy negative review seemingly without actually attending the play, he questioned how it was acceptable to question the character Frank played without writing a word about how he played it. 'Recipe for a dramatic critic,' Frank noted in 1942. '1. Don't see the show. 2. Quote the words of writers long dead. 3. Do it decisively and if possible, in a foreign language.'

When reflecting on a mixed bag of reviews for *Twelfth Night* at the Royal Shakespeare Theatre in Stratford in 1975, Frank remained as bemused by critics as ever:

> A detailed study of all these notices would reveal more about the critics than about the actors. What would a theatrical historian make of the fact that at least four of the principal actors, Nicol Williamson, Jane Lapotaire, Ron Pember

and Frank Thornton all receive notices ranging from 'excellent' and 'the best of all in the production' through 'merely competent' down to 'terrible' and 'the worst'? Can anyone say who was good and bad in absolute terms?

Of the public spat between producers and press for *The Hidden King*, Frank adopted a somewhat more resigned tone:

The three weeks' run were enlivened by the press controversy which became a good publicity stunt and brought us good public support. Despite everything, however, the actions of Messrs Tynan and Robson, who are not often in agreement, were probably the final thing that prevented us venturing into the West End.

With *The Hidden King* at an end, the search continued for Frank. He was getting frustrated and turned to his old company boss Donald Wolfit for advice.

'I don't know, by the time you were thirty-eight you'd done all your Shakespeare, including Hamlet in the West End, you were an actor-manager and you were a success,' he began. 'I've fiddled about for eighteen years, including four in the air force, and although I've kept going, I feel a failure.'

Wolfit would hear none of it. 'Frank, my boy,' he countered. 'You're a success, you're still in it. Think of your contemporaries who were in my company twenty years ago. Where are they now? Post offices and shops.'

A change in agent from MCA to Max Kester undoubtedly improved things for him. He estimated that in the fourteen months he had been with MCA he had found only thirty-five pounds' worth of work, his own personal representative getting him no actual work and only one audition as an eighty-year-old man in a musical. His time with Kester was considerably more successful. The impact was immediate, Frank getting an interview with Basil Appleby of Sapphire Films that resulted in one of his most substantial television roles to that point, a three-month contract on *The Four Just Men*. The relationship with Kester only came to an end in 1981 when Max retired leaving Frank to join forces with Simon Cadell's father John.

With the change in agent, Frank was still canvassing the BBC for more work himself, appealing to the children's television department to expand his scope of work there, while also maintaining his continual search for dramatic work. He even sent in pictures of his performance as Mouche in *The Empty Chair*; 'I may not be as pretty as Alan Badel but I need the money more,' he joked. Kester also blitzed the BBC with requests for work, but Frank would soon find himself getting the biggest break of his career and forging one of the strongest friendships he would ever know – all courtesy of one of the biggest flops he was ever involved with.

4

Where Will It Lead?

ON'T SHOOT WE'RE ENGLISH WAS A COMIC REVUE that had been a
big success on its tour around the country. It had been born from
a television show commissioned in 1958 called *After Hours*,
essentially a late-night chat show with intermingled comedy sketches
broadcast in the Midlands and hosted by former Goon, Michael Bentine.
With a host of future stars within its cast including Dick Emery and Clive
Dunn, such was its success that the idea of converting the best of the
comedy routines into a stage revue was mooted by some wealthy backers.

At the helm of the revue was Richard Lester, who bravely tried to keep
control of a production that had a hefty thirty-three sketches to wade
through. Bentine himself recalled its opening night in Newcastle as being
a night like no other in his stage career, with only three of the scenes
going without a hitch. Included in the disasters was the departure of one
of the spotlight operators after a row with Lester. Lester himself took the
spotlight for the first performance, missing almost all of Bentine's
entrances but, perhaps to Lester's relief, also missing chaotic scenes off
stage. Clive Dunn recalled, 'From the side somebody dropped a stage
weight and the recipient was heard to say in a broad Geordie accent,

"That was my fucking foot." With impeccable timing Mike said, "From time to time you may hear some technical terms bandied about."'

Despite its opening night horrors, critics were largely kind with their reviews. This was after all a stage production from one of the Goons, from whom chaos would surely be a key ingredient of the zany comedy. Amazingly, through audiences believing the show's problems to be all part of the act, and the stoic efforts of its quality cast, *Don't Shoot We're English* was deemed a success, with exceptional box-office takings.

The opening-night dramas, however, were too much for Lester, who pulled out after only a few performances; but, with pressure from the backers, impressed at how good the returns were, the cast soldiered on and embarked on an eleven-week tour. When it came to its final venue in Bournemouth, the offer of a West End residency was made.

At this point, Frank was in London after returning from a tour of Cyprus where, in a five-week stay, he appeared in a revue with Peter Jones, Ollie Halls and Hugh Lloyd among others. With the troubles there at the time, Frank's experience was a mixture of positive reviews and swimming in the Mediterranean in December all under the watchful eye of armed escorts during the height of emergency.

Michael Bentine, meanwhile, was exhausted having carried responsibility for *Don't Shoot We're English* as well as appearing as the compère; so when it transferred to the Cambridge Theatre in London's West End, Frank Thornton was added to the cast on the recommendation of old pal Clive Dunn.

Frank was still in London and looking for work after the failure of what he would later describe as a 'fortunate flop', *The Golden Touch* which told the story of an Armenian shipping magnate and his daughter, Cee Linder and Eveline Kerr respectively, who clash over what to do with a Greek island they arrive at. It had opened in early April 1960 and arrived at the Piccadilly Theatre with some significant backing, but aside from a few tolerable musical numbers, it had very little going for it.

Reviews were kind to the dancing, but not a lot else. In the musical play, Frank had the unlikely part of Bishop Zog of Nixos, the island's bishop who decides to introduce commercialism and curb the freedom of the islanders. Some reviews did their best to find the good points in

The Golden Touch, invariably focusing on the dancing talents of the cast, but critics were harsh about Kerr's vocal talents, despite previous success in *Gigi*, and takings were poor.

Jane Thornton recalls commenting, 'Well, that's not going to last very long, is it Daddy?' and she was proven right – the show closed after just twelve performances. In his 2010 reflection on post-war musical theatre *A Tanner's Worth of Tune*, Adrian Wright noted that, 'There is, so far as I know, no evidence that audiences booed *The Golden Touch* and its like, but it was probably a close call.'

Wright's comment may have been accurate, but the reason for that lack of vocal disapproval could have been down to the number of people who merely left the theatre early, if some reports at the time are to be believed. *The Golden Touch* had been presented by renowned producer Michael Codron, who, in frustration at curtailing the show's West End run so early, vented his angst to the trade publication *The Stage*, bemoaning that, 'I would very much have liked to nurse *The Golden Touch* for, say, six weeks. I had faith in it. And it seems to me with a less destructive approach by some of the critics, this would have been possible. But the production was killed at the outset.'

The production wasn't the first to fail at the Piccadilly and, if nothing else, it did give Frank the opportunity to do his bit for recycling! In years previous, Peter Jones had had stationery printed headed simply 'Piccadilly Theatre, Denman Street, W.1.' He had the expectation of a long run in a show which actually ended in a matter of a few weeks. When Frank was settling into the Piccadilly for *The Golden Touch*, Jones passed the many unused pages on to him with the expectation that if he didn't get through them, he would in turn pass them forwards. The play having ended so swiftly, Frank of course had plenty of this high-quality dark blue paper left, and so he eventually handed it over to Henry McGee in 1997 when he appeared with Peter Bowles in *School for Wives*. McGee made Frank and Beryl his first correspondents, writing, 'I have high hopes that we'll last a mite longer than a fortnight but as I barely write more than a half dozen letters a year, I'm never going to get through it all so I'll just pass the box to some likely lassie or lad with the requirement that the one who finishes the box must get some more printed. I foresee gaps of fifty to a hundred years!' The box having already survived over forty years by 1997, one can only speculate where the stationery went next!

With *The Golden Touch* closed, director and producer Paddy Stone jumped ship and was placed in charge of *Don't Shoot We're English* after Richard Lester had escaped the production. It was he who, acting on the Clive Dunn recommendation and clearly impressed enough with his efforts in the defunct musical, approached Frank to see if he would join the cast. Stone was able to match his existing wage of twenty pounds a week; largely as an understudy but, with a wife and daughter to support, refusal wasn't an option. And besides, Frank thought there was enough about his new job to enjoy, with one sketch in which he had no dialogue but dominated as a snooty bank clerk opposite a timid little man with a piggy bank.

With the tour of *Don't Shoot We're English* taking in all the seaside resorts that one would expect from a touring comedy, the decision to transfer to London was a risky one. By now it was 1960 and it seemed that London's theatregoers wanted more bite to their comedy than the revue had to offer. *Don't Shoot We're English* was dismissed by critics on its arrival in the West End as it continued to suffer the pains of its early nights on tour. The *Evening News* review of the opening night at the Cambridge Theatre focused almost entirely on the failings of the production crew, while taking a swipe at Stone for being 'content to bring his dancers and even some of his routines straight from the defunct *The Golden Touch*'.

Bentine's humour was never in doubt, but with the production chaos the show was on an express journey to closure. Things even went wrong when Frank, along with Bentine, Emery and Dunn, appeared on the BBC's *Wednesday Magazine* to promote the show. After a Bentine interview with David Jacobs and an improvised sketch from the quartet, Frank recalled, 'Michael with his typical unselfishness gave the principal spot to me in the Piggy Bank Sketch – ruined by the director putting the cameras in the wrong place with unnerving accuracy.'

Don't Shoot We're English was largely ignored by the public, leading to its inevitable cancellation after only two and a half weeks. 'The old-fashioned, established critics did not really understand Michael's sense of humour and said so,' recalled Clive Dunn. Both he and Frank bemoaned the closure – 'alas for the loss of some lovely comedy material'.

Despite joining the cast at such a bad time, Frank had unknowingly opened the door to his future in television. What he and his fellow cast members didn't know at the time was that seeing past the intrusive song and dance elements and the production failures were some eager young prospects with an eye for anarchic comedy.

Almost immediately after the show had closed, Bentine was approached by Denis Norden and Frank Muir. They liked the approach Bentine took to his comedy with the mock-documentary style. Since they were comedy advisers at the BBC, they persuaded Eric Maschwitz, Head of Light Entertainment at the corporation, to green-light a pilot using some of the more recyclable elements of *Don't Shoot We're English*. With that opportunity, Bentine surrounded himself with the same cast as had been so unceremoniously rendered unemployed after the stage show's cancellation, and so *It's A Square World* was born.

Bentine, when asked what kind of programme *It's A Square World* was, simply described it as, 'mad, mad, mad'. It was left to the writers at the *Radio Times* to elaborate to the guide's readers that the show, from what they witnessed at a run-through, was a mixture of *Panorama*, *Sportsview*, *The Goon Show* and *Underwater Adventure*. The resultant pilot was deemed sufficient to commission a full six-part series, albeit delayed somewhat due to Bentine's health, suffering a three-month lay-up after burning himself out keeping *Don't Shoot We're English* from going under.

Once the series arrived in the spring of 1961, producer Barry Lupino said of the pilot:

> The programme was immensely popular... It has been called a diversion for the low in brow – but I wonder? The topics are lofty enough. What could be more uplifting than the opening of the Royal Academy? That happens around the time of our first programme and Michael Bentine is taking appropriate action. Nor, of course, shall we overlook the situation in Volcania, of the effects of children's television on the adult viewer, and the arrival and departure of distinguished personages in the great metropolis.

For Frank, this was a career-defining moment. After the years of bit parts and exhausting tours, supplementing his income with the photo-graphy operations from his flat, there finally seemed to be a break in the clouds; as he wrote in his journal:

> It seems appropriate, having reached the end of this first volume, to reflect that *The Golden Touch* and the fact that it did not run has proved a great stroke of luck for me having landed me with Michael Bentine. As can be seen from the *Telegraph* notice… a series is planned. This will be my first ever – where will it lead?

Reviews for *It's A Square World* were instantly positive. The *Daily Sketch* described Bentine's lengthy supporting cast as 'his circus of Performing Nitwits' as they noted that 'their crazy antics make many other comedy shows seem more jaded than they really are'. Benny Lee, Clive Dunn, John Bluthal, Peter Reeves and Bruce Lacey along with Bentine himself and Frank were a hit.

The pilot episode having gone so well, it was no surprise that the BBC commissioned a series on the strength of it. Frank having found some-where that felt like home was very fortunate to be able to appear in the subsequent series. Bentine's exhaustion and slow recovery meant that his planned filming schedule was shelved, allowing Frank to complete his theatrical obligations. A man of good conscience, he would have wrestled with his own thoughts when it came to deciding whether to honour his commitments or join the show that he clearly loved.

Two theatre commitments posed a threat to Frank's availability for Bentine. The first of these came in the form of a play called *Hassan*, which opened in the Dublin Festival in the autumn of 1960 ahead of a brief tour. More lengthily titled *The Story of Hassan of Baghdad and How he Came to Make the Golden Journey to Samarkand*, it was supported by the music of Delius.

Frank and indeed Beryl were huge poetry fans, so this adaptation of the narrative poem, while not hugely successful, left Frank quite contented. Revived by Basil Dean, who had produced the original in 1923, *Hassan* suffered it seems from a lack of budget to allow the grandiose settings that the author James Elroy Flecker had imagined. Frank's own notices were good, and he was kind to Dean, of whom he noted: 'Basil Dean, who has earned a reputation of being a somewhat tyrannical figure in the directorial seat, was unchangingly quiet, jovial and kind to us throughout the production.'

The second commitment in late 1960 was *Naked*, by Luigi Pirandello, in which Frank starred opposite Diane Cilento, with a comparatively unknown Sean Connery at the bottom of the bill. The play was simplistic-ally described in *The Stage* as being about Pirandello's belief that 'people are not what they seem'. Frank excelled in the role of a devious writer.

Frank himself was concerned less about the reviews of *Naked* and more about the implications for his burgeoning television career. *Hassan* had already caused him to surrender a role in *The Sid James Show* in October, something he greatly regretted. Duncan Wood, then Chief Assistant at the BBC's Light Entertainment department, described it as their loss and was keen to ensure that Frank didn't slip through the net again.

Wood, whilst keeping Frank in mind for any future opportunities with Sid, was most keen that he be available for Bentine. The BBC had shown extraordinary faith in *It's A Square World*. It was expected that the show would be produced in January of 1961, and success for *Naked* would have seen Frank miss out. However, Bentine's illness meant that he spent a significant spell in hospital battling double pneumonia. He conceded to some out-of-body experiences as he battled to survive and taking three months to walk properly before even thinking about making the first series.

As *Naked* didn't transfer to the West End, and with recording delayed by those several months, Frank got the role he so desperately wanted: regular work with the man whose comic talents he respected probably more than any other throughout his career and whom he would regularly refer to as the master. Frank's opinion of Bentine was only heightened by a visit to see the ex-Goon as he recuperated, recalling, 'He was sitting with his legs up and recited almost every bit of material for the series. What an amazing man and how I look forward to the series.'

On 17th April 1961, rehearsals finally got under way for the first full series of *It's A Square World*. At various times the core performers would be Bentine, Frank, John Bluthal, Bruce Lacey, Peter Reeves, Clive Dunn,

Dick Emery, Joe Gibbons, Len Lowe, Benny Lee, Leon Thau and producer G. B. Lupino, with Bentine's co-writer John Law.

Emery, Gibbons and Lowe were all ex-Gang Show performers. Frank had of course introduced Emery when he compèred *The Centre Show*. When Emery took up flying lessons during his time on *It's A Square World*, Frank actually donated him his old RAF flying boots as a gift, having liberated them from the forces at the end of his flying duties. 'Why I had bothered I can't think – not a lot of use in weekly rep,' he recalled.

The show involved intense amounts of location filming, costume changes and special effects, while recording six live shows through to the end of that May. It wasn't without its challenges, such as when the artists, make-up, wardrobe, props, electricians and director all arrived at the Theatre Royal, Stratford-at-Bow to film a segment called 'The Titfield Hippodrome'. The camera crew, however, had gone to Stratford-upon-Avon, causing a delay through to midnight. Seemingly insignificant, but with time being of the essence, a somewhat stressful diversion.

It's A Square World was quite the spectacle. Bentine liked destroying things; almost everything on the programme seemed to start with an explosion or end with an explosion. To do that, you had to have something to destroy, in a variety of locations and with a vast array of models.

Michael's son Richard, who carries the glorious laugh of his late father, remembered of the models:

> It might be a sixty-foot Moby Dick going down the Thames or a Chinese junk bombarding the Houses of Parliament or Queen Victoria doing steam launches or the Great Train Robbery that they filmed at Dymchurch in Hythe (the Romney, Hythe and Dymchurch railway being a one-third scale rideable railway line). So, we're talking about production values that were really quite odd and you have to have professional actors that can hold that together. They've got to be able to react to that weird scenario.

It was a sentiment from Richard that echoed his Dad's comments in the press in 1963. When asked why the cast were recording on Sundays, Michael explained that their schedule was put together in order that their performers would get as much time as possible to take on other work – and for very good reason:

> We have to do this in order to get the actors of the quality we want. They've got to be character actors with an enormous repertoire of accents, and they have to be able to suggest a wide range of ages with very little make-up to help them – the longest Jill Summers gets in which to make anyone up is thirty seconds.
>
> Then there's language – we speak six languages between us, as well as the ones we invent which all have to sound real to the ear. The actors have to be ready for anything, excellent at miming and very athletic.

As to the lack of a woman in the line-up, Bentine explained: 'No, we don't have a regular woman member of the team. You see, the show has to look like a sort of balmy *Panorama*, and *Panorama* is presented by a lot of terribly serious-minded men. We're a bunch of serious-minded idiots, and the things that happen to us shouldn't happen to a woman.' ('They shouldn't happen to a dog!' – Frank Thornton!)

The show was a brave one, knowing that during the week they would shoot twelve or thirteen minutes of material on location where they couldn't rely on the weather. Rehearsal for the studio recording was a day at most, but sometimes purely on the same day on set. Then Bentine himself would knit it all together with his various intros and outros.

Bentine was an incredibly generous performer, especially given that *It's A Square World* was his creation. He had assembled a cast around him that he trusted implicitly. 'Once they started working with Dad, whatever script Dad produced for them they knew how to perform it,' recalled Richard. 'Dad didn't go around going, "Right, I want you to be an upright British military whatever." Dad gave them the script, he'd give them something that said British ex-army, and that would be it and then whatever persona they came up with, Dad was happy with.'

Richard also recalled that his father was quite content not to be the 'star' around whom the other performers gravitated: 'Dad was quite happy for others to take the lead. He didn't care, he just wanted the whole show to look good... so a script didn't mean that Dad was the one to deliver the punchline, it could be any of them and they enjoyed that.' Michael's thinking was, 'You must have flexibility in a show – in any show – because everybody has so much to contribute. No one man can think for a team. Only the actor himself can tell you how he can do a part.'

This approach to his happy band of performers was one of the things that appealed to Frank: 'It was great fun. The great thing about Bentine is he's so generous, he inspires you and gives to you. He's not the selfish leading comic, so one was part of the team. It was one of the happiest times of my life.'

Frank and Michael became instant pals. Both devotees of comedy hero Buster Keaton, Richard recalled that Frank was exactly the kind of performer that such a chaotic show required: 'Frank never wrote any material, he was always an actor working from a script. He was always so professional... what do you want, what do you need, whatever was required, perfect delivery, always knew his lines. Terribly professional, he was always on time, immaculately turned out – a real old-school performer. They had a deep affection for each other. Apart from anything else they were both very nice people. Frank was a sweet, lovely man always... never difficult to work with, intensely professional. Dad and Frank were gentlemen in the sense that they always went out of their way to say well done to people or say thank you if somebody did something that was helpful. They were two of the nicest people I've ever met.'

That appreciative nature was noted years later by Morris Bright MBE, who along with Robert Ross followed the *Last of the Summer Wine* production on location in preparation for a book on the programme's twenty-fifth anniversary.

'They would come to an event and I'd always get a handwritten card afterwards in the post,' Bright recalled. 'That's something that doesn't happen much any more, or if it did it would come through an agent. Not Frank: it was always lovely writing, written in an ink pen, slightly italicised. That was Frank, he always took the time.'

Richard's recollection of the politeness of Frank was exemplified in June of 1963 when somehow Sammy Davis Jr came to appear on *It's A Square World*. Sammy was already known to the Bentines. He and his then wife May Britt had dined with Michael and Clementina and, when Mrs Bentine remarked on how much she liked the pepper pot, Sammy promptly scooped it up and smuggled it out under his jacket, the pot still being in the Bentine family to this day and simply referred to as Sammy Davis.

After finishing his own live show in town, Sammy dashed across to Television Centre to record a short sketch as an aspiring singer doing an audition for pub entertainers, failing to reach the required standard. After the session, Sammy was piloted upstairs by top bosses at the BBC where he was given a champagne reception. None of the *It's A Square World* cast were invited, not even Bentine, but Frank was not especially put out by the snub in terms of missing out on the event itself. His concern was that the impression given to Sammy would be that the *Square World* cast were snubbing him by not attending after he had done them the honour of appearing in the show. Ever the one for appropriate behaviour, Frank and Leon Thau took it upon themselves to visit Sammy in his dressing room at the Palladium to apologise for the bad manners of their employers. 'He is charming and understanding,' Frank fondly recalled of the encounter.

Aside from the quality of the ideas pouring forth from Bentine, there were two main reasons why *It's A Square World* worked so well. Firstly, with the possible exception of Emery, who – while openly appreciative to Michael for helping his career – didn't quite match the level of amiability of the other members of the collective, they were all lovely people. Richard recalled: 'It's very unusual in any form of entertainment industry, where you survive basically on the bones of the people you can clamber over. That's what the vast majority of people do. Out of that whole crew that worked with Dad, all of the rest were lovely people.'

The second important ingredient was appreciation of the chaotic humour. Richard, only a youngster at the time of filming, remembers being winched out of the way with a bottle of pop and some crisps to watch the filming and, even at such a tender age, he could see that this collection of fine performers was having a ball. Frank himself recalled with joy: 'One of the more hilarious days occurred while filming in a Virginia Water sandpit for "the memoirs of the director of the Army School of Music" representing war in the Western desert. Barry Lupino personally let off about five hundred smoke bombs between 9am and midnight, forcing the camera team to wait to pounce like hawks on any fogless moment here and there in which to film the actors.'

The craziness of *It's A Square World* was exemplified by an entry Frank made in his journal in April 1963:

A whole week of pre-filming for the series including racing up and down a field on farm tractors; a motor-mower race; sloshing round a farm in muddy clothes; having our trousers blown off while advancing on enemy guns; a day on the Woolwich ferry as idiot sailors and Frank Thornton the Prince Consort; in the mud at Leigh-on-Sea and then in a disused army camp near Guildford all dressed up as a NAAFI food dump for dangerous old puddings etc. A strenuous if stimulating week.

Frank, and indeed Bentine, couldn't have imagined how positively *It's A Square World* would be received. It spanned forty-three episodes over four years, attracted as many as sixteen million viewers and earned Bentine a Writers' Guild award. Bentine was genius at playing to the strengths of his performers, such as casting Frank as an American military commander from Texas who needed Bentine's British interpreter character to translate from Dick Emery's British general, Clive Dunn's German general and Bruce Lacey's Turkish commander-in-chief. The pay-off of a misunderstanding of words was when Frank's character lost his mind and launched a nuclear weapon, leaving Emery to decide that impending oblivion still afforded them time for a nice cup of tea.

'It was great fun; we did it all before the Pythons,' Frank later reminisced. Alas, the dreaded BBC programme wiping, so rife in the 1960s, gives modern audiences minimal opportunity to test Frank's theory, but there was certainly the same level of zaniness across the performers and sketches. One particular favourite of Frank's was the game of drats. He recalled, 'Michael invented that from a misprint in the paper for a game of darts, and he invented this absurd game for country yokels and buckets of goats' milk and the lurker – that's George, he lurks by the door [said Frank in his thickest West Country accent]. People actually wrote in for the rules to play!'

The pinnacle of the show's success was in 1963 when the BBC were invited to submit an episode for the Golden Rose of Montreux award. Having already won a BAFTA the year before, it now took the Grand Prix de la Presse award, but it failed in its attempt to get the coveted Golden Rose.

Frank was already unimpressed with the BBC's approach to the festival. Although entering *It's A Square World*, and despite Bentine's show being widely tipped as Golden Rose winner, they also chose to show an episode of satirical programme *That Was The Week That Was*. While not entered into the contest, as a sideshow screening it was received poorly. Tom Sloan, then head of BBC TV Light Entertainment, was quoted as saying, 'It's a great pity that this was sent to a professional festival,' and promised to raise the issue within the corridors of power.

Frank was more scathing, recalling that, 'When *It's A Square World* had built up such a fund of admiration for the BBC, Donald Baverstock had to destroy it all by a showing of his brainchild that either bored or offended everybody within sight with its smut and bad taste.'

Whether the sentiment really turned against the BBC enough to cost *It's A Square World* its shot at the big prize seems unlikely as there were a number of other theories afoot. The show lost out to the forty-eight-minute CBS special *Julie and Carol at Carnegie Hall*, a musical comedy vehicle showcasing Julie Andrews (ironically Richard Bentine's god-mother) and Carol Burnett. The announcement of the winner was met on the night by a chorus of booing in some quarters of the room. Bentine's prize on this occasion was merely a special mention for originality. Frank gave his take on proceedings, thoughts which were echoed in the press at the time:

> Expected by all at Montreux to get the 'Golden Rose', our show was beaten by politics. The UNO sketch showed Krushchev, Kennedy and MacMillan too doing the twist. For this reason, the Russian, Hungarian and Romanian judges refused to agree to an award, wishing to give first place to the Czechoslovak programme. Politics had to be met with politics, so Western European judges vetoed this. Eventually the prize went almost by default to the American show, a photographed stage production that would not have offended even the most touchy political puritan, being completely innocuous and adolescent in content, though splendidly performed. The award was very unpopular. *Square World* came away with all the acclaim of the Press Award and the sympathy and admiration of all around. Scandinavian papers described the result as 'a scandal'.

Despite the controversy of Montreux, the whole experience was a positive one for Frank. His first series had been a success, while also establishing a lifelong friendship with Bentine. Jane Thornton recalled of this happy time: 'Clive Dunn was there; he'd known Clive for donkey's years. He absolutely adored working with Michael.'

On top of the shot in the arm for his career, Frank described *It's A Square World* as, 'Altogether a happy and stimulating show to be with.' It was one of his happiest professional times and he was delighted when, at the end of the third series, his last with the group, the special effects team at the final-night party presented each of the cast with a modelled 'Bumbly' – each one made in some way characteristic of the person to whom it was given.

For all the work Frank did on *It's A Square World*, with Bentine's plan to leave room in his cast's diaries to do other work it left him still available for dramatic roles. He wrote once more to the BBC and even used the varied nature of characters in Bentine's crazy sketch show to demonstrate his breadth of talent: 'The show by nature has demanded quite a range of character acting – not just a row of variety comics "being funny" – and I have enjoyed the experience immensely. It is however very important to me that I should be thought of, not as just a vaguely light entertainment body, but as an actor.'

During his run in *It's A Square World*, Frank appeared in another BBC show that was hardly going to add weight to his argument that he was more than a light entertainment performer. While this role possessed no specific comic lines, it was one that he would arguably become most famous for outside of future successes *Are You Being Served?* and *Last of the Summer Wine*. It was time to reunite with Sergeant Anthony Hancock.

When Frank had first seen Hancock in action during RAF Gang Show auditions, he had liked what he'd seen. A subsequent visit to see him on stage found him performing an entirely different character, not one Frank thought would work, but Hancock had subsequently returned to the pompous failure to great success and now, in his final series at the BBC, he turned to his old RAF colleague for someone to play against. It was of course the famous 'Blood Donor' episode, where Frank would get the unwanted attentions of Hancock as he looked for a badge of recognition for having donated 'very nearly an armful' of blood for his country. Even when Hancock was at the reception desk quizzing June Whitfield when signing in, Frank was still in shot, peering over his newspaper with that already superior expression. It was Frank's disdainful look at its best.

'I thought it was a wonderful script that any competent actor could do well with,' he told author Richard Webber. 'But with Hancock and his particular talent, he made it a great show, despite the use of autocue.' What he was referring to was Hancock's need to have the script on autocue, leading to the line of his vision almost always being slightly askew from the person he was in conversation with. It certainly made sure that the supporting cast were word perfect to avoid Hancock losing his place.

'The Blood Donor' became the quintessential Hancock piece, and as such it also cemented Frank as the ever-reliable straight man in a comedy scene, which wasn't entirely what Frank wanted. Agent Max Kester pleaded with Bush Bailey at the BBC that while their Drama Department seemed to believe Frank was only suitable for comedy, 'he is an absolutely first-rate straight actor, having appeared with Donald Wolfit in Shakespeare, with Peter Ustinov in *The Empty Chair* and in *Naked* for Frank Hauser'. As good an agent as Max was, his impassioned pleas that echoed Frank's own desire for dramatic work fell on deaf ears.

For a man who was now twenty years on from appearing on the West End stages with Wolfit and Gielgud, one can see why the comedy shows, while enjoyable enough work, were not enough to satisfy Frank's acting bones. Mixed in with his *It's A Square World* and *Hancock* appearances were recordings for commercials: a beer advert that included John Bluthal and a cartoon dog ('everybody delighted but the people who make the beer') and a tinned food advert ('I make five guineas stuffing Heinz spaghetti into my face). There was even a documentary about drains with Warren Mitchell and a cartoon character called Mr Flexpipe, filmed at a muddy building site in north London and a small hut in a Wimbledon playing field. Combined, these roles kept income coming in but were hardly the things Frank was trained for at the London School of Dramatic Art.

Perhaps Frank might have felt differently if his next comedy attempt had been taken up. Shortly after the airing of 'The Blood Donor', he was called up by *It's A Square World* producer Barry Lupino to appear in a comedy pilot for the BBC called *The Man in the Bed*. Frank described it as a wonderful opportunity, but it was never given the chance to succeed by the corporation.

The man in the title was Bernard Braden who spends all his days in bed being waited on by his butler. Somewhat inevitably, Frank is perfectly cast as the butler and by the use of his imagination and a screen, the man in the bed is taken anywhere he wishes. Frank recalled:

> It would seem to have scope for interesting ideas and Hobkins, who in fact employs Braden to be his master so that he can continue to follow his vacation in spite of a large pools win, is a lovely part for me, being one of the only two that go throughout the series. But it never gets past the first one and even that isn't transmitted, so a lovely chance is gone, sunk without trace somewhere in the upper reaches of the BBC planning department.

As much fun as the comedy was, and with a two-month notice served on their flat that would take effect on Christmas Day of 1961, it was safe to say that Frank Thornton was still waiting for the role to elevate his career further, and the 1960s seemed destined to leave him standing as every comedian's straight man.

5

Not The Frank Thornton Show

AS THE THORNTON FAMILY MOVED INTO THEIR NEW FLAT over the 1961 Christmas holidays, Frank's career seemed to be at somewhat of a crossroads. Dramatic roles on screen were limited to minor parts such as guest appearances in *The Avengers* and *Dangerman*. Comedy successes in *Hancock* and the still ongoing *It's a Square World*, while enjoyable, were pigeonholing him into being the straight-man authority figure for the great and the good of comedy to bounce off or rebel against. The stage was where he was happiest, but that was the least well-paid medium, leaving a relentless array of commercials and voice-overs to pay the bills on the new home. Robertson Hare may have been right in predicting that Frank would not find fame or a persona until he turned forty, but where he now was in his career didn't really match his original acting ambitions.

With *The Man in the Bed* not even making it to screens with its pilot, Frank had hoped for better when appearing in two *Comedy Playhouse* efforts. Tom Sloan, then Head of BBC Light Entertainment, had commissioned writers Alan Simpson and Ray Galton to come up with ten shows with the brief that they were to write exactly what they wanted to write, with no particular star in mind. Frank had appeared in the very first episode, which seemed to stand a decent chance of going to series given the standard of actors employed. Eric Sykes led the way in 'Clicquot et Fils' as Pierre Clicquot, an undertaker for a small French country town. It's 1926 and business is poor. Frank played a strike leader amongst actors hired to impersonate the relatives at a fake funeral. Despite the best efforts of Sykes and with a strong cast that included Warren Mitchell, Joan Hickson and Charles Lloyd-Pack, father of Roger of *Only Fools and Horses* fame, the show failed to get the nod.

In early 1962 Frank had a second shot at success with the closing episode of the ten showpieces, 'The Channel Swimmer'. With old pal Barry Lupino at the helm again and in his element, the cast headed down to Dover for filming in a choppy sea with a cold wind – February was not an ideal choice for such location shooting.

Frank and his co-stars Warren Mitchell, Sydney Tafler and Bob Todd felt bad enough wrapped in clothes; but playing Clive, the eponymous channel swimmer, Michael Brennan suffered in only bathing trunks and two layers of grease. Frank recalled in sympathy: 'His dresser, Joe, was most solicitous for his health and began filling him up with Bacardi rum to keep out the cold. After the first two large ones I don't think Michael cared whether he was cold or not and by teatime I have never seen such a paralytic swimmer!'

As if Brennan's tale of woe wasn't bad enough, Frank himself suffered when they came to film the studio elements: 'The first time I've nearly been seasick in the studio – sitting in a rocking boat with heavy sea on back projection on two sides and cameras on all sides to help the effect.' As comical as the filming scenario was, only one of the first series of *Comedy Playhouse* pieces went to series: 'The Offer', which became known as *Steptoe and Son*, in which Frank became the most frequent guest star.

Frank's performances, all while being seen in his multitude of guises on *It's A Square World*, were certainly getting him noticed. A further *Comedy Playhouse* was another one-off, 'Our Man In Moscow', which starred Robert Morley as the British ambassador to Russia, dealing with a temperamental tuba player seeking asylum for not being allowed to play Strauss. Frank's role was as the secretary to Morley's ambassador.

'Frank Thornton looked his imperturbable, superior best,' said *The Stage* as his stock continued to rise.

As he started performing with Benny Hill, and with Terry Scott and Peter Butterworth in *Hugh and I*, the latter of particular significance given the involvement of a certain up-and-coming producer by the name of David Croft, Frank was getting heavily utilised. Unusually not attributed to a particular publication within Frank's scrapbooks, a report appeared on 'last night's TV' which praised Frank's talents to new levels:

> The name Frank Thornton is still comparatively unknown, but this actor might well have a rapid rise to fame. He is the tall, slim character who helps to prove Michael Bentine's geometrical theorem each week and he has also assisted in many other comedy shows. The new Bentine series is giving him more opportunity to show his versatility, particularly in dialect humour. Perhaps he will follow the example of Dick Emery, another talented former inhabitant of the 'square world', in developing his own show.

The idea of Frank being the star of the show wasn't one that he entertained. He felt that the moment you hit the top you were destined to fall. In an interview with John Sandilands, he clarified that, 'Being principally a supporting person I feel that I'd be better able to carry on than if I was given say, *The Frank Thornton Show*. The great fear is, you know, that they'll get fed up with you. If you're on the screen for three years in a series, you're no longer an actor, you're that character. One chap I know earned seven thousand pounds a year for three years, then, when the series ended he picked up just two hundred and fifty pounds in the following twelve months.' Perhaps Frank's cautious approach to stardom explains why he was so excited that at the age of forty-two, he proudly bought his first car, a one-year-old Volkswagen 1500 for the tidy sum of seven hundred pounds!

A few years later, as Frank was popping up all over the place in such programmes as Terry Scott's *Scott On...* series and a three-person sketch show with Kenneth Griffith and Sheila Steafel called *Some Matters of Little Consequence*, he was asked again about whether he harboured any ambitions of his own show. Again, he shot the idea down: 'I am very happy in a supporting role, as part of a team. I'm just not the right type to take the lead. Most actors lack confidence. They're hiding behind their part.'

Further *Comedy Playhouse* opportunity came along in the form of 'Good Luck Sir, You've Got a Lucky Face', a Marty Feldman-penned piece starring Graham Stark and Derek Francis; but undoubtably Frank's best crack at regular sitcom success came in the form of *HMS Paradise* as he jumped ship from the BBC for one of the commercial television companies.

Frank attended a first reading for *HMS Paradise* just after Christmas of 1963, recording the pilot a few weeks later. The show was Associated Rediffusion's attempt to create a successful sitcom along the lines of the huge radio hit *The Navy Lark*, which had been running successfully on the BBC airwaves since 1959. Perhaps the comparisons were too obvious, maybe not helped by the lead being taken by Richard Caldicot, who also appeared in *The Navy Lark*, but it seemed that the knives were out ready to sink *HMS Paradise* before it had left harbour.

The pilot episode offered enough to convince the decision makers that the show could be a success, so a series of thirteen episodes was commissioned for the spring of 1964. It gave Frank just enough time to record an episode of *The Villains*. Also a commercial production, this time for Granada Television, he was delighted to be given the opportunity to be something other than funny. *The Stage* review was largely unimpressed with the programme, but highlighted Frank's performance as a bright spot: 'Frank Thornton's seedy solicitor was a brilliant character study, proving – if anyone needs to have it proved – that no casting director need fear that Mr Thornton's *Square World* image will get between him and any strong part he is offered.'

The comment didn't go unnoticed by Frank, who felt that the review 'highlights the attitude of the BBC which affects many besides me. Any actor used by the Light Entertainment Department is automatically written off by the Drama Department as no longer being an actor. Granada take a less blinkered view.'

After recording *The Villains*, it was back to comedy with *HMS Paradise*. With a lengthy series secured, production went ahead with a six-strong cast to spearhead what ITV felt sure would be a hit. Frank was playing Commander Fairweather, a man allegedly in charge of a naval base on the fictitious Booney Island, somewhere off the Dorset coast. Booney is nicknamed 'HMS Paradise' due to the fact that its residents are seemingly living the good life courtesy of being a haven for fiddlers and work-dodgers. Frank's character is once again the authority figure, although rather than playing him as a superior ranking officer, he is more placid in nature and happy to focus on fishing rather than thwart the schemes of his subordinates. It's an island life that frustrates Captain Turvey, played by Caldicot, who is the onshore authority figure who disapproves of the rather anarchic goings-on within the base, but cannot get control of things as his arrival on the island never goes unnoticed by those on the lookout.

On the face of it, *HMS Paradise* ought to have been a success, with a strong cast and perhaps an element of *Bilko* about the premise. The Royal Navy gave its full assistance in production of the show, and producers Associated Rediffusion were so convinced that they had a success on their hands that they had eight episodes in the can before commissioning a further thirteen, taking the total to twenty-six episodes approved before the public had even seen a moment of the show.

Publicity was extensive – Frank and his castmates were on the cover of *TV Times* in the show's first week of release and Frank himself was called on for a host of interviews, allowing him the opportunity to remind the world that he was actually a dramatic actor trained as a member of the Donald Wolfit company. He also continued to insist that, as was the case with his new show, being a member of a successful ensemble was preferable to being the headline act, telling Elsie Smith in a syndicated interview at the time:

> Television stardom is the only job where you can work yourself into the Labour Exchange by being good at it. You can be a star for three or four years. Then the public gets tired of you and says, 'Let's have a new face.' One can name several to whom this has happened. Now the man who sets his sights a bit lower can go on much longer.

Despite his own misgivings about fame, Frank was now a very frequent face on British screens. In the *Evening News*, James Green even wrote that 'Thursday night is Thornton night' as the BBC continued showing new episodes of *It's A Square World* shortly after *HMS Paradise*

Frank's parents, Bill and Rosina Ball

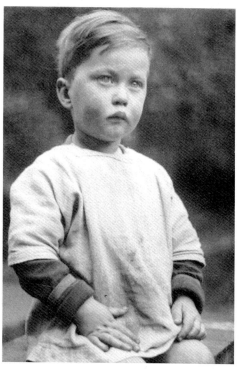

The Peacock stare in its infancy

Youthful Frank, always reading

The family group: parents Rosina and Bill,
siblings John and Joan

Performing Uncles,
Harry (left, viola) and
Frank (right, cello)

Marry Me Then,
one of many home
productions for
family gatherings

Frank exercises his
musical talents with
the attention of Mick,
the family's Dalmatian

OF LITTLE OR NO INTEREST

‖

being a record of the attempts of the above-mentioned individual
to justify his invasion of the theatrical profession - after deciding
that his sojourn in the insurance world was not lucrative
enough to compensate for the boredom thereof.
(Sounds good, anyhow) 1940.

‖

April 1940 to August 1960

The beginning of Frank's journals in 1940
as he leaves insurance for the stage

One of Frank's earliest portrait shots

Frank and Beryl found sanctuary on
what they named Beryl's Island in Ullswater

Reading remained a solace for Frank
after his RAF call-up

Frank as Mosca in *Volpone* when part
of the Donald Wolfit company, 1942

Frank as Angus in Gielgud's
Macbeth, 1942

Frank marries Beryl Evans
in June 1945

Top left: proud parents Frank and Beryl with their only child, Jane

Top right: in *The Dancing Years* (1947), a show that Frank thought was his last due to the unexpected arrival of a speech impediment

Above left: Frank had minimal interest in sport, but was proud of his snooker skills, on show here in the late 1940s

Above right: a rare capture of Frank's first television appearance, hosting *The Centre Show*, 1950. Dick Emery looks on

Left: backstage of *One Wild Oat*, 1949

As Mouche in *The Empty Chair*, 1956

A dedicated shot with Dan Dailey from one of Frank's many appearances in *The Four Just Men*, c.1959

Frank's photography skills enabled him to supplement his acting income, along with personalising his Christmas cards, here with Beryl and Jane

As Bishop Zog of Nixos in *The Golden Touch* (1960), a flop that freed Frank up to join Michael Bentine's group of performers

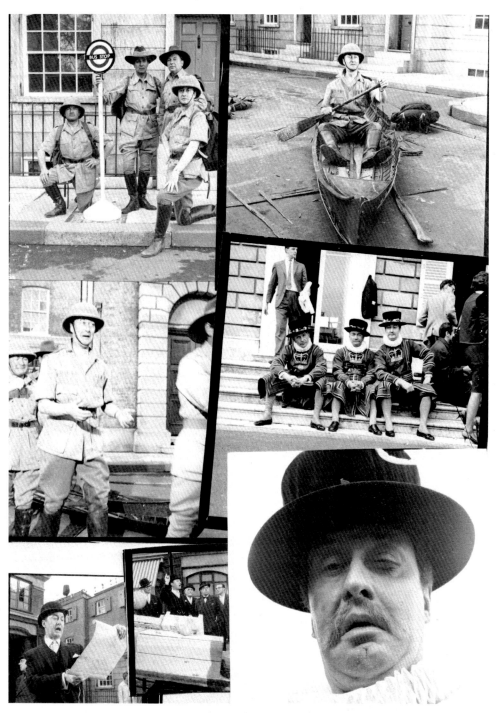

A selection of shots from Frank's time in the ever-zany *It's A Square World*, c.1961

Frank with his comedy idol Michael Bentine between shots on *It's A Square World*, c.1960

One of Frank's most famous guest spots, innocently waiting to donate blood in *Hancock*, 1961

Frank worked with almost every British comedy
great, here in a scene with Harry Worth, 1967

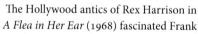

As Commander Fairweather in Frank's first attempt
as a sitcom headliner: *HMS Paradise*, 1964

The Hollywood antics of Rex Harrison in
A Flea in Her Ear (1968) fascinated Frank

As the BBC in *The Bed-Sitting Room* (1969), Frank continued a frustrating pattern of gaining little to no credit, despite in this case being used in most stills and recording the trailer voiceovers

Never afraid to dress in ridiculous outfits, Frank poses with *Scott On...* regulars Terry Scott and Peter Butterworth, 1970

Frank found a kindred spirit when performing as lugubrious Eeyore in the stage adaptation of *Winnie-the-Pooh* in two successive years, here in 1972 with John O'Farrell as Christopher Robin

Eeyore meets Eeyore as Frank shares a dressing room with the gift made by his daughter

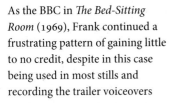

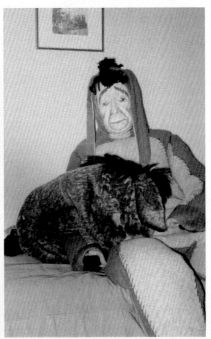

As his most famous character, Captain Stephen Peacock, in *Are You Being Served?* (1973) alongside Mollie Sugden and lifelong pal Trevor Bannister.

Grappling with Mollie Sugden as Mrs Slocombe in the stage version of *Are You Being Served?*, 1976

The full *Are You Being Served?* cast in the only external shot used in the budget-friendly movie version of 1977

Peacockmania ensues on a publicity tour of Holland in 1977

A welcome return to Shakespeare for Frank as Gremio
in the 1980 Jonathan Miller adaptation of
The Taming of the Shrew

In character as Sir John
Tremayne opposite Robert
Lindsay's Bill Snibson in
Me and My Girl, 1984

A contented Frank backstage during his happiest run in theatre, *Me and My Girl*, 1984

Back as Captain Peacock in 1992's *Grace and Favour*.

Frank had a remarkable skill for sleeping at will, here in evidence waiting for rewrites of *All Rise for Julian Clary*, 1996 (courtesy David McGillivray)

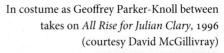

In costume as Geoffrey Parker-Knoll between takes on *All Rise for Julian Clary*, 1996 (courtesy David McGillivray)

Keen not to detract from the long-standing cast, Frank keeping in the background at the unveiling of a 25-year plaque dedicated to *Last of the Summer Wine*, 1998 (courtesy Morris Bright MBE)

Hopes of a discreet appearance at the 25-year event were shattered when Michael Aspel surprised Frank for *This Is Your Life*, 1998 (courtesy Morris Bright MBE)

Sharing thoughts between takes with fellow veteran Peter Sallis on *Last of the Summer Wine* (courtesy Terry Bartlam)

As Truly of the Yard in *Last of the Summer Wine*, Frank would enjoy his longest-running sitcom role (courtesy Terry Bartlam)

Frank Thornton, 1921-2012

was aired on ITV. But for all the pre-airing bluster, the critics mauled *HMS Paradise*; and perhaps Frank's belief that stardom risked a very short career was backed up by the fact that the show, not any of its ensemble cast, was the target of the chorus of disapproval.

The *Evening News* led the way, bemoaning that:

> It fell between two gangplanks in that it was neither lower-deck vulgarity nor upper-deck wit. Any series that starts as this did with the original and excruciatingly funny joke of hitting your thumb while hanging a picture signals doldrums ahead. It continued with verbal jokes about the Virgin Islands and visual ones of commanders stepping off ship and into the sea (twice).

While a handful of reviews hoped that the poor scripts could develop in the hands of Caldicot and Frank, most considered the material so poor that even they would be powerless to keep it afloat. 'Little short of a disgrace to all concerned'… 'Absolutely the worst comedy show I have ever endured'… 'I feel quite miserable at having to report that of wit, humour and visual gaiety there is not a sign. Sunk, in fact, without trace.' It's safe to say that *HMS Paradise* was set to run aground in garish reviews and puns!

Writer Lawrie Wyman wasn't put off by the reviews, banking on his belief that 'if the critics love you, usually the public doesn't and vice versa', but it proved to be that neither were taken by his new show.

Frank certainly enjoyed the filming of the series, along with the remuneration such a well-backed production brought with it. And he reported that there were almost more laughs to be had during filming than from the programme's script.

The Royal Navy cooperated with location filming for some onboard sequences. The cast were in full naval costume filming on a ship moored off Portland in Dorset. A South African frigate arrived, and her captain gave the order to begin to tie up alongside while filming was taking place on the other side of the naval ship.

On another day, producer Sid Colin recalled that life imitated art in the filming of an episode called 'The Ferry That Didn't Want to Know'. Colin had forgotten to warn ferry authorities that they were filming in the Solent. The cast of the show in their navy attire were alarmingly ignored as they waved from their small boat with no oars or rudder, with the script requiring four-day beards from the adrift crew who would be shouting and gesticulating at passing vessels in the hope of rescue. At the time, Colin recalled of the passing Isle of Wight ferry, 'The passengers merely looked at them in a mildly inquiring way, then shrugged and went on minding their own business. A wonderful example of British phlegm.'

During location shooting for episode twenty-three, Frank noted that he swiftly left after a day's filming to be in the audience for the recording of *It's A Square World*, which he had left to pursue a comedic life on Booney Island. It was probably the one poor choice in a largely impeccable run of successful career moves; although the film *Gonks Go Beat*, which involved four days of work for Frank before the *HMS Paradise* finale was filmed, was hardly the cultural high point of his career. It was a bizarre futuristic musical take on *Romeo and Juliet* that even Frank described accurately as an extraordinary piece, but its redeeming factor was that it paid for his first holiday in seventeen years, a long trip to Greece! Comedy historian Robert Ross actually used the film as a means of introducing himself to Frank in the 1990s:

> I didn't want to be that hundred and twenty-seventh person of the day to say, 'I loved you in *Are You Being Served?*' so I thought, let's try and find something to make him think, who is this whippersnapper? And so I said, 'I really liked you in *Gonks Go Beat*.' His eyebrows went up and he said, 'Good God, you've seen *Gonks Go Beat?*' – then a great comedy pause – 'And you liked it?'

HMS Paradise came to an end by taking to HMS *Eagle* for the final episode. This particular chapter in Frank's career didn't bring the success he might have hoped for, but thankfully didn't tarnish his reputation, and he enjoyed the gracious behaviour of the servicemen as they filmed on board: 'Great fun and wonderful hospitality from the Navy despite the fact that it was not a very strong show.'

Wyman would have better success writing for Frank when shortly afterwards he created the radio show *The Embassy Lark*, a direct spin-off from *The Navy Lark* as opposed to a pale imitation. Frank and his colleagues had toured Downing Street in preparation; although he did find that, while it was an interesting experience, 'The prospect of bumping into Harold Wilson around a corner is not quite so exciting as, say, Winston Churchill or Disraeli.'

HMS Paradise never resurfaced for repeats and all episodes were seemingly lost at sea, so we will never know whether critics were unkind or accurate.

With his television ventures on the high seas at an end, Frank found comfort back on stage in 1965. He received high praise for his performance as an aging El Cid in *A Juan by Degrees* from Greville Poke, who co-founded the English Stage Company. Poke gushed:

> I think my main reason for feeling so enthusiastic about it is that you made the old man absolutely real. I believed in him as a person and from that person sprang the humour which you gave it, and by your timing you extracted the maximum laughs out of it. In doing so, however, you never went out of character.

An impressive analysis to mark exactly twenty-five years since Frank's stage debut and a comfort that his reputation was untarnished by the poor reception of his most recent television comedy.

A few weeks later saw Frank begin rehearsals for the Charles Wood play *Meals on Wheels*, directed by the infamous John Osborne. Despite having an angry reputation both in his personal and professional life, Frank was somewhat surprised at Osborne's demeanour. The production was clearly failing in rehearsals, but Frank recalled Osborne's refreshing approach:

> A very different man from his public image – quiet, shy, good humoured – and very generous when, to counter mounting depression, he takes the whole cast and stage management, after drinks at his sumptuous Chester Square house, to the Ken Dodd Show at the Palladium and then back to supper with such things as plovers' eggs no less. The depression is, alas, justified as the play is universally loathed by the critics and ninety-nine point nine per cent of the few members of the public that visit us during our run – shortened mercifully from four to two-and-a-half weeks. From the actor's point of view, however, the play had great fascination and was a very stimulating exercise – particularly the bits we understood! Poor Charles!

Alas, Frank was right about the dislike shown towards *Meals on Wheels*. Opening night had a decent reception, but he recalled that it was in stark contrast to the boos and a slow handclap from the English Stage Society members at the dress rehearsal the night before; there's no business like show business, he mockingly reflected!

Film opportunities continued to arrive, ensuring that Frank remained very much one of the most recognised faces in British comedy, even if he did still consider himself a straight actor who was good at comedy. He appeared alongside Norman Wisdom in *The Early Bird*, and ran a clothing shop in *Carry On Screaming*, playing opposite Harry H. Corbett and Peter Butterworth.

He was also amongst an array of comedy faces to appear in *A Funny Thing Happened on the Way to the Forum*. His role as Brutal Slave Driver involved screen time with Michael Crawford and Zero Mostel, along with future *Are You Being Served?* star Alfie Bass. Alas for Frank, although he did get to meet Phil Silvers, his two weeks of filming did not manage to secure him an encounter with his comedy hero, Buster Keaton, making his final screen appearance.

Frank's compensation, in a schedule that found him somewhat lonely staying at the Motel Osuna outside of Madrid, came in the company of Bass and Roy Kinnear. His own comedy moment was at the expense of Roy, who, when Frank and Bass returned home, was forced to remain due to an abscess on his tooth that 'blew his face up into a passing resemblance to Quasimodo', Frank recalled. 'I shall never forget the sight of the unit director (I suspect, the local vet) plunging a jumbo-sized hypodermic syringe full of penicillin into Roy's jumbo-sized backside!'

Frank would encounter Zero Mostel once again filming *Ride of the Valkyrie*, a short comedy about a singer in a Wagner opera trying to make their way from the airport to Covent Garden Opera House in time for their performance. Although rehearsals for the shoot consisted mainly of driving around Regent's Park while Mostel climbed in and out of the windows of a Vauxhall Victor, when it came to filming, done entirely on location, Frank had a rather more challenging time behind the wheel.

Aside from almost having a nervous breakdown, Frank was given a warning by police on the M4 and was booked on the A4 for carrying a dangerous load, the load being Mostel dressed as the female opera singer. The potential for prosecution was eventually addressed, with the film company admitting they had not given the authorities proper details of their plans, so in the eyes of the law, the driver was responsible – Frank! Legal implications averted, Frank admitted that, 'Apart from this, however, an interesting experience to work with two such contrasting characters as Peter Brook [director] and Zero Mostel and my three-week guarantee is profitably extended to a fourth week by Zero catching bronchitis while travelling on the roof of the car in a dressing gown.'

In 1966 Frank took a role in the now fondly remembered Children's Film Foundation series, playing Sergeant Bull in *Danny the Dragon* alongside old pal and *Carry On* favourite Peter Butterworth and Patrick Newell, Sally Thomsett leading the child actors. Frank was never above children's television; acting jobs were acting jobs and throughout his career, his children's television roles mirrored his adult audience ones in as much as he worked on such a remarkable array of programmes.

After a few guest appearances in *The Adventures of Charlie Quick* opposite Clive Dunn, Frank even put pen to paper and wrote to Dorothea Brooking at the BBC's Children's Department as he looked to extend the scope of his work on children's television. He was unsuccessful with his plea at that point, but *Danny the Dragon* offered a full series. It was a little more strenuous than he had anticipated, the scripts being rewritten somewhat after Newell caused filming to be suspended when he wrapped his car around a lamppost. On one day's filming when Newell was due to spend six hours riding a bicycle, the activities were switched to Frank instead due to Newell's injuries. His final scene found him sitting fully clothed in a bath full of water in the middle of a muddy farmyard – quite the challenge when he had to dash off to the Savoy to appear opposite Andrew Cruickshank in *Alibi for a Judge*!

On a visit to Australia during the height of *Are You Being Served?* fame, Frank was touted for a potential series built around him, which all fell apart due to louder voices than his in the boardroom of the relevant television company. He knew he didn't have the dominant nature to throw his weight around to have things his way, unlike some actors. Frank's resistance to the implications of being star material would give him a lesson in the temperament perhaps needed to be such a single-minded performer in the summer of 1967. In May of that year, he flew off to Paris for a test for the role of Charles, a worried manservant in the Georges Feydeau farce *A Flea in Her Ear*. The main name on the bill was one Rex Harrison, at the height of his fame after *Doctor Dolittle* and the earlier *My Fair Lady*, but whose reputation of wanting things his way went before him.

Frank was in a whole new world as he worked with the Academy Award winner, and he was most intrigued by it:

> Fascinating to be in the big league for once and see the international star go about his business – Mr Harrison certainly knows his business brilliantly and goes about it with a single-mindedness that is stunning to watch but dangerous to tangle with – like a train at full throttle. One does not act with him, merely in the vicinity. However, the star is the star is the star and the difference in salary precludes any arguments. A superb professional, nevertheless, and unfailingly charming to me at all times.

Directing the film was Jacques Charon, who had previously directed a stage version in London at the Old Vic. Frank had every sympathy with the Frenchman, who steadily watched as those around him took over the movie with rewrites for Harrison and interference from other quarters: 'A wonderful actors' director, he was totally crushed under the combined weight of Rex, the director of photography and the editor all telling him how to shoot a picture or rather how they were going to shoot it.'

The movie on release was not well received. Despite being set in Paris and somewhat impressive to look at, the French didn't like it, *Le Monde* suggesting that 'if you put a grain of sand in a mechanism it may break down. The adapters, in this case, have thrown a shovelful of gravel'.

Frank may have been intrigued by the experience of working 'in the vicinity' of Harrison, but he conceded of the poor reviews, 'I was not surprised. They had taken a farce written for a team and turned it into a light comedy vehicle for a "star". It was bound to fail.'

A few years later Frank was working for Billy Wilder in a minor role in *The Private Life of Sherlock Holmes*. As Frank sat on the set wishing he could have had a better role working for such an exalted director, he was spotted by one of his *A Flea in Her Ear* co-stars, Louis Jourdan, who had come to see Wilder. Jourdan greeted Wilder and confirmed, 'Frank and I made a lousy picture in Paris – and we knew it!'

For all Frank's fascination with how the Hollywood star operated, his own lack of interest in being a show-business personality per se came through during the filming. Despite being given a pleasant flat in the suburbs of Paris with its own garden, Frank took every opportunity to dash back to help turn the house in Westmoreland Road in Barnes – to which he and Beryl had moved not long before – into a home: the place they would call home for the rest of their lives. It also gave him the opportunity to take back tins of baked beans, upon which he was desperate to dine after tiring of expensive restaurants, even if the bills were on Fox's expenses!

In 1968 Frank joined the cast of seemingly the whole comedy acting industry – as he called it, the Dick Lester repertory company – for the bizarre apocalyptic comedy *The Bed Sitting Room*. The original play from which the movie morphed was co-written by Spike Milligan, for whom Frank had just finished work on *The World of Beachcomber*. Although a success, that particular show Frank didn't think loaned itself to television: 'It just didn't come off the page. It was too much a literary work.'

In the film version of *The Bed Sitting Room*, London has been reduced to rubble and the movie follows the small number of people who have survived a nuclear holocaust, seemingly around twenty in number, in their varying levels of sanity. Frank's opening day of filming was at Chesil Beach, with the dome of St Paul's Cathedral protruding from the water. His miles continued to rack up during the week, taking in a soggy gravel pit in Corby, a burnt-out carwash near Kettering, splashing about in a clay quarry in St Austell in four inches of water wearing a pair of plimsolls, an unfinished reservoir near Staines doubling as Downing Street after the bomb, and finally Guildford Street in the rush hour, doubling as Downing Street before the bomb.

Frank's performance was impeccable. Dressed in shredded rags from the midriff down but in his best dinner suit and bow tie upwards, Frank's role is that of the BBC as he continues to speak in news reporter fashion, not in front of a camera but simply by putting his head through the shell of an old television set.

The full cast is like a who's who of comedy at that time, with Milligan joined by Peter Cook, Dudley Moore, Arthur Lowe, Marty Feldman, Harry Secombe, Jimmy Edwards… the list goes on and yet somehow it represents one of the oddities of Frank's career – the lack of credit for his work.

In the majority of movie posters for the film, Frank in the television frame is the only actor present. In the official trailer for the movie he is interviewing the Prime Minister on the steps of Downing Street as the dreaded bomb falls. He is subsequently the first person to be seen in the post-holocaust scene, welcoming Michael Hordern with the words, 'Good evening. I mean that most sincerely. I am the BBC as you can see, and here was the last news,' after which he sets the ground for the film as he reveals that a nuclear misunderstanding led to the Third World War, the shortest in living memory at two minutes and twenty-eight seconds.

Remarkably, the voice that brings us the whole trailer, along with the most memorable image of the movie, the bow-tied BBC speaking mostly with a television on his head, or on the head of those he speaks to, goes effectively uncredited. The trailer scrolls through them and Frank is not mentioned. He is the sole human image on the posters and yet his is not among the twelve names listed. It's a remarkable snub that remains mystifying to his fans and family to this day, even more so given that director Richard Lester was a firm friend.

It wasn't the first time Frank was lost to strange publicity approaches. Photos for *The Embassy Lark* didn't include him or Derek Francis, despite them being the two main star names of the series. There followed a long exchange between agent Max Kester and the BBC, with the blame eventually being put on the *Radio Times*.

The ultimate irony of the *Bed Sitting Room* snub was that Frank was actually called back specifically to pose for poster stills and record the voice-over for the trailer, despite not appearing on the bill or being credited on the trailer; especially perplexing given his role was significantly greater than some of the names listed!

It also wasn't the last time Frank would be left off the billing despite being a significant part of a show. In 1969, he received the call everybody in British showbusiness wanted: to be a guest on *The Morecambe and Wise Show*. As ever, he was the strait-laced character to be bounced off, on this occasion as the boys went to a restaurant to persuade a well-known figure to be a guest in one of the plays wot Ernie wrote, Frank playing Richards the waiter.

Initially the star being courted was Susan Hampshire, but Eric was unwell in rehearsals. It wasn't quite with the drama that the tabloids reported, the newspapers suggesting Eric had collapsed during rehearsal. In fact, fellow guest Deryck Guyler had got the flu, Ernie then missed two days and finally Eric was sent home with the same bug. By the time they came to rehearse again, Hampshire was no longer able to take part, being heavily pregnant, and her place was taken by Diane Cilento. Despite the quality of his performance, Frank wasn't mentioned in the show's opening credits as other guests were; he wasn't even mentioned in the very comprehensive list of performances in Graham McCann's otherwise excellent biography of the boys. The only saving grace, aside from the honour of working with the legends, was that he did have the pleasure of awaiting Janet Webb's arrival routine at the end of the show!

For now, it was back to the stage in the form of *The Young Visiters*, a musical based on a best-selling book by Daisy Ashford, a nine-year-old of Victorian times when she wrote it. The production was troubled almost from the outset. Director Philip Grout left after three weeks of rehearsal, with Martin Landau to take over. Frank was already sceptical, not of Landau's talents but of the demands of dual roles, Landau now being both director and production manager: 'Although he whipped the production into technical shape, we inevitably missed the firm hand of a full-time director. Rehearsals seemed to go on for all hours but to no great effect.'

Ten days of indifferent business for the pre-West End run at the Bristol Hippodrome resulted in plenty of cuts and changes and by the time the show returned to London, there were production problems and money was an issue. The biggest bone of contention seemed to be with the musical numbers. RCA had the recording contract and wanted some of Ian Kellam's score replaced by contracted writers. Given that the new numbers were far more 'pop' in style than the show was suited to, Frank was appalled at the immorality of the approach. In the end, two numbers were replaced by offerings that he considered banal beyond belief.

Music was set to be the key to the show's success, but with the new numbers also came changes to the existing ones. 'What Does a Gentleman Wear' was a four-person harmony that was eventually cut down to a one-person song for Anna Sharkey, which then meant that the number was considered too visual for putting on the show's album release. Eventually, the mediocrity of the soundtrack meant the show didn't capture an audience and it closed in February of 1969.

Scandal was something Frank could never be accused of. His shows were more often than not an unqualified success and, while there was the occasional questionable role, these were more often than not signs of the times rather than anything genuinely controversial. So, when Frank began rehearsals in the spring of 1969 for *Staircase*, he was most likely not expecting to stir up any controversy.

Staircase was Charles Dyer's story of an ageing gay couple, Charlie and Harry, who manage a barber shop in Brixton. Their lives have changed significantly since their younger days, in particular Charlie's who was previously a married actor and who has a grown-up daughter.

The play was entirely a two-hander, Stanley Beard starring opposite Frank under Trevor Danby's direction. It was being produced of course only two years on from homosexuality being decriminalised in the UK, but such headlines as 'Play About Loneliness of Two Homosexuals May Shock Audiences' in the *Richmond and Twickenham Times* suggested not all areas had embraced the change in the law and, as Frank himself noted, were hardly calculated to drag the whole of Richmond into the theatre. The subsequent article sat rather on the fence with its content, still suggesting that a play about two homosexuals would 'be enough to make quite a few regular patrons throw their hands up in disgust'.

Danby was quoted as having said that Dyer's play was 'primarily a play about the loneliness of these two men. They are real people, not caricatures.' Frank and Beard were both largely praised for their per-formances, particularly for not camping them up. The *Thames Valley Times* praised them for being 'well contrasted as the odd couple, continually abusing each other in the hope that their interdependence is not too obvious'.

Despite the reality of the play being as much about loneliness as anything else, it was inevitable that there would be some reaction. There had been warnings of a possible protest, something that had made both Frank and Beard nervous and in Frank's eyes had unwittingly meant that they had possibly overplayed the comic elements of the play.

Then as the second act began at one Wednesday performance, cries emerged from the audience. National Front members had decided to make their position clear, protesting against 'the propagation of filth' and a 'decadent spectacle detailing the degradation of two middle-aged sex perverts'. The curtain came down and the 'Hallelujah Chorus' was blasted out in order to drown the abusive chants.

First on the scene was reportedly the theatre's eighty-year-old usherette, Constance Pearce, who tried arguing with the protesters before leading one outside. More staff came to clear the others; and after the interruption, Frank and Beard reappeared to a rousing round of applause. The closing of the evening resulted in five curtain calls, and it was at least of some consolation to those concerned that the theatre audience had nothing but anger and contempt for the protesters.

In 1970 Frank was chosen by none other than J. B. Priestley himself for the role of Councillor Albert Parker in a revival of his stage comedy *When We Are Married*. Priestley was seemingly a huge fan of *It's a Square World* and *The World of Beachcomber* and singled Frank out as his preferred option in the role.

The first read-through of the production was actually carried out in Priestley's presence under the direction of Laurier Lister. Rehearsals continued without any great incident, but Frank noticed that star name Fred Emney was starting to rewrite his part of Henry Ormonroyd to suit what Frank described as his style of short, throwaway lines. Although the original part was intended to be spoken in a Yorkshire accent, Emney being the star of the show began to adapt the role to himself rather than adapt himself to the requirements of the role.

Frank was not overly convinced that the benefits of such a name in the show would outweigh the negatives of the alterations being made. His concern was the damage that could be done to the balance and character of a play that he considered to be as fresh and living as it was when it was originally staged in 1938, a production that teenage Frank had actually seen.

That being said, Frank delighted in one glorious moment that Emney gave them during rehearsals:

> Nearing the end of rehearsals a run-through for the author was called. We assembled with a certain degree of nervousness. On the stroke of 10.33 the producer and the author entered the auditorium and silently took their places in the middle of the stalls. We commenced. Act One – pause – Act 2 – pause – Act 3 – pause. The producer and author rose and silently left the auditorium. A further short pause as we gazed silently at their backs disappearing through the door. As it swung to, Fred uttered the deathless line which could stand alone as evidence of his genius: 'Well, if he didn't like it, he shouldn't have written it.' The glorious illogicality of this pronouncement was compounded by the fact that Fred's Henry Ormonroyd owed more to his own invention than to Mr Priestley's carefully constructed script.

Priestley himself was particularly pleased with Frank's performance, writing to offer him praise:

> I was delighted by your Albert Parker at Leeds, which is now well up to the standard set by Raymond Huntley originally. It was all the greater pleasure to me because casting you was entirely my idea, on the strength of some amusing performances on TV – so that this was rather a gamble. But it has paid off, for which many, many thanks.

The show opened to a fine reception, with an element of over-enthusiasm from one particular audience member who had come to see his pal on opening night after their recent work in the *Scott On...* series of comedies: 'The loudest laughter, clearly audible and encouraging to the cast but a trifle disturbing to some of his neighbours, came from Terry Scott!'

Sadly, Scott's laughter was probably the peak moment for the show as it went into something of a downward spiral very quickly. Peggy Mount was quick to insist that the producer was changed, so out went Laurier Lister. His replacement, Robert Chetwyn, made his own mark on the show by overseeing wholesale casting changes. By the time it arrived in the West End, *When We Are Married* had gone through so many changes in style as well as staff that Frank's conviction that it would run for at least a year in the Strand Theatre dissipated.

What frustrated Frank more was that the younger members of the cast were the ones who were holding the production together as more experienced performers let the show drift. He noticed one of his co-stars nod her head sixty-three times during the last ten minutes of the play, two others keeping a nightly tally!

Another star barely went with any of Priestley's original words, choosing her own lines instead. Tricky enough for co-stars, but as Frank noted, much of the comedy was lost. What irked Frank so much was that the guilty parties put their own needs ahead of the play, something he never entertained:

> They are up there on that stage to be loved and loved they are determined to be! Oh God, how this lovely comedy was thrown away and battered out of shape. And all the producer said when his attention was drawn to it was, 'It's not too bad.' An ultimately disappointing engagement considering that I had cherished the hope of playing Albert Parker ever since seeing the original production by Basil Dean. The theatre is not what it was.

In 1971, after dabbling in a number of children's productions since *Danny the Dragon*, including spending significant time sat in a pond for *The Double Deckers*, Frank started rehearsing for what was his first venture into children's Christmas stage entertainment.

Although Frank recalled it as such, he had actually appeared in panto once back in 1960 as Will Atkins in a production of *Robinson Crusoe* at Windsor. He would recall a near-miss that could have ended his career before it had barely started, or at least wiped out a member of the orchestra. He recalled the occasion in an after-dinner speech he made years later:

> I had survived a sword and dagger fight as Laertes to Donald Wolfit's Hamlet and in the panto I had to duel with Robinson Crusoe. It was just before the interval and at one point Robinson, played by Patricia Michael, disarms me, knocking my cutlass out of my grasp.
>
> One night the cutlass flew back over my shoulder as planned but bounced neatly and disappeared point-first into the orchestra pit.

I feared the worst and as soon as the curtain came down, I rushed down to the band room to see if I had killed anyone or at least smashed somebody's valuable instrument. I was assured all was well. As the orchestra leader made a down stroke thus forming a triangle – the bow, his arm and his violin – my cutlass had passed harmlessly through the hole and onto the floor. What timing!

However, as you may or may not know, the orchestra for the Windsor panto is recruited from army bandsmen from across the road in Windsor Castle. As I made my first entrance after the interval I glanced down into the pit and there was the leader calmly playing his fiddle as required but wearing his regulation army steel helmet!

Thankfully there would be no such dramas in *Winnie the Pooh*, which was being adapted into a musical stage production at the Phoenix Theatre, opening nine days before Christmas. With his history of lugubriousness, there was only one person that could possibly be right to don the skin of the permanently depressed Eeyore: Frank Thornton.

Eeyore proved to be quite the challenge. For four-and-a-half weeks Frank would have a solo song and dance number, 'Pooh has Found a Tail'. Not only that, but he would also be performing these numbers, his first time dancing on stage, in a hefty grey donkey suit.

The show was a great success earning rave reviews, including from the children in the audience who seemed to warm more to Eeyore than the other characters. Frank was singled out by the press as the standout performer, and it wasn't lost on him. 'On no previous occasion have critics been so generous in their praise,' he wrote. 'It appears I have to disguise myself with a skin, hooves and grey make-up to rate such words. As my friend Eeyore would say, "Typical! Absolutely typical!"'

Winnie the Pooh was so successful that it was staged at the same theatre again a year later. Original Pooh Jimmy Thompson was replaced by Ronald Radd while the original Christopher Robin, Vivian Stewart, was replaced by ten-year-old John O'Farrell, who would of course go on to become a best-selling author. It would be O'Farrell's first and only stage performance.

O'Farrell remembered being somewhat in awe of Frank as he was the most famous face in the cast and was frequently seen on television:

I remember him being very funny and getting a great response from the audience. Even at ten I thought I was going to be making my life in comedy and I had a good eye for who had good comic bones and who didn't, even then, and I could see he had great comic bones. Playing depressed is quite hard – playing sad and miserable and getting laughs is not an easy thing to do, but he got a great response. I remember him being very professional, very focused on his work. Frank Thornton was up there on a pedestal for me – older, famous, serious and shy.

Throughout the 1960s and into the early 1970s Frank's career had followed a steady path. The pivotal involvement in *It's a Square World* had opened up a host of television roles, primarily because every working comedian and their writing team could see the value in Frank's talents. An actor of impeccable professionalism, with immaculate comic timing, he could even understand the production values that went into television comedy.

When filming the first series of *The World of Beachcomber*, the BBC replaced the safe hand of Duncan Wood with a first-time director who had been taught at the corporation. Frank was dismayed by the fact that the way the new director had been taught to shoot comedy was to have 'a succession of big fat close-ups of the person actually speaking at the moment. Comedians no longer need legs, arms or bodies.'

Frank expanded on what he saw as an increasingly ill-advised trend when a reviewer harshly commented on an appearance on Tessie O'Shea's *Show of the Week*, which had said that 'neither her smile nor her singing were designed for the close-up world of TV and they are probably more easily enjoyed at the Opera House, Blackpool'. It was a cruel piece of criticism and only backed up Frank's belief that British directors were falling behind their American equivalents in as much as they were too interested in focusing on the face of the actor actually speaking unless they were forced into something else. He used the great Tommy Cooper as a prime example:

The scene – a music hall stage, straight man trying to recite; enter comic wearing hat; cut to waist shot of comic: he puts his hat on sideways, one hand in his jacket and one over his eye.

COMIC: Who's this?

	Cut to waist shot of straight man.
STRAIGHT MAN:	I don't know.
	Cut to waist shot of comic.
COMIC:	Nelson.
	Cut to waist shot of straight man.
STRAIGHT MAN:	I don't wish to know that.
	Cut to waist shot of comic, his hands in the same position.
COMIC:	Who's this?
STRAIGHT MAN:	I don't know.
COMIC:	Half Nelson.

The studio audience laughed but I failed to see the joke. Ten days later all was revealed. The splendid Tommy Cooper, 'doing his impersonations', put a hat on sideways, one hand in his jacket, one over his eye. 'Nelson!' Then he KNELT DOWN. 'Half Nelson!'

Unlike the studio audience at the former show we, the viewers, had not been permitted to see the comic in the act of kneeling down and when we did see him it was from the waist up, alone and not in relation to the standing straight man, so we NEVER KNEW he had knelt.

We have some excellent comedians in this country, many of whom can be as funny with their hands and feet as with their faces. Let us simply sit back and see them at work instead of having our noses forced up against theirs in the unnecessarily 'close-up' world of television.

Safe to say that at this point in his career, as he moved into his fifties, Frank had become the most rounded of performers. He could sing, dance, do the heavy stage plays as adroitly as farces and children's television, and he knew how to get the best from comedy more than anything. His career goal of staying in constant employment rather than achieving the lonely stardom of the leading man seemed safely secure. But in 1972, a shocking world event would force the BBC to dust down an unused comedy pilot episode from the shelves and in so doing, catapult the careers of Frank Thornton and his new co-stars to a whole new level.

6

It Will Ride Up With Wear

BY 1972, FRANK THORNTON HAD BEEN PLYING his trade on stage, radio, film and television for over thirty years. He had worked with almost every comedy great on television and was one of the most reliable sources for an authority figure against which to rebel. His stage career was solid, but he still found television to be a source of frustration, drama work not coming his way and comedy roles merely feeding others.

In the space of a few months in the spring of 1972, Frank took part in two further episodes of *Comedy Playhouse*. The shop window of potential sitcoms, *Comedy Playhouse* was essentially a selection of pilot shows to see what could make it into a series. Since Frank's first appearance in 'Cliquot et Fils' in 1961, *Steptoe and Son*, *Till Death Us Do Part*, *The Liver Birds* and *Up Pompeii!* had all blossomed into successes in their own right after an initial showcase on *Comedy Playhouse*, but plenty of others with significant names in starring roles and quality writers behind them fell by the wayside.

The first of these pilot episodes for Frank in 1972 was 'Are You Being Served?' which came from the pen of Jeremy Lloyd and David Croft. Croft was rapidly gaining a reputation as the man with the golden touch for comedy at the BBC. Lloyd was largely untried, his only credit of note at this point in his career being as a contributor to American sketch show *Rowan and Martin's Laugh-In*.

Lloyd had worked as a suit salesman at Simpson's department store in Piccadilly when in his twenties. Starting at the bottom of the hierarchy that dominated such an establishment, he was adept at observing how the pecking order behaved.

Twenty years on and times were hard for Lloyd. After a nervous breakdown, he wrote an outline of a potential comedy show about his shop-floor experiences under the advice of his then wife Joanna Lumley. Lloyd then fired it off to a range of television executives. He also included David Croft on the list of recipients, who had met him when Lloyd was appearing in the short-lived comedy *It's Awfully Bad For Your Eyes, Darling!* after being brought in to try to rescue the fate of the already doomed flop. He thought Croft would be a useful person to try and comment on his fledgling idea.

Croft liked what he read. He worked his magic, taking the core story Lloyd had written about the menswear department and expanding it to include the controversial arrival of the ladies' department on the same floor to intrude on the space of the gentlemen.

Croft had an uncanny knack of casting the right person from previous experiences, and given the success that *Dad's Army* was achieving, the BBC had no reason to challenge him on his choices for characters within *Are You Being Served?* including Frank.

Frank had worked with Croft in *Hugh and I* and by now had gained a reputation as being the perfect actor for a 'smell under the nose' sort, as Frank often described his role in the show. He seemed perfect for the role of Captain Stephen Peacock, floorwalker of the menswear department at Grace Brothers' department store.

'David Croft thought the world of Frank,' recalled Croft's usual writing partner, Jimmy Perry, years later. 'He had reality because he never pulled faces, he didn't do jokes – he didn't like doing jokes. He had that sort of acid look on his face and his timing was excellent.'

Lloyd recalled that in such department stores, the senior salesman would register when a potential customer appeared from the lifts and

It Will Ride Up With Wear

would await the nod from the floorwalker, who would offer the phrase 'Are you being served?' while the senior salesman would make a quick assessment as to the possible affluence of the person concerned. The more likely they were to have money to spend, the more senior the member of staff that would be assigned to them. It was how life was for Lloyd at Simpson's and it was this hierarchy that was used to great effect in *Are You Being Served?*

In the role of senior salesman was veteran repertory actor Arthur Brough. Finding the right combination of grumpy old man and respectful amiability, he played Mr Grainger to such a fine standard (despite his challenges with remembering lines) that after his death the producers eventually gave up trying to find an effective replacement. Behind Mr Grainger was Mr Humphries and then, at the bottom of the pile, Mr Lucas.

Mr Humphries would become the most successful, if controversial, character in the show because of his excessive campness, exaggerated to the maximum by relative newcomer John Inman.

Mr Lucas was played by Trevor Bannister, arguably the most successful sitcom actor in the cast at that time having come fresh from three series of ITV hit *The Dustbinmen*. Bannister was seen as the top billing in the programme alongside a certain other coloured-haired actress.

The ladies' counter had one fewer staff member: just senior saleswoman Mrs Slocombe, played so memorably by Mollie Sugden, and junior member Miss Brahms, a breakthrough role for Wendy Richard. With Nicholas Smith playing the department head and Harold Bennett the skirt-chasing company boss, Young Mr Grace, *Are You Being Served?* seemed to be a prime candidate for success… but the BBC hated it.

Comedy Playhouse was supposed to offer an array of pilot episodes in the knowledge that some would succeed in finding an audience while others would fall by the wayside. The BBC disliked the product so much that they had no plans to even air it to test its audience reception.

The unfortunate circumstances surrounding the eventual dusting off of the *Are You Being Served?* pilot are now well known. The Munich Olympics of 1972 was thrown into chaos when members of Black September, a militant Palestinian organisation, took members of the Israeli team hostage. After negotiations and a rescue operation were botched, eleven hostages were killed. It was the Olympics' darkest day, and the games were suspended.

Insignificant though it was in the grand scheme of things, the BBC found itself with an empty schedule. More than ten hours of time in its programming had been devoted to *Olympic Grandstand* and *Today at the Olympics*. Out of sheer desperation and some cajoling from David Croft, they decided that a poor sitcom that probably wouldn't get watched anyway would be a better option than nothing at all.

As Frank waited to see the reception of *Are You Being Served?* he committed to another *Comedy Playhouse* effort, 'The Birthday', written by Eric Davidson. The programme was described in *Radio Times* as 'The party – Sodom and Gomorrah with sandwiches. But nobody comes. The answer? Rentabird.'

It was hardly the most encouraging description and barely one to suggest a successful morphing into a series was on the cards, but the star of this particular show was Gordon Peters. Producer Dennis Main Wilson was optimistic. Frank recalled that Wilson 'assures me that Gordon will be the next big star, comparable with Hancock. Time alone will tell. I'll not hazard a prediction.'

Despite the uncertainty as to whether the Gordon Peters episode would succeed or not, it did get taken up for a series simply entitled *The Gordon Peters Show*. Frank was magnanimous enough to admit that he had been wrong about its chances when recording in April of 1973, but he remained unconvinced about its long-term prospects: 'I have to admit that when I did the pilot I thought the show would be sunk without trace. I was wrong, but the *Times* critic seems to share the opinion.'

That particular critic questioned both Peters and the script, suggesting that Peters 'lacks the mobility and the gestures to carry it through… Suffice it to say that even such stalwart supporters as Frank Thornton and Barbara Mitchell could scarcely squeeze from it the ghost of a subsidiary smile.'

Alas, Peters would not come anywhere near the heights of Hancock. *The Gordon Peters Show* survived only one series and although he carved out a solid living on the sitcom circuit, including occasional appearances with Frank in *Are You Being Served?* and later *Grace and Favour*, Dennis Main Wilson's predictions fell short.

Comedy was now becoming Frank's expected television presence. A week after recording the pilot for *Are You Being Served?* he recorded another pilot, this time for Thames, called *By Jeorge*. It was another dabble in children's television, Frank playing the manager of a television station dealing with a rogue ventriloquist, Jack Riley, and his puppet Jeorge who takes over the studio with the help of a prop man and puts on a live show despite only working in the station's property department. That failed to materialise into anything more than a pilot, but elsewhere the CV of comedy greats he was appearing with was expanding all the while as Frank appeared in *Sykes* and then spent a day filming with Spike Milligan in the Jim Dale movie *Digby, the Biggest Dog in the World*.

Quite bizarrely, amongst all the comedy guests and comedy pilots, Frank was employed to spend a few days dubbing over the role of Kamaswami in the Conrad Rooks adaptation of *Siddhartha*, a 1922 novel by Herman Hesse. The film had been shot on location in India with an Indian cast, and the resulting product was being edited back in England.

Remarkably, it was deemed cheaper to have another actor dub the original lines rather than bring the on-screen talent over to the UK. Frank did what was asked of him in dubbing over the original actor's voice. It's the sort of thing that would never happen today and although it was nothing unusual in the early 1970s, Frank was somewhat despairing of the approach: 'The Indian actors were perfectly good... such is the economics of the film business and its effect on the performances and careers of actors.'

It's testament to Frank's skill at accents that as an understandably uncredited role, such a performance has gone unnoticed... but a viewing now with that knowledge shows it is unmistakably Frank!

Frank's workaholic approach in the spring of 1972 was all the more remarkable given that he had spent some time in hospital in March. For almost a year he had been without his sense of smell. He had been born with a slightly deformed septum which had given him a history of nasal congestion, and the loss of smell convinced him to take action.

In Frank's own descriptive terms, surgeon Maxwell Ellis 'bashes out the septum's bumps and bends and snips away about a pound of sprouts!' For many subsequent weeks his nose was tender, but his breathing had improved: perfect timing for the amount of work he was taking on.

Alas, the joy was short-lived as by the autumn of that year the returned sense of smell departed once again, leading to allergy tests that provided a host of possibilities, but ultimately the trouble would stay with him leading to multiple polypectomy operations during his career. It also meant that the damage to his sense of smell and taste remained.

In 1983 he revealed that through her cookery skills, Beryl would try to compensate for his compromised senses by emphasising the visual texture of good food, both of which became of increased significance to Frank.

'One of the things I often dream about is the rich smell of freshly ground hot coffee,' he bemoaned. 'Now I prefer piquant food – there's some compensation there because I think I can recall the taste, and I like to see plenty of lemon wedges on my plate just like with curries and especially pepper steak, the taste of which is easy to imagine.'

With so much going on in Frank's career, he could have easily been forgiven for forgetting about the pilot for *Are You Being Served?* which is rather what the BBC seemed destined to do.

After its initial airing in September of 1972, nothing further emerged. Co-writer Jeremy Lloyd had originally given the option to commercial television; it was David Croft who had convinced him to get the rights back in order that he try his luck with the BBC under the *Comedy Playhouse* umbrella.

Ironically, the BBC were nonplussed by the show, and felt that ITV represented a better fit, given what the corporation saw as the lower-brow humour of sitcoms like the opposition's then big success, *On The Buses*. Croft, however, disagreed; so when the BBC suddenly found themselves with a gap in their weekly schedule caused by a delay to the production of new episodes of *Till Death Us Do Part*, he convinced Head of Light Entertainment Bill Cotton to give him the nod to put *Are You Being Served?* into a full series. The executive took a bit of persuading as he disliked the campness of John Inman's character. Reluctant as Cotton was to allow the show to go on with Mr Humphries, Croft insisted that much of the comedy would be lost without him and that the presence of Humphries was non-negotiable. Cotton succumbed.

The arrival of a full series was intriguingly heralded in the *Daily Express* in the same week as rehearsals began. Describing the upcoming series as 'a show without stars', James Thomas wrote: 'TV comedy seems to be swinging away from the outrageous and back to the safe situation with which Mrs Mary Whitehouse will find no quarrel. I am not sure this is a good thing, for new patterns are only exploited through experiment and I doubt if *Are You Being Served?* will come anywhere near that category.' Perhaps Mr Thomas was unprepared for the upcoming twelve years of camp comedy, suggestive shop displays and jokes about Mrs Slocombe's pussy!

Of his new creation, Croft almost underplayed the show, reflecting that, 'In a way we shall be identifying with the past. It is a very close look at a very small world in which everybody has his place. But it is a world we all come up against, buying new underpants or a cigarette case, without the faintest idea of the curious relationships which exist behind the scenes. It's almost like the theatre.'

Are You Being Served? was indeed like the theatre. Frank recalled:

> We tried not to do too many retakes because it would upset the flow; after all it wasn't as if we were playing Shakespeare. And we didn't use canned laughter. So it was more like playing to a theatre audience. We had to film well in advance to fit in with people's theatre arrangements. John Inman always had a pantomime and a summer season to do, so he was available only in the spring and autumn.

The sets were basic enough – the main shop floor and the adjoining office of Mr Rumbold, with only the occasional visit to the canteen appearing as any other regular set. Rehearsals would take place for five days ahead of filming at the weekend. Felix Bowness, another regular member of the unofficial David Croft repertory company, was the warm-up man and, after his routine, filming in front of the studio audience would commence.

Croft had five cameras at his disposal, but by the time *Are You Being Served?* reached its later series Frank was finding that the heavy lighting and the length of time it took to get cameras sorted – ten in the morning until 6.30 at night – while standing on a cream-coloured, reflective, hard floor meant it was akin to being out in full sun for eight hours. The only way he felt he could stop himself from ending up with a blinding headache was by wearing dark glasses and a panama hat!

The premise of the opening episode, aired in colour on its reappearance, established the rivalry between gents' ready-made and ladies' apparel. Mr Grainger was being forced to surrender some of his floor space to allow the ladies to be moved in, something about which he was less than impressed.

Captain Peacock was the floorwalker who actually did nothing of particular use, merely noting when a potential customer had arrived and summoning a staff member from the appropriate counter by calling to them, 'Are you free?'

The futility of his job was not lost on other members of staff; 'Anyone can stand there with their nose in the air looking stupid,' protested Mrs Slocombe when being rebuffed at the idea of taking over from Peacock in a later episode.

The pilot episode introduced the viewer to much of the character that Frank would develop over the years. After reprimanding Mrs Slocombe for not putting the new Beauty Belle display in a prominent position and Mr Lucas for his untidiness, Captain Peacock delivers for the first time one of his death stares as he looks to Mr Humphries for support on which kind of writing implement should be stored within the breast pocket; 'Ballpoints, Captain Peacock,' was the line to get the admonishing glare in return.

The highlight from Frank's point of view in the first episode is his teaching Mr Lucas how to arrange his handkerchief appropriately: 'We place it, so. We then take it in the middle like so, we flute it, so. We bend over the bottom, so… and tuck it back, so.'

Throughout this description, of course, from the suggestive manner of fluting to bending over the bottom, Mr Humphries is looking on with a mixture of shock and enthusiasm, but Frank carries off his delivery impeccably with his faultless physical humour. Peacock's admonishing of Mr Lucas would become a mainstay of the seven years that Bannister was on the show.

'I remember asking Frank where he got the character of Captain Peacock,' recalled Richard Bentine, who remained lifelong friends with the Thorntons. In traditionally modest fashion, Frank offered full credit to Jeremy Lloyd: 'He said he was described down to the way he dealt with the cuffs on his jacket, his mannerisms, everything: Jeremy absolutely painted the portrait of this man and Frank said, "That's who I became."'

Frank was of course firmly of the belief that a good actor could do comedy without trying to be funny, which was fundamental to his underplaying the comic element to Peacock. Years later he would recall the words of the great farceur Ralph Lynn who at a casting conference in 1954 said of an actor whose name had arisen, 'Oh no, not him. He tries to be funny. You mustn't try to be funny. I don't try to be funny,' (pause) 'but, by God I *am* funny.'

Frank's reason for citing this memory was to express that, 'One must remember that the character doesn't think he or she is funny: that is for the audience to decide.' And Frank's reasoning was put into practice perfectly. Throughout the show's ten series, barely a smile drifted across Peacock's face, and yet once one looks beyond the pussy jokes and the campness of Mr Humphries, much of the programme's success hinged on Peacock maintaining a humourless tone of inflated superiority… and that was down to Frank.

Peacock himself was a pompous character, hanging onto his military rank and lording it above his subordinates. 'He had no right to use his title when he was demobbed,' Frank recalled. 'Only senior officers could do that, but he did it in order to give himself a feeling of superiority.'

Peacock despised reporting to Mr Rumbold, a buffoon in many ways, and over the years there would be many occasions whereby Rumbold would get completely the wrong end of the stick in conversations, allowing double meanings to flow at remarkable pace.

The military history of Peacock was highly questionable and there would be frequent jibes at the Captain's expense suggesting that the staff all knew his claims were not backed up. This would come to a head in series seven when the search for a new member of the menswear department unearthed Mr Goldberg (Alfie Bass), who recognises 'Corporal' Peacock from his own military days. 'We both got a cushy job in the cookhouse,' Goldberg reminds him at his interview! Rumbold protested that Peacock fought hand to hand with Rommel's army, but Goldberg would blackmail Peacock to get the job with photographic evidence of Peacock's military exaggeration.

Although the pilot episode lacked some of the more obvious seaside postcard humour, the first of the newly filmed episodes dived right in. Subsequently, the second episode, 'Dear Sexy Knickers', set the tone for all that followed it, with a suggestive invite from Mr Lucas intended for Miss Brahms falling into the wrong hands and leading to a series of misunderstandings.

In those early episodes there were plenty of missed lines and the sight of the boom microphone in shot was a regular one.

The press were largely horrified at what they had seen. The *Times* said of the opening episode, 'What could have been rich play between Mollie Sugden's hoity-toity chief of ladies' wear and the men, led by Frank Thornton as Captain Peacock, the head floorwalker who fusses over a display handkerchief like a butler with a bottle of vintage port, was ruined last night by vulgar knockabout and silly jokes – old silly jokes.'

The *Mail* was no kinder: 'What could have been a success in the vein of *Dad's Army* is only Grade Two comedy exploiting the willingness of most of us to laugh at anything we recognise immediately as funny.'

The BBC wasn't particularly kind to its new show, but then it was never one for treating *Are You Being Served?* as well as it treated other shows. Having been reluctant to even air the pilot, the first series was given an unenviable slot opposite *Coronation Street*, ensuring a lukewarm response from viewers.

But those who watched it, liked it; and, like the rest of the cast, Frank felt that there just might be hope for the widely dismissed show: 'It is perhaps interesting that while critics such as these are very scathing about the show, the public reaction has been very enthusiastic, with shop assistants coyly saying, "Are you free, Captain Peacock?", even a policeman calling, "Are you being served?" from his car and wanting to know when the show would be on again.'

Despite the uncertainty from the first series as to whether *Are You Being Served?* would return to the air, Frank's journals show an astonishing amount of work in the interim. British sitcoms being of only limited runs compared to their American equivalents, as well as being poorly paid, meant that even a successful television programme needed to be supplemented with other work across the year.

Frank openly admitted to a single day's work being his standard for most jobs as the parts he was getting were minor; but he had become such a reliable asset that the demand from the cream of the British talent at the time was relentless. It is also intriguing to see how he reacted to some of those stars.

He made several recordings for Tommy Cooper. Now revered as one of the iconic performers of the 1970s, Cooper had already had Frank appear on his show in 1969, but Frank recalled that Tommy had gone over his time with his solo spot by eight minutes. Something had to go, and it couldn't be the host, so inevitably Frank's guest spot was cut, frustrating for all as it had seemingly been a very well-received sketch. Frank nonetheless worked for Cooper again in 1973, with the somewhat inevitable result – Tommy overran again! This time fifteen minutes had to be cut, but thankfully only one of Frank's two sketches fell in the editing, so one out of three overall sketches made it to viewers' screens.

Frank also appeared with Dudley Moore in *It's Lulu, Not to Mention Dudley Moore*. Dudley was of course a great giggler, so it's interesting to note that Frank mentioned, 'I maintain my reputation for imperturbability when all around me are dissolving into giggles,' doubtless involving chief giggler Dudley. Corpsing was indeed not something Frank usually suffered from, later citing Danny La Rue as the only man ever to cause him to corpse when appearing together in *Our Miss Fred*.

Regular appearances on *Scott On...* and *The Reg Varney Revue* were squeezed into Frank's schedule. He particularly enjoyed his time in *Scott On...* as it gave him a chance to sing, saying that it was something he wouldn't have dared to do without Terry Scott and that increased his self-confidence. It was somewhat ironic therefore that alongside a picture from *The Reg Varney Revue* where he is gathered alongside Varney, David Lodge, Pat Coombs and Elizabeth Counsell, he jokingly noted that, 'That bugger insisted that I join in the chorus!'

Frank even found time to appear in a radio incarnation of *Dad's Army*. As much as he enjoyed the occasion to be with other David Croft favourites like Arthur Lowe, John Le Mesurier and his old pal Clive Dunn, he wrote with some sadness of the absence of James Beck, by now very seriously ill.

Just a few months later Frank noted, 'An attempt at doing a one-hour comedy programme all on film location [*The Village Concert*]. The finished result was alas very unfunny. An unhappy story associated with this production is that Ian Lavender had taken over James Beck's part when he became ill. Jimmy's cremation service took place while we were filming. He will be missed – a good actor and a nice fella.'

The Goodies was one of the less likely shows for Frank to appear in, but given his penchant for being the authority figure to rebel against or mock, perhaps the anarchic trio of Graeme Garden, Bill Oddie and Tim Brooke-Taylor actually provided the perfect home for him.

He made his first appearance in this busy time as a waiter in 'Farm Fresh Food', trying to persuade the three to order all manner of processed food. When he appeared again as a punk rocker in a later series, Frank was sent up along with a number of other guests as punk rock gripped the nation.

'I recall his performance as the MC at the Punk Ball,' remembered Graeme Garden. 'In a tattered costume festooned with tat and safety pins, he mooched about the set with that wonderfully lugubrious face expressing extreme disapproval. But when it came to the performance, with that booming voice and military bearing, it was clear that he was having a whale of a time. He appreciated silliness and had impeccable comic instincts.'

Those impeccable comic instincts, along with the talents of his co-stars and doubtless some persuading from David Croft, eventually convinced the BBC to persevere with a second series of *Are You Being Served?* which began rehearsals in February 1974. This time the corporation gave it a more fighting chance of finding an audience by putting it after *Top of the Pops* on a Thursday evening. It had the desired effect with viewer numbers increasing almost as a polar opposite to the critical reception.

For all its success and that vast body of work Frank was accumulating alongside the greatest in British comedy, he still yearned for more dramatic roles. For all his comedic talents and funny bones, he was at heart a trained actor; but as Peacock and his subordinates gained in popularity, so he started fearing drifting into the world of typecasting. Calls for dramatic roles at the BBC had dried up.

Frank went from one extreme to another in 1974 as on the completion of recording the second series of *Are You Being Served?* he went to the Royal Shakespeare Theatre for a stint as Sir Andrew Aguecheek in *Twelfth Night*. Director Peter Gill, who had worked with Frank on the troubled production of *Meals on Wheels* in 1965 as John Osborne's assistant, initially wanted Frank to play Malvolio. It was also what Frank himself would have preferred, but Nicol Williamson wanted that part and since he was also booked for *Macbeth*, Williamson took that role leaving Frank with a choice of Sir Andrew or nothing.

Frank felt he was somewhat miscast due to his age: 'In the event it wasn't perhaps quite as bad as that, though my notices were quite extraordinarily mixed. Alas the predominant note was "faint praise".' It was a gruelling schedule, rehearsing for eight weeks before arriving in Stratford for further dress rehearsals and six previews.

Notices were indeed mixed, but Frank as ever was gracious in acknowledging the skills of the cast and protective as much of them as he was of himself. Williamson, who had carved out a reputation both within the profession and with outside observers as one of the leading lights among Shakespeare performers, was dismissed by Frank Marcus in the *Sunday Telegraph* as having no talent for comedy, while ironically in sister paper the *Daily Telegraph* John Barber hailed Williamson's performance as brilliant. Barber noted that his Malvolio was 'a silver-haired invalid as comical in his pomposity as he is pathetic in his conceit'. One can see why Frank felt that role would have suited him, given the success he was now finding with those attributes of Captain Peacock.

In defence of his colleague Frank recalled, 'Mr Frank Marcus doesn't seem to like anything or anybody. It is always interesting when a critic says, as he does, that Nicol has no talent for comedy. What then, in the name of reason, were they laughing at? I would like to hear him and John Barber discuss Nicol Williamson's performance.'

Now back at home with the bard, Frank moved seamlessly from *Twelfth Night* to *Macbeth*. In comparison with working for Wolfit, Frank was intrigued at how times had changed when it came to a production cutting its coat according to its cloth as he gained his first experience with one of the major subsidised theatres:

Certainly they know nothing of how to trim your budget to the resources of the box office in the way that Donald Wolfit had to do in presenting Shakespeare. Certainly, there was overstaffing and certainly when inflation began to enforce some economy it was not all the overstaffing that was cut down – it was, inevitably, the actors. Instead of getting rid of, for example, the publicity director and his staff (for, I ask you, what theatre in the world needs less publicity than Stratford?), Trevor Nunn decided to put on *Macbeth* with a cast of only thirteen actors, making an artistic virtue out of thirteen actors playing all thirty-odd parts. Now he may have been perfectly sincere in his artistic endeavour, but it didn't half save on actors' salaries. So it was actors who signed on at the Labour Exchange.

And of course, for those kept on it meant a heavier workload. For Frank himself, that meant taking on the roles of Duncan, a ghost in the cauldron, Edward IV of England, the Scottish Doctor and a walk-on in the final scene.

As frustrating as it was for Frank to see his fellow cast members axed ahead of personal assistants and advisers, he did admit that the whole experience was a happy one across the two productions; and what made it all the more enjoyable was the comfort of having his beloved Beryl alongside him for the entire season. They had found themselves a shepherd's cottage to rent in nearby Kinwarton, a spotlessly clean two-up, two-down property surrounded by tranquillity. However hard Frank was prepared to work, and he was, he was never happier than when he had the company of Beryl and a comfortable home.

As the Stratford season rolled on, Frank found himself in the bizarre scenario of getting down to Acton to rehearse and record a third series of *Are You Being Served?* at the same time as holding down his roles in one or other of the Shakespeare plays, life made somewhat easier when *Twelfth Night* and *Macbeth* transferred in toned-down versions to the Aldwych; his involvement in *Macbeth* being now down to Duncan only, he was only on stage for twenty minutes, meaning the company were still finishing when Frank had his feet up with a glass of whisky in hand! There was even time to squeeze in a few days' filming for the movie *The Bawdy Adventures of Tom Jones*, 'involving an exit upstairs with dropped trousers, no underpants and a cunning arrangement of camera tape!'

An invitation for Frank and Beryl to attend the BBC Light Entertainment department's 1974 Christmas Party at Television Centre was a first for them; but as much as it was a reflection of how well *Are You Being Served?* was gaining traction, it also signalled a continuing trend that, at the BBC at least, Light Entertainment was where Frank was to be pigeonholed, whether he liked it or not.

Like it or not was a dilemma facing the critics over *Are You Being Served?*, but the public following was growing significantly. Despite commanding excellent reviews for a role in George Bernard Shaw's *Doctor's Dilemma*, the public were now starting to see Frank Thornton as Captain Peacock first and foremost.

Success for the show had its offshoot benefits, of course. Frank had recorded a multitude of commercials to help keep money coming through the door, including a safety advert with his onscreen co-star Larry Martyn (maintenance man Mr Mash). With *Are You Being Served?* making its stars so recognised, Frank was asked to wear a pair of neatly fitting incisors and perform as a somewhat joked-up Dracula in adverts for Smiths Crisps' Horror Bags opposite Nicholas Smith: 'I thought it would never see the light of day... but experience will show that it and the nasty product became a great success with the children.'

Just as Frank was happy to turn his attention to most adverts offered to him, equally he was prepared to make personal appearances. Far less glamorous or well remunerated as they would be in later years, in 1975 his first 'in person' event as Captain Peacock came in the form of opening a new department at Medhursts Department Store in Bromley.

The chauffeur-driven Rolls Royce in which he arrived only had to transport its honoured traveller from the rear of the store to the front, Frank having parked his Volkswagen round the back. After a speech, ceremonial ribbon cutting, photographs, autographs, tour, sherry and most importantly, the pay cheque, he was back in the VW to head to Elstree to film a scene in the Leslie Phillips movie *Spanish Fly*. A whistle-stop personal appearance the like of which would become more frequent as he became ever more ingrained into the public psyche.

The next set of adverts to be filmed demonstrated the absurdity of fame. Frank and Beryl packed up for an overseas trip, beginning in

Canada where he would make six promotional films for the Ontario Pork Production Marketing Board, apparently designed to promote various national recipes all using pork. It made for some unusual-sounding takes on well-known classics, including pork bourguignon, pork cannelloni, pork stroganoff and pork and kidney pie!

Like so much of Frank's work, the adverts were a huge success, so much so that within the year he was asked back to portray a whole new set of characters for Ontario Pork. His second trip started with a slightly more awkward conversation as he tried to dissuade the Pork Board official from having Frank portray Rhett Butler. It was an argument Frank lost; but, 'Thanks to a film clip for study, a superb make-up man and a modicum of ability on the part of F. T. it went very well indeed.'

The second set of films were as much of a success as the first as Frank ran the character and accent gamut in five days, this time playing a butcher, switching from Canadian to Irish to Mexican with funny hats and fake moustaches, Napoleon and Josephine, a Latin lover, and a French waiter to a German customer!

Frank and Beryl left Canada on that first trip and were then destined for New York, first making a stop at Niagara Falls to include dinner with old friend Frankie Howerd, another comedy great Frank had added his gravitas to. According to Beryl, Frankie once commented that she always seemed to be behind Frank pushing him along. One can only imagine now the spectacle of seeing these stalwarts of British comedy in such a setting, with Frankie, hands on hips, saying, 'Yes, we can see who wears the trousers in that household!'

Once safely ensconced at the Hotel Elysee on 54th Street, the Thorntons set about seeing the sights and shows around Broadway; and, after several days, they took in supper at Sardi's restaurant. During their evening, Richard Burton arrived with a few guests, one of whom was British actor Brook Williams. Frank knew Brook but also knew that it would be very poor etiquette to engage him in conversation, particularly as it may look as though they were trying to engineer an introduction to Burton.

He needn't have worried as Brook spotted Frank and Beryl and brought Burton over to introduce them. They exchanged pleasantries and had a brief chat before Williams and Burton returned to their table.

Frank was subsequently amazed at how he and Beryl now went from complete anonymity to the focus of all eyes – after all, they must be important if Burton goes over and stands at *their* table!

Shortly afterwards, a man in a lounge suit appeared, introduced himself as owner Victor Saidl, and immediately laid on the VIP treatment. He subsequently introduced them to Richard Watts, drama critic for the *New York Post*, even though he still had absolutely no idea who either of them was.

Before they finished their evening, Zero Mostel and his wife arrived, greeting them loudly across the room with a roar and following it up with a bear hug. They shared drinks with Frank's former co-star at Mostel's table before Zero took them home in his and his wife's cab. It was a taste of fame somewhat bemusing, given that to this point adulation had come solely in England with shouts of 'Are you free, Captain Peacock?' from punters in the street.

For series four of *Are You Being Served?* the first personnel change occurred as Larry Martyn said farewell as he was committed to the ITV sitcom *Spring and Autumn*. He had been starring in that show with Jimmy Jewel in tandem with his Grace Brothers appearances but backed the wrong horse as *Spring and Autumn* ended in 1976. He was replaced at Grace Brothers by Arthur English as the new head of maintenance, Mr Harman.

English would later recall nothing but immense pleasure during his time on the show. As Mr Mash before him, Mr Harman was continually reprimanded by Captain Peacock for being on the shop floor during opening hours, reflected in the recording sessions on the Sunday evenings. As opposed to the warm-up man introducing the whole cast, he would simply introduce English, who would then proceed to introduce the rest of the cast himself. He recalled, 'I would introduce Frank Thornton by getting down on my knees and salaaming to him.'

Series producer David Croft developed a penchant for creating stage shows from his most successful television shows. *Dad's Army*, *'Allo 'Allo!*, *Hi-de-hi!* and *It Ain't Half Hot Mum* were all given the stage treatment, each with immense ticket sales in their summer seasons even if, perhaps expectedly, not greeted with critical acclaim. *Hi-de-hi!* and *Dad's Army* even made successful transfers to the West End.

In 1976, Croft was in overdrive. *Dad's Army* was nearing the end of its days, but *It Ain't Half Hot Mum* was in full flow and *Are You Being Served?* had become equally popular. Despite its ageing cast, *Dad's Army* had been turned into a stage show in readiness for a season at the Opera House in Blackpool. Impresario Bernard Delfont rather liked the idea of *Are You Being Served?* being brought to the stage too, so in May of 1976 Croft and Jeremy Lloyd set to work on getting Grace Brothers' staff to tread the boards. As the basis of the show, they used one of the television series storylines, Grace Brothers being closed for refurbishment resulting in Mr Grace packing them all off on holiday together.

The stage show was produced in the theatre immediately next door to *Dad's Army*, a veritable treat for any holidaymakers in Blackpool for the summer of '76. Of course, *Are You Being Served?* had always contained a large chunk of seaside postcard humour, but now that they actually were beside the seaside, Croft and Lloyd really went for it.

According to Frank, budget didn't run to including Trevor Bannister, nor did health concerns permit the appearance of Arthur Brough given the exhausting schedule of sixteen weeks, twice nightly. Pam Bannister, however, recalled that, 'Trevor turned down the stage show because he thought it was going to be awful. Frank did it but, I think, bitterly regretted it.'

With no Bannister or Brough, nor for that matter Harold Bennett, much of the interplay between departments was gone, leaving gaping holes for the innuendo to fill… It was ramped up significantly and therefore, somewhat inevitably, Mr Humphries and Mrs Slocombe became pivotal to the success of the show. Inman himself recalled at the time that the writers had 'dirtied it up for the Blackpool audience'. With Inman and Mollie Sugden becoming far more central to the dirtier jokes, Captain Peacock was reduced to more of a comic feed than a comedy character of his own.

The change in dynamic was not lost on Frank, but it was something he would have to get used to. 'This is the first time I signed a contract for a play before it has been written – and the last!' he bemoaned of the undercurrent of change. 'This may very well prove to be a good commercial proposition, but it would have been nice to have been told about the drastic shift in balance… However, the salary is good so I shall grin and bear it.'

When interviewed for PBS in 2000, Nicholas Smith recalled that the show was struggling in its early days despite good takings. 'We couldn't get laughs,' he recalled, 'except in the second act where John wore a woman's nightie and popped two balloons he was wearing underneath it. Frank said, "I've been an actor for thirty years and I can't get a laugh here."'

Despite not being involved, Trevor and Pam Bannister still attended one evening. She recalled, 'We popped in to see them all and everybody was saying, "Oh my God, it was dreadful," but they were committed to doing it.'

Frank was right about the success at the box office, but every expense was spared when it came to the staging of the show, recalling:

We open officially on 18th June 1976 in one of the cheapest and most crudely painted lot of sets it has ever been my misfortune to meet. For example, one front-cloth scene of a Spanish hotel has a large window showing out onto the swimming pool etc. The designer gave the painter a holiday brochure and told him to copy it. He did – right down to the lady climbing out of the pool! There she is, frozen for sixteen weeks! Whatever I may think, the piece is a smashing success with the public and our business is far and away better than any of our competitors either here or elsewhere. It is almost unknown to have the first house sold out so often.

David Croft was proven correct in his approach, at least from a fiscal standpoint. He acknowledged that the play was 'broad comedy' from the first minute, but it seemed that this was exactly what the audiences wanted. *Are You Being Served?* took more in four days than its neighbouring production *Dad's Army* did in a week, and capacity estimates range from 95% to 98% across the entire summer, a remarkable return.

With a sixteen-week roaring success at Blackpool under its belt, *Are You Being Served?* was only becoming more popular. At its peak it was commanding viewing figures in excess of twenty million. It was no surprise that rehearsals for a fifth season began in early 1977. Audiences had taken Arthur English to their hearts as Mr Harman and so the cast remained as tightly knit as it had ever been. 'We were very lucky on that show,' Frank recalled. 'We were a bunch of actors who all got on very well. Underneath all the petty jealousies and rivalries of the characters, we got on like a house on fire.'

The rapport among the cast came across exceptionally well. As the show had gone on, Captain Peacock's disdain for Mr Rumbold's running of the floor had gradually ingratiated him into being 'one of the team' rather than the hierarchy, except on the odd occasion when power went to his head. Rumbold was his superior in rank, but in no way his superior as a person.

The show would have a long life overseas as well, being so remarkably English, and in 1977 the whole shop-floor crew were invited over to Holland for a range of interviews with local media, along with a boat trip, some autograph signings and a shop opening; the kind of thing they had each become accustomed to on a more individual basis back at home.

The trip seemed innocent enough. After arriving at a hotel in Utrecht, the quintet of stars plus some of their companions were greeted by flowers, drinks and a lunch before being whisked off by a pair of Rolls Royces to open a leisurewear store in town. It was a market day so the already narrow streets were even more so, especially as people knew that British television stars were in town.

A gathering crowd had reached huge numbers, thousands in Frank's estimation. The cast hastily started signing preprinted photos to hand to their adoring public, but police were needed to hold back the crowd behind barriers and in the end it was decided that, for safety's sake, they would instead repair to a first-floor balcony and throw the signed pictures from above.

After a brief visit to Amsterdam, the British visitors were then treated to a canal boat trip courtesy of the magazine who were accompanying them on their whistle-stop tour. Here each was picked off for more individual chats with the reporter, named – somewhat aptly given the Croft and Lloyd reputation – Ruud Kok. Frank and Beryl squeezed in a visit to the Rijkmuseum in Amsterdam and a brief tea and cakes with a local bank manager before the end of a hectic day... but something troubled Frank about the boat journey.

Courtesy and ethical behaviour were a must for Frank. They were elements of his personality built into his British gentleman nature and he understandably hoped for reciprocal behaviour in others. As it was a first trip to Holland, Frank felt it only right to learn an element of the language. However rudimentary his Dutch was, a combination of the smoothness of the group's reporter companion and the limited amount of understanding of the published article led him to think all was not as it should be. As such, he sent the article away for a more accurate translation. He was right to have been suspicious.

The translated article was perfectly nice about Frank and Beryl, noting that unlike Captain Peacock, Frank was 'courteous, friendly and not at all high hat'. Mollie Sugden was also spared any derogatory comments, although the quotes made do depict her as somewhat more of a starry-eyed housewife than she doubtless was. For Trevor Bannister, most of the focus was on how often the reporter caught him with a gin and tonic in his hand, while their line of questioning was more about his marriage split at the time, Bannister having been married once before meeting Pam.

John Inman didn't fare terribly well. The translation shows that they quizzed him as to whether it was true that his now deceased fiancée forced him into acting. Inman had actually first appeared on stage as a child.

'I've always wanted to be an actor, even when I was a small boy,' the translation read. He looked at a photo being waved at him. 'Is the picture of a girl you're showing me supposed to be my fiancée?' he retorted. 'I don't even know the woman. Pure nonsense. It's all made up.'

The reporter also prodded and poked enough to establish that Inman was doubting his ongoing involvement in the series. 'This is how you get to learn about things if you tour Holland with the leading players of this very funny and enjoyable television series,' the article boasted, as if the acknowledgment of the show's quality and success was enough to recompense for the unpleasantness within.

The person who emerged the worst of all was Wendy Richard. The article depicted her as a sullen, grumpy and demanding woman who was there under duress and had more time for showbiz tantrums than the duties they were there to perform. One subsection of the article is simply titled, 'Miss Brahms is bad-tempered.'

The article went on to suggest that Wendy stamped her feet when not in the Rolls that she wanted to travel in and that she was forever ordering her future husband Will Thorpe around. 'She looks angry again to show that she's fed up with me,' the article closes with. A thoroughly unpleasant and unwarranted character assassination.

The team had always been protective of Wendy Richard. During that period she led a troubled life where relationships were concerned and there were occasions when the make-up department had to work especially hard to cover up bruises from her most tumultuous partnership.

Frank's translation received, he was both justified in his pursuit of an English version and horrified at having his suspicions confirmed:

> Boat trip on the canal during which more photographs and more interviews for a magazine that resulted in a surprisingly unpleasant article containing snide comments on several of us by the smooth-seeming interviewer with the truly appropriate name Ruud Kok. The mag' printed it all plus colour photographs. Can't newspapermen be nasty bastards sometimes? The question is 'why?' Is it that unpleasantness sells more copies than the opposite?

Frank was always protective of his castmates, whether it be functional or reputational. During *Shut Your Eyes and Think of England*, despite Frank's desire to get home to Beryl he would wait for co-star Jan Holden after every performance in order to drive her to the railway station and see her safely on board for her trip home to Brighton. He was also in defence mode in 1975 when appearing in a new production called *Play-By-Play*, with some heavy-hitting cast members alongside him.

The play was by Robert Patrick, who was fresh from success with *Kennedy's Children* and so the assembled cast had names like Sheila Hancock, Christopher Benjamin and Hugh Paddick alongside Frank. Robin Askwith, who was becoming known for the *Confessions Of...* films, was amongst the younger names in the cast.

Play-By-Play was being produced at the King's Head, Islington, which was what Frank described as 'a pub with an air of imminent physical collapse, unbelievable lavatories, a small stage and one communal dressing room which is in fact the passage behind the stage'.

Despite saluting his enthusiasm, Frank noted of American Dan Crawford, who ran the King's Head, 'He refuses to install such modern things as decimal currency and central heating. He prefers to retain the old fire grates but unfortunately the Clean Air Acts won't let him put fires in them!'

The play was about a Shakespeare company with characters who were actually saying what they really thought of each other – an early take on *Noises Off* in some ways but set in the world of Shakespearean actors. Frank played one of two clowns opposite Askwith. It was a clever play, perhaps too clever. Frank had already taken issue with one critic who dismissed the production as camp and parochial, where 'everyone behaves as if they were screamingly funny. They are wrong.'

Frank was disappointed by the review, as he said: 'Hugh, Sheila and I are too old in the business to be guilty of "trying to be funny", and being on the stage every night are in the unique position to know whether the audience think we are funny. They often did.'

The reviews didn't stop coming in. One even threw a back-handed compliment to Frank in an otherwise scathing critique, suggesting that 'I suppose a play can be said to have a distinction of a kind if it prevents Mr Thornton from getting a wholehearted laugh.'

Particularly riling Frank was Milton Shulman, who, while leaving Frank's name out of his scathing *Evening Standard* review, took the whole company down with his belief that 'Actors are a limited lot. They weight their parts, can rarely tell a good play from a bad and judge success by the volume of noise they arouse.'

Frank was seething as he wrote:

> Completely without exception the critics, while acknowledging that Sheila, Hugh and I probably by this time know our jobs pretty well and that the youngsters aren't half bad either, entirely fail to realise why we accepted the engagement. We all know the play was a piece of pretentious rubbish and we all decided to do it because of the opportunity to work together and produce, if possible, something approaching a silk purse from a sow's ear. The form of the play provided the rare opportunity of improvising within a character, capitalising thus on any mistake, dry, fluff and so on to produce laughter from the audience, something the author wanted but did not provide the material for.

Frank wasn't always comfortable with straying from the script. Madeline Smith remembered his look of horror when Donald Sinden improvised by smashing a telephone into the audience in *Shut Your Eyes and Think of England*, a piece of improv' that subsequently stayed in the show. But *Play-By-Play* was a very different production, with the intimacy of the King's Head and the punters enjoying dinner during the show.

As Frank rightly highlighted, he, Hugh Paddick and Sheila Hancock were too long established to be overly concerned with the reviews, which incidentally were not entirely echoed by audience numbers once the play had settled into its rhythm. But he was concerned about the 'youngsters' as he referred to them.

The clowns that Frank and Askwith played were extras engaged in a constant game of one-upmanship, endeavouring to outdo the leading players. 'I used to irritate the hell out of Frank, but I never knew if it was for real,' recalled Askwith. 'Invariably, people had had enough at half-time. They'd had their dinner, thought, what the fuck is this? and walked out.'

Askwith had recently won the Outstanding Newcomer category at the *Evening Standard* film awards so was seemingly in a good place, but the critics to some degree went after him as he was appearing in a great many shows on stage and screen at the time:

> After I won the award, I went on stage with it to prove I was the better clown. The audience loved it, they cheered. Frank and I got on incredibly well, but that was the nature of the characters. In the end I brought on a bigger award every night for about five nights.

The disheartening sight of people leaving the show was particularly dispiriting for Askwith, however:

> People were walking out in their droves, particularly when Frank and I were on stage. I sat backstage and I was very distressed while Frank was doing his *Daily Telegraph* crossword in the interval. I said, 'Frank, I'm not going to go out there again,' and he said, 'Oh you've got to go out, dear boy, you've got to...' I said, 'But Frank, they're walking out,' and he said, 'Ah yes, but did you see their faces?'
>
> I think that summed him up completely, that sort of absolute stoic optimism. His way of getting through it was to believe that everyone was loving it.

And in reality, the quality of the ensemble was strong enough not only to see the run through, but the cast actually got a pay rise and the run was extended as the little theatre was being filled as it rarely had before!

Back then to Blighty and once home from Holland it was safe to say that Frank was in *Are You Being Served?* overload. The trip had happened in the early hours of a Saturday morning after an 8pm filming of a series five episode on the preceding Friday. Just a few weeks later, the whole cast, reunited with Arthur English, Harold Bennett, Nicholas Smith and Arthur Brough, would begin filming probably the low point of the show's entire history – the movie version of *Are You Being Served?*

Just as Croft and Lloyd had successfully mounted stage versions of their work, so now they turned to the established practice of getting their characters on the big screen. This trend spanned a much wider range than just Croft and Lloyd or Jimmy Perry. *Porridge*, *Steptoe and Son*, *Bless This House*, *Rising Damp* and, most profitably, *On The Buses* were a few among many TV sitcoms that made the transfer to the cinema, some with remarkable box-office returns.

It seemed the British public couldn't get enough of the bawdy comedies that appeared on their television sets, and they turned out in their droves to send the movies to greater box-office success than some of Hollywood's biggest hitters of the time. Frank's character acting even brought him into the fold, appearing in *Steptoe and Son Ride Again* as well as the *Bless This House* and *Till Death Us Do Part* cinema releases.

Are You Being Served? was a far inferior vehicle to most of its sitcom rivals when it came to its film version. Frank didn't want to do it, and the money on offer was derisory, but the team were so entrenched in their 'all for one, one for all' approach to the show that none of them wanted to be the one to rock the boat. The script was a rehashed version of the stage show, but what was popular for a Blackpool summer show certainly didn't transfer well to the cinema screen.

'Mistakes that we ironed out in Blackpool were still in the film script,' bemoaned Nicholas Smith.

For the third time, the story of Grace Brothers closing for redecoration and therefore Young Mr Grace sending them all to a dubious holiday destination at his expense was wheeled out. The gang are forced to spend their night in tents outside the main hotel and their arrival at the Costa Plonka is particularly badly timed as a revolution is taking place, culminating in them getting caught in the crossfire between revolutionaries and the authorities.

The addition of Andrew Sachs, between the two series of playing Manuel in *Fawlty Towers*, is almost certainly the only redeeming quality of the film. 'It was dreadful,' remembered Pam Bannister. 'Trevor said, "Oh good, it's going to be set in Spain," but the farthest they got was Gatwick Airport to get on this dummy plane.'

Sure enough, the budget didn't stretch to any location shooting. The only outside shot was indeed the filming of the Grace Brothers staff climbing the steps into a jet. Everything else was back in the studio. 'No money is spent,' Frank noted. 'Crowds of three people and the result is quite awful.'

When the filming was over, more turmoil was waiting for the cast of *Are You Being Served?* as they said a tearful farewell to one of their most beloved cast members, while facing the prospect of the show getting axed at the height of its success.

7

The West End or the Mechanics' Institute

WITH THE STAGE AND MOVIE VERSIONS OF *Are You Being Served?* complete and the fifth series airing to an ever-increasing audience, there was seemingly little that could derail one of the BBC's most successful series.

Inevitably the critics continued to disparage the show, but Frank remained as protective as ever of its success. The freelance journalist Douglas Kynoch wrote a particularly barbed piece for *The Times* in which he claimed to test the 'crudities' of *Are You Being Served?* on a ten-year-old boy. The supposed boy was questioning what was funny about Mrs Slocombe's cat getting clipped and shampooed and Mr Humphries giving an organ demonstration. Once it was explained to him that these were all jokes because the words used had other meanings of a sexual nature, in Mrs Slocombe's case the 'female genital area', the boy questioned if the programme was a sex education programme and pondered why they filled it with sex things at ten to seven in the evening if it wasn't. 'I really can't say, darling. Why don't you write a nice letter to the BBC?

Perhaps the Board of Governors can explain.' The fictitious mother was clearly unimpressed.

Frank was even less impressed and despite knowing how *Are You Being Served?* had been dirtied up for the Blackpool run, he took to his writing desk to defend the programme on behalf of his colleagues:

Dear Sir

When I was very young, my elders were briefly amused by the 'Knock! Knock!' 'Who's there?' routine. One in particular baffled me completely. It went on:

'Paralysis.'

'Paralysis who?'

'Paralysis in the family way.'

I puzzled over it for a while but soon turned to more important things like my Meccano set. If only I had known how deprived I was! If only Douglas Kynoch had been around at the time, he could have explained in detail how poor Alice had permitted a man to give 'an organ demonstration' in her 'female genital area' thus producing a state of pregnancy etc etc etc.

How it would have opened my blinkered eyes! I could have given up building model cranes and the Forth Bridge and led a useful and productive life looking for the dirty bits in *Tiger Tim* and *The Magnet*.

Perhaps in next Sunday's issue Mr Kynoch would like to bring his fearless probing mind to bear upon that piece of seaside postcard filth that up to now has given pleasure to innocents of all ages. It's called *A Midsummer Night's Dream* and is about a fellow named Bottom (!) who is turned into an Ass(!) and at one point he lays his head in the lap (female genital area) of a fairy (!!) named TITania.

It was ironic that as Frank was protecting the show, it was about to enter its rockiest moment thus far; but for now he was happy to return to the stage. He had a brief tour, the briefest of his career (by the producer's intent, not box-office failing), taking in just Scunthorpe and Preston in a production of *Roger's Last Stand*, for which he received glowing reviews. During rehearsals, Frank became a grandfather at the age of fifty-six. He and Beryl would become grandparents to three boys, Jonathan, Andrew and David. They weren't cuddly grandparents, but it was noticeable that amongst Frank's first-night cards were frequently to be found pictures drawn for him by his grandsons. The boys clearly meant the world to Frank, but his generation just weren't good at showing it.

Frank was back on more familiar ground in September of 1977 in the farce *Shut Your Eyes and Think of England*. The show starred Donald Sinden, with whom Frank would remain friends for the remainder of Sinden's life. It was Sinden who suggested to producer John Gale that Frank would be a good option for the part of Sir Justin Holbrook. He was a particularly awkward character to play, switching not only mood but also character as he shifted from a straight bully to an erring husband to a Jimmy James style of drunk.

Sinden's insistence, for Gale was not as convinced as his star, paid off. Frank was of course magnanimous enough to suggest that Sinden's own performance was the reason for the show getting a year-long run at the Apollo Theatre in Shaftesbury Avenue: 'Very, and at times outrageously inventive, sometimes making his fellow actors blanch with fear, he went blithely over the top but never too far for his audience.'

It was round about midnight one night during rehearsals for *Shut Your Eyes and Think of England* that Frank received a phone call from an unlikely source. It was a call that a younger Frank would have dreamed of before he became a star: 'This is Hoyt Bowers speaking, from Paramount Studios, Hollywood.'

It seemed that the American market was ready to embrace its own incarnation of Grace Brothers, but they had a problem. Casting was not, so they believed, a problem for all but one of the characters. They couldn't find the right actor for the floorwalker and so casting director Bowers decided that rather than risk a miscasting, Americans not having the greatest history of portraying well-spoken English gentlemen, they would go to the original source.

Of course, American shows run for significantly longer than their British equivalents, so talk of a possible six-year deal was startling to Frank. He calculated that even ignoring residuals, a deal contracting him to twenty-six episodes a year for six years would bring in the monetary equivalent of working for the BBC for fifty-two weeks a year – for forty-five years: 'I may not be greedy for money, but it was interesting to say the least!'

It was a theory borne out by the fact that years later, Frank reflected on the financial benefits of *Are You Being Served?* as he cheekily recalled that the smallest cheque he ever received for the show was for thirty-eight pence, and that American broadcasts earned him around a penny per episode!

Frank wrote to David Croft, who was of course involved in the potential export, with his concerns about the complexities of being released from *Shut Your Eyes and Think of England*. As ever, he wasn't just concerned about the financial impact of contractual breaches. With Sinden having stuck his neck out to get him the part, and John Gale having acted on Sinden's recommendation, he felt an element of loyalty was required in return.

Discussions were ongoing for many months. Gale was co-operative in being prepared to release Frank from his stage obligations for the pilot, but he didn't want to release him from the play, allow an understudy to work for a few weeks, and then have Frank resume his role. Frank for his part was prepared to take the chance that the pilot would be picked up, so Gale began making attempts to replace Frank long term.

Frank was dignified in his correspondence with Paramount and Croft, insisting that, above all else, time was the key courtesy that Gale should be afforded. Alas, time was something Frank himself ran out of. The Screen Actors' Guild would not sanction his entry into the country, despite him being a fully paid-up member of both Equity in the UK, and the Assoc-iation of Canadian Television and Radio Artistes. He noted jokingly:

> It seems that you have to have documentary evidence signed by God Almighty to the effect that you are an international star – or alternatively drop a few thousand dollars into the right hands. We could not provide the former and my agent [Max Kester], being an upstanding British Gent, didn't think of the latter. The producers had to engage an American actor at the last minute. Knowing the situation, he stung them for a pretty sum!

The missing permission only stopped Frank appearing in the pilot, so the option remained that if the pilot produced the offer of a series, he could be called upon once again. However, the subsequent offer never materialised. The doomed American version went ahead as *Beane's of*

Boston. Jonathan Hillerman took the role of Peacock. Although being a Texan by birth, Hillerman became very successful with a British accent, most notably as Higgins in *Magnum PI* which was of course a huge success in the 1980s. *Beane's of Boston* was screened in early 1979 and sank without trace.

While Frank was being considered for the American incarnation, another member of the cast was being wooed. Mr Humphries had begun as a comparatively minor role, but as time went on his involvement became ever more integral to the success of the show; and, to satisfy the demand, Croft and Lloyd played to their audience's requests.

John Inman had met with some resistance from the very first episode over his portrayal of Humphries, seen by some to be merely reinforcing the stereotype associated with homosexuals in the 1970s: effeminate mincing, over-the-top outfits, the colour pink. For all that, however, he had become a successful mainstream gay character (although Croft denied specifically defining him as such) in a prime-time comedy show, not something seen before.

With Inman's popularity rising, Thames Television came calling, cheque book in hand. They offered Inman a three-year deal for his own starring vehicle with them. The idea that the two series could co-exist was not an option, ITV and BBC being direct competitors in the fight for viewers.

What they created for Inman was *Odd Man Out*, in which he would be the star, supported by Josephine Tewson. He played a fish-and-chip-shop owner who leaves his business to take up the running of his late father's Blackpool rock sweet factory. The co-owner is his half-sister (Tewson), whose existence was to that point unknown to Inman's character. Vince Powell, the man behind plenty of sitcom success stories like *Bless This House* and *Nearest and Dearest*, wrote the show and there was support from the wonderful Peter Butterworth in the cast.

Odd Man Out was aired while Frank was in rehearsals with Sinden for *Shut Your Eyes and Think of England*. With the Thames contract for Inman being an exclusive one, the question was: what would the absence of Inman mean for *Are You Being Served?* Frank felt that just as shop staff come and go, the programme should be able to survive the departure of a principal actor, including himself, given that it was an ensemble piece:

'I suggested to David Croft we should be able to survive the departure of Mr Humphries. But David and Jeremy Lloyd having a weather eye on John's bandwagon, decided instead to dump the rest of us and end the show.' It was quite the turnaround for Inman, given the BBC had originally wanted the show to proceed only if Mr Humphries was not included!

So it seemed that this should have ended the *Are You Being Served?* story after five series, and Frank was already being quoted in the press as being critical of the BBC's belief that without Inman they had no choice but to cancel the programme. He confessed:

> To me it seems a strange commercial decision. A successful situation comedy is hard to come by so you don't deliberately drop one which still has life in it. Even actors quitting would have presented no problems. They could simply have been written out of the script by leaving the store, being fired or moved to another department.

The decision to end after five series exemplified the problems that Frank perceived the BBC to have at the time:

> The BBC is like a Post Office department. Programmes are an irritation to them. In recent years all economies have been on the production side so there are now about three office workers to every one creative person. It was summed up for me when Michael Bentine received a chastening memo after we caused uproar in the reception area while filming *It's A Square World*. The memo said: 'In future, please do not use the Television Centre for entertainment!'

The cast of *Are You Being Served?* were now preparing for life after Grace Brothers, but what nobody had anticipated was how badly *Odd Man Out* would bomb. Alan Coren also referred to the Inman bandwagon in his *Times* mauling of John's new vehicle, but suggested that he should have held out for a better script:

> One could forgive him for stealing *Are You Being Served?*, since the major crime was not the theft but the show itself, but how can one forgive him for agreeing to mouth the scripts of this new abomination? I hold no personal grudge against Mr Inman, but does he not owe us some explanation for his part in dragging situation comedy to a new low?

Coren's judgement was brutal, but not uncommon for *Odd Man Out*. The show indeed had little going for it; if the gay community had a problem with Mr Humphries, in ramping up the campness to previously unseen levels Inman's new character of Neville Sutcliffe would only intensify the objections, and with weak characters all round and a bizarre closing monologue to the camera at the end of each episode, the show was a disaster.

In his brutal review, Coren advised that John would do well to think again; and whether it was he or Thames that pulled the plug, *Odd Man Out* lasted no longer and nor did Inman's contract.

Frank, while not being happy with Croft and Lloyd's decision to axe the show without Inman, bore no grudge against his friend and took no pleasure in recalling, 'Unhappily for John, the show nosedived in the ratings. Since it is always the actors that are blamed for such failures, even if the script was rubbish or the director a blockhead, the usual procedure was adopted, and John's three-year contract was quietly dropped.'

Rather than being shunned for leaving the Grace Brothers gang in the first place, Inman was welcomed back with great eagerness by the writers. He returned to the fold and the staff of Grace Brothers were back in business, but sadly not for the full cast.

Frank worked with Arthur Brough in February 1978 on a commercial for an Australian clothing company, another of the offshoots from the success of *Are You Being Served?* Brough kept getting the name of the manufacturer wrong, and after being repeatedly corrected by the director simply responded with, 'Does it matter?'

It was a typical Mr Grainger style response and part of the charm that endeared him to all who worked with him. He was a genuine favourite among his castmates; 'a darling', according to Pam Bannister. Frank felt Brough to be superb, despite his frequent gaffes during recording of *Are You Being Served?*, and he later recalled a typical moment from the studio sessions during a speech honouring Inman's forty years in show business:

> I want to tell you a little story about a man that both he [Inman] and I loved: Arthur Brough. Something like half the profession worked for Arthur when he ran the Folkestone Rep with its famous matinee teas.

As well as running the company, Arthur also played a number of parts and consequently never really had time to study the lines properly. We first came to know him when he played the wonderfully cantankerous Mr Grainger in *Are You Being Served?* At one recording with the audience in the studio, we moved from the main shop set to do a canteen scene. We were arranged along the table with Arthur in his usual place at the end.

The scene went without a hitch except for one line, of which Arthur made an absolute porridge. He calmly carried on and the rest of us managed to do the same without laughing. At the end the floor manager called, 'Thank you, hold it studio, there is just one retake.'

Almost as if they had rehearsed it, Mrs Slocombe, Miss Brahms, Mr Lucas, Mr Humphries and Captain Peacock turned to the end of the table and said, 'Well, we know which one that is, don't we?'

Arthur had learnt his lesson from Bernard Shaw's Sergius Saranoff: 'I never apologise.' Knowing full well that the writers, producer, director etc. were all in the gallery and could hear every word uttered on the studio floor, Arthur gazed at us and said, 'That's the thanks I get for trying to improve a rather indifferent script.'

You have to admire such magnificent gall.

Just a few weeks after Frank's appearance with Brough in the clothing commercial, Arthur's beloved wife Elizabeth died after which he announced his immediate retirement. The heartbroken actor passed away just two months later. The normally stoic Frank recalled the sad day in May of 1978: 'A brilliantly funny man... a dearly loved friend that the whole cast will miss tremendously. Irreplaceable. Such men do not pass this way often.'

Series six had been written with Brough still very much in the writers' plans and, with Inman's ill-fated stay at Thames at an end, filming could begin once a replacement had been found for Mr Grainger. That came in the form of James Hayter who would play another long-serving Grace Brothers employee, Mr Tebbs.

Frank felt that Hayter was a superb option and that he was proof that the departure of a beloved character need not be the death knell for the programme. He did, however, acknowledge the challenge facing Hayter: 'He is an actor of no mean comic ability faced with the difficult task of taking over scripts written for Arthur and trying to make them his own with the minimum of rewriting.'

However, Inman's return was not a case of crawling bashfully back to the fold. The belief remained with the writers that Inman was now too integral to the show to risk losing again, and so there was a significant change in the billing.

When it first arrived, *Are You Being Served?* had been an ensemble piece but with Trevor Bannister and Mollie Sugden very much top of the bill; but Inman's perceived value and near-departure meant that the billing was now reshuffled. At the end of the show, the 'You Have Been Watching' segment saw him promoted to top billing alongside Sugden, shuffling both Bannister and Frank down the pecking order.

Frank was too honourable to complain. Billing and the correct treatment of actors was always an important thing for him, but the team at *Are You Being Served?* were such a tight-knit group that what might have caused him to rebel went unchallenged. The stars were simply too close to allow such things to splinter the group.

Frank's friendship with Trevor Bannister was particularly strong and it wasn't their only working partnership. They had appeared in a number of other productions together since first working on the same bill in 1965 in *A Juan By Degrees*, even a commercial for a brand of Australian cigarettes. Frank, in full Peacock regalia, was seen elegantly holding the cigarette while offering his finest floorwalker sneer at Trevor, with the appropriately placed captions, 'Quality befitting a gentleman' and 'The bargain price suits me'.

In later years, as we will learn, Bannister was involved in getting Frank into *Last of the Summer Wine*, and the pair's careers were always of interest to one another. Pam Bannister remembered, 'If anything came up to do with work, he would say, "I think I'll have a word with Frank and see what he thinks."'

The friendship didn't apply solely to work. Eagle-eyed viewers may well have spotted in Frank's *This is Your Life* in 1998 that Trevor, forced to send a video message due to working overseas, wished Frank and Beryl – 'The Queen Mum' – a wonderful evening. A mild titter at best from the audience as they would have had no clue as to the context of that quip, and had Michael Aspel queried it, the resultant story would have been hastily edited from the final version!

Beryl Thornton had a reputation for dignity and elegance. While Frank became known as the quintessential English gentleman, Beryl was every bit as much the definition of a lady, well-spoken and always immaculately dressed and well mannered. During the research for this book, as much as the word 'lugubrious' was constantly associated with Frank, so it was that so many interviewees commented how beautifully turned-out Beryl was. But of course, when somebody is the pinnacle of decorum and elegance, any slip becomes so much more memorable.

Wendy Richard was getting married and, as the cast were so tightly knit, the remaining Grace Brothers staff were of course invited. The Bannisters and Thorntons were travelling together, Trevor swinging by to Barnes to collect Frank and Beryl.

Everybody was impeccably dressed for the occasion, but the traffic on the way to the event was horrendous. 'Oh Christ, this fucking traffic!' exclaimed Trevor as it became clear that their prompt arrival was in jeopardy.

Pam Bannister was horrified and she immediately turned from the passenger seat to Beryl, apologising profusely: 'Oh Beryl, I'm so sorry, you've not to mind my husband's language.'

'Oh, don't worry about that,' replied Beryl, her comic timing sharp as a tack as ever. 'We can never go from Barnes to the West End without Frank calling someone a cunt!' With traffic at a virtual standstill, Trevor opened his car door and feigned falling out.

'Oh, what's the matter? Did nobody tell you about my language?'

'It's not so much that,' retorted Trevor. 'We just didn't expect it from the Queen Mum!'

This is Your Life mystery solved. From that day on, cards and good wishes were always signed or addressed to Frank and the Queen Mum. Pam recalled being shocked to the core: 'She would never normally have said that word, though Frank would; but we never stopped laughing at that. It's ingrained in my memory. We were all great mates.'

Beryl, and indeed Frank, also liked a tipple, despite Frank saying in a number of interviews that he didn't drink. Pam also remembers Beryl's talent for putting away the alcohol:

> She was so fun; she could drink anybody under the table. I remember going to see Alan Bell to celebrate Alan's birthday and for some reason they all got

delayed. She had left a message with the restaurant to bring us champagne on arrival – we had more when the rest arrived, more during the meal and Beryl was matching everyone glass for glass when she was pushing ninety… and then I think she had a negroni afterwards, and you would never have known. She never got drunk, but my God she could drink.

On the periphery of the core *Are You Being Served?* quintet was Nicholas Smith. As Mr Rumbold, Smith spent many years gamely playing a role where his famed facial features of premature baldness and larger-than-average ears were mocked in almost every episode. Looking back, one cannot help but feel that the relentless 'jug ears' jokes were perhaps a little too frequent. Even with Smith, however, Frank struck up a bond. His daughter, actress Catherine Russell, remembered that even though her father often struggled to make friends, Frank was one person in the cast that he did become pals with.

With the reordering of the billing left to go unchallenged, the friend-ships remained tight, and filming continued. However, series seven of *Are You Being Served?* saw another casting change.

People with a keen ear may note that James Hayter's voice was somewhat familiar. He was actually the voice of a certain manufacturer of 'exceedingly good cakes'. Frank recalled that unfortunately for the producers of the show, 'James Hayter is in the happy position that Mr Kipling's cakes are prepared to pay him not to do the show again but to sit quietly in his little hacienda in Spain. And so again a last-minute replacement is sought.'

Frank recalled with relish his lasting memory of Hayter's brief time on the programme:

> One wonderful memory survives for us all. At rehearsal, members of the cast would sometimes suggest a gag or bit of business and David would say yea or nay. One day, without any prior warning, Jimmy came out with the line, 'I'm taking my wife on holiday to North Wales: I'm going to Bangor.' This is a mildly uninteresting line to read until you know that what he actually said was, 'I'm going to bang 'er.'
>
> The assembled cast exploded, and the line was written into the script forthwith. I shan't forget the look of satisfaction on Jimmy's face at the success of his gag and the realisation that he was now firmly 'one of us'. How sad it was that he did not continue after his first series.

The replacement for Hayter's Mr Tebbs arrived in the person of Alfie Bass as Mr Goldberg. Like his predecessor he had to adapt material not written for him, with the exception of the opening episode which hinges on his wartime acquaintance with Captain Peacock.

This acquaintance is revealed at the interview for a replacement for the retired Mr Tebbs, as a selection of misfits are paraded in front of the staff, the only one with any hint of employability being Mr Goldberg.

Unfortunately for Peacock, Goldberg served with him in the military, knowing him only as Corporal Peacock. Frank employs his most appalled facial expressions as Goldberg reveals a few more details about Peacock's military past than he would have liked, including some photographic evidence, in order to ensure he gets taken on at Grace Brothers.

Seeing Peacock's past clarified in that first episode was an entertaining twist but, much to Frank's disappointment, it was a storyline that failed to continue:

> An excellent comic situation smelling of blackmail that could be well developed. But the writers don't wish to junk five or six episodes already written and so that situation is simply forgotten, and we are back to fun and games plus funny entrances and funny clothes for Mr Humphries. John of course doesn't complain and neither does the costume designer but to me it seems a good opportunity missed.

Frank's comments were indicative of the seeming demise in quality of the scripts for *Are You Being Served?* Mr Goldberg was a good character, somewhat shifty and underhanded and a different challenge for Peacock, but the show was leaning towards relying heavily on pantomime-style elements.

It was a tricky balancing act for Frank. While the nation was watching him as Peacock trying to stop staff spreading news about a boil on his behind, he and Trevor Bannister were battling works of a different kind: Frank as George in the hefty Tom Stoppard play *Jumpers*, Trevor as Owen in Michael Frayn's *Clouds*, successive plays at the Leatherhead Theatre.

Frank's playful friendship with Bannister remained as he remarked, 'It's interesting to note that the previous production to us was Michael Frayn's *Clouds* with Trevor Bannister, who predicted that the Agatha

Christie-loving Leatherhead would find neither that play nor *Jumpers* to their taste. "I'll half finish the place old boy," he said, "and you'll finish it off." '

Despite their fears, audiences were mostly engaged with the fare they were offered, and Frank was happy to concede that he and Trevor's mischievous expectations had been wrong:

> So due tribute to the authors and casts of both plays and indeed to the Leatherhead audience. In the spirit of accuracy and truth, of course it must be admitted that one or two elderly ladies gave up the struggle with Tom Stoppard's obliquities and did not return after the interval. But they were only a few, thank God, for I shudder to think what it would have been like giving the university lecture that forms a large chunk of George's part to a half empty house.

In May of 1980 Frank finally received something he thought he had seen the last of: the offer of television work from the BBC's drama department. While theatre audiences were mostly prepared to see beyond Captain Peacock, especially when he wasn't sporting his Peacock moustache (sometimes grown, sometimes fake), Frank always found that the BBC could see no further than light entertainment for him. On this occasion it was Jonathan Miller who convinced the BBC of his value, and so he joined the cast of Miller's production of *The Taming of the Shrew* nearly forty years on from his Shakespearean exploits under Donald Wolfit.

Leading the cast were John Cleese and Sarah Badel in the roles of Petruchio and Katherine. Frank had worked with Cleese once before on the judicial comedy *Misleading Cases* prior to *Are You Being Served?* fame. He had performed a three-minute scene with Roy Dotrice, one of the leads alongside Alastair Sim, but it had ended up being another occasion where his performance was lost in the editing process. It had seemed to get significant laughter from the studio audience, but a few days later Frank received a call from John Howard Davies informing him of the decision to cut the segment in its entirety. It was a frustrating cut for Frank, who bemoaned the reasoning behind the cut: 'One of the causes of overrun was a scene with John in the witness box that he wrote himself to twice its original length and half its original comic effect – and then proceeded to deliver at a somewhat funereal pace that didn't exactly have the audience wetting their knickers with laughter: he will get his repeat fees!'

There was no genuine animosity with Cleese. When they came to work together in *Taming of the Shrew*, Frank could see the similarities between himself and a fellow actor so completely associated with one very successful comic creation in sitcom land:

> I can't say I have always agreed with [Miller's] ideas in the past but perhaps I have to thank his unconventionality for thinking of me. Certainly, John Cleese is not everybody's first choice as Petruchio. In the event I thought his performance well-suited for the box – a quiet man who decides that unreasonable ranting is the method to use in quelling Katherine's fires.

The only thing Frank didn't agree with in Miller's production was the interpretation of Tranio, which he saw as a Sam Costa cockney talking posh: 'JM thought it immensely funny, but Shakespeare very plainly states that though he is of lowly birth, he has been given the education of a gentleman and can therefore confidently pass himself off as one. It is very difficult to say, "I know you to be a gentleman" to someone who quite obviously wasn't.'

Frank's return to Shakespeare was otherwise one that he revelled in. He found Miller himself charming and stimulating to work with, while he and of course Beryl ingratiated themselves into the company. They even found time to join in a session of anagramming the *Shrew*'s creator; the runaway winner was apparently Beryl's contribution who turned the bard himself into Amelia Palewhiskers, which from that moment on was how Cleese apparently referred to him.

The reviewers loved the production, though Frank couldn't help noticing that, 'The press cannot resist linking John and myself with our better-known personas – as if we could come on looking and sounding like, say, The Two Ronnies!'

With *Are You Being Served?* still getting the viewing figures, despite seemingly being on the decline in quality, Frank was soon to be packed off down under where more TV producers wanted to capitalise on the Great English Gentleman persona now synonymous with Frank and his alter ego.

There was just time for one brief production, one that came to Frank with great relief as he had been without work for some months since the screening of *Taming of the Shrew*; 'Thank God, I'm working again,' he contentedly reflected as he began rehearsals for Ionesco's *The Chairs*.

It wasn't just that he was working again that Frank was grateful for. He found the piece so different from what he was better known for that he couldn't turn it down. Seen as an absurdist play, Frank shared the bill with Gwen Nelson as an old couple recalling their lives, with chairs appearing on stage representing the attendees arriving to hear their final words of reflection.

This particular performance was staged in the round at the Royal Exchange, Manchester and Frank found it strange and difficult, but ultimately fulfilling:

> It's a strange enough play to start with… our rehearsal period is quite remarkable given that Gwen Nelson and I disagreed quite radically with a great deal of Richard [Negri]'s ideas – which were often, to say the least, on a multi-physical level that no actor – or certainly not this one – could hope to get across to an audience even if he wanted to. This led to a great deal of discussion, even argument, but quite astoundingly no loss of good humour and friendliness. The play needed quite a lot of cutting if it was going to keep the house interested for there was an inordinate amount of repetition in it. After all the amicable battles, each side winning a proportion, we arrived at what we were going to do.
>
> I'm inclined to agree with those critics who think *The Chairs* has had its day. It was a great exercise and a great challenge, and the management seemed pleased with it. I'm not exactly wedded to theatre in the round as one can only act in one direction at a time, which means the performance has to be shared out among the three-hundred-and-sixty-degree audience: nobody gets all of it. The critics were right about one thing: Gwen Nelson was terrific and a real joy to work with.

Years later Frank would congratulate Richard Briers on his own good reviews for *The Chairs* in 1997. He admitted that his own efforts had amounted to 'a rather confused stab at it', but joyously reflected that, 'My most abiding memory of the engagement is that almost every time that Gwen had occasion to bend over, she farted. I never plucked up the courage to ask her if it was part of her characterisation!'

Towards the end of *The Chairs'* run in November 1980, Frank made a dash down from Manchester to have lunch with the management of the Adelaide Festival Theatre who were keen to talk to him about performing in the Alan Bennett play *Habeas Corpus*. Once *The Chairs* had completed its run, he and Beryl were subsequently whisked off to Sydney where they not only looked forward to Frank being in the Bennett play, but were also given the opportunity, or so they thought, to discuss a possible sitcom series down under.

The very rough theme was 'A Pom Hits Australia'. Frank was no stranger to the comedy value of the Englishman abroad. His few solo routines had included work on a piece with Peter Jones that he had regularly visited over the years, but he also crafted a piece of his own about the stranded Brit, first performing it to a national audience in December 1962 on the radio show *Midweek*.

Frank's own version targeted the ignorance of the Brit when overseas as opposed to the hosting nation, noting that his new phrase book, which had promised to offer him 'Everything You Need in France', actually offered opportunities to understand how an Englishman behaves when on the continent:

> You see, at home, like so many people during and after the war I've been educated into an attitude of grovelling humility when talking to people like shop assistants, bus conductors, taxi drivers, waitresses and so on. I mean, when there's seven-and-sixpence on the clock, with a sort of ingratiating leer, I hand the driver another four bob, hoping it'll be a large enough tip. And waiters terrify me. When they pour that little drop of wine in your glass and glare at you, I never have the courage to say I don't like it, even if it tastes like inferior boot polish. I just smirk in acquiescence.
>
> But obviously that's not the way to behave in France. Seemingly, one has to show a bit of the spirit that won the battle of Waterloo. In my ignorance, I looked for such phrases as, 'Thank you driver, are you sure the tip is large enough?' and 'Those escargots were delicious – and so cheap – my compliments to the chef,' apart from such routine chatter as 'You are very beautiful, mademoiselle, but my wife would not understand.'
>
> But there was nothing like that. Let me read you the apparent way to deal with a taxi driver:
>
> 'Don't drive so fast – drive carefully – go faster – I want to get out here – what have I to pay you? – I haven't any change – your meter appears to be

out of order – I shall not pay this amount – I will give you x francs, I will not pay more! – I am giving you a great deal too much – let us call a policeman.'

That should settle his hash shouldn't it. Similarly, at the hotel. Don't stand any nonsense. Here goes:

'Ask the head waiter to come here (that gets you off on the right foot for a start) – I don't like this table – give me a table near the window – it is too warm in this room – a little more ventilation is needed (then as soon as you get it)   shut the door please, there's a terrible draught.'

Drawing a veil over whatever happens about the food we come to the end of the meal:

'Give me my bill (you get it) – this bill isn't correct (straight from the shoulder, you see) – we did not have this – this must be a mistake – you have charged too much for this – I want to speak to the manager (he comes) – I'm leaving tomorrow morning after breakfast, I want my breakfast at seven o'clock!'

And finally, when you've got absolutely nowhere there comes the final cry from the heart – 'Is there anyone here who speaks English?'

Yes, there is! The waiter, the wine waiter, the head waiter, the manager, the receptionist, the commissionaire and even one of the taxi drivers. They were all absolutely charming – I had the time of my life!

With the prospect of a starring vehicle, Frank along with his host on the trip and creator of the idea of the show, Harvey Spencer, attended a lunch at the Channel 10 executive suite.

Eight people gathered around the table, seemingly to discuss the comedy idea, but that never happened:

There is no conversation because the whole time is monopolised by some big mouth whose name I have mercifully forgotten telling the Channel 10 bosses of his achievements in booking American stars for Australian television and what he can do for Channel 10. At one point Harvey's partner in the project makes one attempt to bring up the subject we are supposed to be discussing but he is soon talked down by Chattie Charlie. I sit amazed, sipping my Perrier water, saying nothing. Perhaps I should have told him to belt up, but I was playing the part of the quiet, good-mannered Englishman.

The meeting broke up without any conversation taking place about the possibility of Frank being involved in his own show.

As much as he loved being wined and dined around Sydney, taking in the tourist sights and the wildlife, he was having doubts about the merits of the journey: not just the seemingly doomed 'Englishman abroad' plans, but also about *Habeas Corpus. Are You Being Served?* was hugely popular in Australia and so John Inman and Mollie Sugden had already both appeared in successful farces down under. *Habeas Corpus* did not fit the same bill as that of his beloved co-stars, but that wasn't going to dissuade the producers of the show from marketing it in much the same manner. The publicity posters horrified Frank, seeing them as second-rate seaside postcards: 'all leering doctors with stethoscopes chasing scantily clad girls with big tits!'

A few days later Frank met with Don McKay, who he described as 'a pleasant man but with a frequent, braying laugh that bodes ill. No man who laughs like that can have a sense of humour: and so it turns out – and he's been picked to direct an Alan Bennett comedy!'

Frank's misgivings were justified, but he was determined not to be the pushy Pom there to show the Aussies how to do it. However, the play was such a disaster that he couldn't help trying to challenge McKay's approach.

McKay was also the artistic director of the Victoria Arts Council, however, and so Frank had to accept that making progress on a small scale with some of the more receptive talent in the show was the only way he could improve the piece. McKay was after all key to bookings for the show's run.

The poor show along with the dubious advertising meant that initially positive bookings quickly tailed off. Frank recalled despondently:

> Those who expected farce and a star performance from yours truly are somewhat disappointed, and those who would like Bennett's sophistication tend to stay away because they have got the wrong impression from the advertising. What a pity! What was really needed from me was a touch of the Rex Harrisons – a ruthless determination to get things done the way I know they should be and to hell with anybody's feelings. But it needs a courage I don't possess. So we, as it were, continue to compromise and try to keep everybody happy – but that's not the way to make theatrical history.

Despite enjoying a long tour and all the joys of the wild, sea and birdlife in the country, plus the fact that Frank and Beryl managed to spend time staying with his old pal from the RAF, Johnnie Ladd, when their tour hit Melbourne, the stay wasn't entirely smooth sailing.

In order to help publicise *Habeas Corpus*, Frank and a few of his co-stars took part in the Moomba Parade, the culmination of a community four-day festival. They were driven in the parade in a green Bentley with adverts for the play on its sides. Suddenly a painted clown danced up to the car and slapped a charity sticker on it. While grinning and waving to the crowd, the clown put his face into Frank's and hissed, 'Bloody Pom – taking money out of Australian actors' mouths,' before prancing happily away. Frank was left stunned.

There was a certain irony in the clown's bizarre protest, which was only backed up by the rules of Australian Equity.

While in the country, Frank did many promotional television pieces for conservation efforts, including protection of the bettong, a species of small kangaroo, and a piece on the infestation of European carp that, having been released into the artificial Lake Burley Griffin, were now dominating at the expense of other species of fish and their dependent birds.

Bizarrely, while happy to use Frank for more noble causes, when it came to filming commercials, Australian Equity sided with the parade clown. It was a somewhat short-sighted approach.

An advert for Illawara Building Society was due to be filmed, and so Frank and the crew packed up their things on a Sunday morning and flew to New Zealand. Having shot three commercials, they stayed at a hotel that evening, rising early the next day to be back in time for Frank to be on stage for *Habeas Corpus*. Instead of paying one British actor and everyone else involved being Australian, to avoid breaching Australian Equity's rules the commercials were completed using almost entirely New Zealanders as cast and crew, and the adverts were still legally shown in Australia.

Frank would return to Australia in 1983 for another *Habeas Corpus* production, but it suffered similarly disappointing returns. He was convinced on that second visit that it would be his last, believing that the Australian promoters brought current stars over on the crest of a wave and then would move on to the next big import. But his frustrations with Australia's acting laws remained.

They wanted a British name to sell tickets, meaning more employment for Australians, some of whom in the *Habeas Corpus* cast also held down day jobs, but they wouldn't permit more than one British performer per production. 'One is faced with being unable to take either a leading woman or man in a vital partnership role or a director to shape the production properly,' Frank noted frustratingly. 'You jump off the top board into the deep end with your eyes shut and your hands tied behind your back. No wonder the results are often less than brilliant.'

The Australian trip may not have provided Frank with quite the theatrical plaudits or television breakthrough he might have hoped for, but across the three months of that first visit he had a blessed time, full of all the things he and Beryl found important in life: good company, good people, and being able to witness nature at its best.

Once they touched down at Heathrow there were barely a few hours before Frank was expected to arrive at Acton's rehearsal rooms in preparation for the eighth series of *Are You Being Served?*

That eighth series was notable for the show's most significant casting change. Having originally been one of the two headline names, Trevor Bannister had left the programme. A change in studio recording dates to a Friday meant that he could no longer accommodate the sitcom's schedule due to his stage commitments, and he reluctantly bade farewell to Grace Brothers. Frank was less than impressed with the producers' decision, but he soldiered on as Mike Berry took over the junior salesperson role: 'A pleasant lad, but Trevor is a distinct loss.'

The early 1980s, the Australian tours aside, were proving largely frustrating for Frank. He was still a solid performer for comedians. He appeared a number of times alongside Kenny Everett and also on *Kelly Monteith*, the self-titled comedy hit from the likeable American who had his own show on the BBC after being discovered on Des O'Connor's chat show. Frank thoroughly enjoyed Monteith's efforts and, watching them now, he turns in a faultless speech in the manner of *Yes Minister*'s Sir Humphrey Appleby with as much aplomb as the great Nigel Hawthorne did when he spouted sentence after sentence of nonsensical phrases to Paul Eddington's bemused Jim Hacker.

In one of his Kenny Everett appearances, he played a BBC staff accountant determined to replace him in his own show as Kenny was considered too smutty. Frank couldn't help but be amused that only a few days before, the BBC had indeed admonished Kenny for just such an offence on radio. Frank even kept a clipping of the gag Kenny made that got him his ticking off: 'When Britain was an empire, we were ruled by an emperor. When we became a kingdom, we were ruled by a king. Now we're a country we're ruled by Margaret Thatcher!'

Frank had the offer of a role in *Doctor in the House* in late 1983 – a good salary, but a play he couldn't face and so he took a role in *Last of the Red Hot Lovers* by Neil Simon, a much smaller salary but a marvellous part that he couldn't resist, reuniting him with Hugh Paddick who was at the helm. The play was performed at The Mill at Sonning, a dinner theatre in Reading. The unusual setting of the actors essentially trapped in the middle of a D was not quite as disconcerting as Frank initially feared.

Frank played the part of a middle-aged New Yorker who after years of marriage decides to have a fling. His ability with accents came to the fore, with a little help from the guidance of a native New Yorker. 'It's vital to get the accent right before you begin to learn the words,' he said. 'Then if you dry up on stage you can at least ad lib in the same accent.'

The show was a well-received effort, but Frank was quick to offer credit to his co-stars rather than claim any for himself: 'We are a great success, thanks in no small measure to Dilys Laye playing two parts in extreme contrast and Linda Jean Barrie as the kookie blonde.'

The success of *Last of the Red Hot Lovers* gave Frank a sense of fulfil-ment, but didn't do the same for his bank account. He knew well that his year would have been considerably more remunerative if he had taken the role in *Doctor in the House*, but he was at the stage of his career that allowed him to be pickier in the roles that he chose. 'I want to do good stuff, by which I do not mean Strindberg and Chekhov all the time. *Last of the Red Hot Lovers* is a modern comedy but it's good stuff. It's the rubbishy farce and panto that I want to avoid; but I wonder, is there any hope for me?'

In the late spring of 1984, Frank and his friends filmed the tenth and final series of *Are You Being Served?* and said goodbye to Grace Brothers. He had pondered in an interview, shortly before filming began, quite how the public would be with him once Captain Peacock had gone from the television screen: 'A new play can start anytime, and in the commercial system that exists it can be stopped anytime due to lack of public interest.

What I also realise very well is that whenever it is decided to stop *Are You Being Served?* it will all change again. Then perhaps I can return to the smaller parts, when they have forgotten about Captain Peacock at least. But it is also possible that I will sink into oblivion.'

Are You Being Served? had been on the rocks for some time. Although Frank felt the final series had offered a tad more than some of those immediately previous, storylines remained rather absurd and rehashed. A new, more anarchic wave of alternative comedy was also sweeping the land and the more traditional sitcoms and comedy styles were being laid to waste. Who wanted to hear jokes about Mrs Slocombe's pussy or the gentleman's drawers when university graduates were busy raising their fingers in disgust at Mrs Thatcher? Seemingly very few, albeit *Are You Being Served?* did well to last as long as it did.

David Croft and Jeremy Lloyd knew that the writing was on the wall, as did the cast, and each time they wrapped a season they were uncertain whether they would return for more. Quite whose decision it was to finally pull the plug is a matter of some debate. Gareth Gwenlan, the new Head of Comedy at the BBC, wrote a very brief note to Frank thanking him for his years of dedication and talent on the programme and saying that, 'I view its "rest" with regret but I'm sure that David's judgement is correct at this point.' David Croft knew the show was past its best, but the decision for it to end was perhaps not on his shoulders as Gwenlan's correspondence with Frank had suggested.

John Howard Davies, Head of Light Entertainment, was even more gushing on the show's demise, writing that, 'I don't quite believe it myself because it seems to be part of the BBC's comedy institution and I can't imagine life without it.'

In return, Frank acknowledged:

AYBS? had become part of my life as they say. In practical terms a freelance actor must go where the work is, whether it's the West End or the Mechanics' Institute. The BBC figures in my files more than any other... when I point the car up Wood Lane the feeling is always that I am returning to the old alma mater. It's a comfortable feeling that won't go away despite the increasing number of new and ever younger faces there are around. And I hope there will always be room in the car park for me from time to time.

It all seemed very amicable. Croft and Lloyd gave the cast a farewell lunch and Croft told the regulars that while the show had come to its end, he hoped to bring the group back one day.

Whether the split was really that amicable between the show's makers and the corporation is less clear. That final series sat on the shelf for a very long time. Six years later in an article in the *Daily Mail* on the occasion of his retirement, Gareth Gwenlan was said to have made axing *Are You Being Served?* one of his top priorities. 'It was smutty, sexist, end-of-the-pier stuff,' he was quoted as saying, adding that the programme made him cringe. In the same sweep, he axed the individual work of the Two Ronnies, in the form of Barker's *Clarence* and Corbett's *Sorry*.

Whatever the truth, *Are You Being Served?* could not have soldiered on much longer. The confines of the store setting had become restrictive on the show's comedy material, with many storylines regurgitated in later years. The doors to Grace Brothers needed to close, and they did so in traditionally strange fashion as the gang appeared as backing singers and musicians to Mike Berry's Mr Spooner as he came from behind the menswear counter to pursue musical fame and fortune.

The question for Frank now was whether there was life post-Peacock. On the one hand, his more traditional acting CV made him an ideal option for producers, bringing punters in based on a television star, knowing that his skills can quickly dispose of any 'that's Captain Peacock' muttering from the audience; even more so given that, for most of the programme's run, his signature moustache was a fake. On the other hand, Inman and Sugden had provided so many years of large summer season and panto box-office takings that they were most likely secure for the rest of their careers repeating the same success.

Work was initially slow for Frank: guest roles in segments of convoluted quiz show *3-2-1*, a medical promotion film as a doctor to Roy Kinnear's patient, a trip to Amsterdam to promote the British Wool Marketing Board, and an Arthurian knight on *Jackanory Playhouse*; substantial offers were seemingly not flying in, even when Peacock's last scenes had still not been aired.

A second Australian tour of *Habeas Corpus* emphasised the challenge of becoming known too well for one particular role.

Frank touched down in Sydney without Beryl – neither could afford to pay for another ticket, despite more than forty years in the business – and was immediately thrown into the rounds of publicity. Once again, he was the box-office name, the Pom over to get the punters through the door.

At the first press conference the Australian public, and indeed producer John Manford, were surprised to see no upper-lip hair – Captain Peacock had no moustache!

Frank tried to reassure Manford that the public would still recognise him, but Manford was not convinced. If he was right, then the usual ploy of using a well-known British television face to sell tickets would fail.

The debate continued into the production of a television advert for the show. In their wisdom, the producers hadn't actually written one, despite being committed to do so.

Frank saw his chance to kill two birds with one stone and set about writing the commercial himself. In it, dressed as Captain Peacock with familiar moustache, he would lose his facial friend, thus showing the potential audience that *Habeas Corpus* was a comedy and that he was indeed Captain Peacock.

Despite being ingenious and funny, it didn't allay Manford's fears. The producer had a moustache drawn onto the publicity material. It seemed a bizarrely desperate move, almost suggesting that either the punters were idiots or that Frank's performance would be sub-standard without facial hair.

The issue was not lost on Frank, who considered suggesting that he could stay in his dressing room and send the moustache out on its own!

Frank's frustrations may seem minor in retrospect, but it demonstrated the potential problems of typecasting. Producers wanted the same face from *Are You Being Served?* to sell a different product, suggesting that once Peacock was gone, Frank could struggle for work.

In October of 1984, when Frank's career could have gone either way, he was given a role that was arguably his favourite of all of his stage performances and one that put him firmly back in the public eye: that of Sir John Tremayne in the revival of Noel Gay's feel-good musical *Me and My Girl*. Robert Lindsay would star as Bill Snibson, the cockney who becomes a lord, although it was only at the third time of asking that he accepted the role as he was quoted as believing that the script was 'a bit twee'.

Starting with a run at the Haymarket Theatre in Leicester, *Me and My Girl* was a big-budget musical, albeit one that could easily have folded before ever making it to the West End. Producer Richard Armitage was frantically trying to secure funding to the very last minute of the three months between its Leicester opening and the transfer to the Adelphi.

A few years later as the show prepared to transfer to Broadway, Armitage recalled to the *New York Times* that he had a noon deadline to come up with the money: 'At five to twelve, I told my most trusted people we'd found no one to do the show, and at twelve o'clock I picked up the telephone, and I didn't know what I was going to say, and I found myself saying to David Aukin: prepare for London.'

Frank's casting as Tremayne was no surprise. As a constant television presence for more than twenty-five years, he was the perfect blend of box-office appeal and acting professionalism, ideal for comparative new-comer Lindsay, who, while a familiar face on television himself as Wolfie in *Citizen Smith*, had no real experience leading a headline-grabbing West End musical company. The company lead was very much in the hands of Frank.

The premise of *Me and My Girl* was a variation on the *Pygmalion* theme as Snibson goes from working class to fourteenth heir to the Earl of Hareford. Being a cheerful cockney, his behaviour is not deemed appropriate, nor is his working-class girlfriend Sally, played by Emma Thompson. Frank's role as Tremayne was as a rather contentedly drunk aristocratic figure involved in transforming Snibson to something more palatable for the circles he was about to join.

Critics and audiences loved the show, even before the transfer. Such was the confidence in its appeal, two extracts were put into the Royal Variety Performance at the Victoria Palace in November 1984 while the production was still in rehearsal. That allowed for Frank to engage in a little comedy business of his own as he appeared as a theatre manager trying to oust Dame Edna Everage from the Royal Box. 'Haven't I seen you somewhere before? Don't you work in a shop?' the Aussie legend quizzed Frank as he tried to evict her!

The ten-week run at Leicester broke box-office records, selling out every night. Between Leicester and the Adelphi there was just time to record a cast album, Frank's own moment being 'If Only You Had Cared For Me', a duet with his onstage partner Ursula Smith. Then on to opening night and a roaring success, recalled by Lindsay in his autobiography:

> We all did the curtain call and we were bowing together when Frank Thornton, who played Sir John Tremayne in the show, made me come forward. People were stamping their feet and Frank knew, being so experienced, that the show was a major hit. He pushed me forward as he gestured to everyone else in the cast to step back. The whole audience was on its feet and I just thought, 'Oh, my God! Oh, my God! This is big!' Until that moment I didn't fully realise what kind of show we had on our hands.

Not everything went swimmingly with the production; and, just as Lindsay had suggested, Frank was once again performing his duties as the most experienced member of the cast to lead the way. The Adelphi was in an appalling state, nowhere near good enough for the cast and crew. The roof leaked backstage and whenever it rained, one stairway by the dressing rooms was frequently awash. One particular night the rainwater flowed down the stairway, through the passage and into the dressing room, soaking a number of costumes. Even the orchestra pit managed to get a drenching.

One night the rain was heavy enough to form a lake outside Frank's dressing room, while his main ceiling began to drip in three different places, including directly down an electric light fitment. Given he was based on the second floor, Frank shuddered to think what the two floors above him were like. With members of the company falling ill with alarming regularity, Frank took it upon himself to act as spokesman, writing to Richard Armitage as well as Equity to protest at the conditions. Armitage agreed entirely with Frank's complaints, especially given the high cost of staging the production at the theatre, and fully supported his actions as he went to Michael Codron to get the ailing theatre brought up to scratch.

For all the physical failings of the theatre in its early run, *Me and My Girl* was, and still is, marketed as 'The Happiest Show in Town' and it was certainly one of the happiest times in Frank's professional life. His friends and family all came to see it on multiple occasions; even an unsteady Sir Laurence Olivier dropped by after the show to congratulate the cast. Good friend David Shepherd was completely hooked, constantly coming back for his happiness fix and racking up an estimated thirty visits, so taken was he by Frank's performance and the show's spirit.

Not only earning critical acclaim in the press, *Me and My Girl* also picked up an Olivier Award for Musical of the Year along with rewarding Lindsay with the award for Outstanding Performance by an Actor in a Musical. The evening following the awards, Frank as company leader stepped forward at the end of yet another standing ovation:

> A lot of people shared in this award: the creative talent; the production teams, both here and at the Haymarket Theatre, Leicester, where this all started over a year ago; those of us you see here on the stage; the orchestra whom you can't see but I am sure you can hear; the technical team backstage and the front-of-house staff. And over the past year we have all shared night after night the award of audiences like yourselves.

Frank was traditionally humble and, having thanked everybody he could on behalf of the company, he proceeded to congratulate Lindsay for his own acting award; and as the audience applause died down, he counted out, 'One, two – one, two, three, four!' before a final reprise of the happiest of all tunes, 'Lambeth Walk'.

Although largely adored by the critics, there were a few who suggested that *Me and My Girl* was now socially unacceptable because it perpetuated a class war. Frank was dismissive of such attitudes:

> People talk about class too much; I think it's a lot of nonsense. I don't say, 'I like you because you are such-and-such a class.' I like them as a person. It was in itself a sort of snobbish thing to say really – that it looks down on the working classes. It's a light-hearted bit of nonsense – cockney meets county and let's have a bit of fun with it. It's *Cinderella*, it's not a deep social document for God's sake.

Happiness was at the centre of the show and Frank knew it: 'Someone came up to me the other day and said, "Oh I did enjoy it, it was so lovely,

I left the theatre feeling so happy – and now I'm going home to watch the television news!"' Frank recalled that meeting with a sagging spirit. *Me and My Girl* offered the perfect antidote to the troubles of daily life and offered way too happy a spirit to be spoiled instantly by the *News at Ten*!

On a personal note though, *Me and My Girl* had proven one thing beyond all else: there was life after Captain Peacock and it began on the West End stage in front of thousands in an award-winning show. Frank needn't have worried about the Mechanics' Institute.

8

Are You Free Now, Captain Peacock?

FRANK HAD PROVED TO HIMSELF, AS IF THERE had been any doubt, that getting typecast in a television comedy need not be the end of any other acting work. *Are You Being Served?* had chalked up sixty-nine episodes across thirteen years, with a film and a stage show thrown in for good measure, plus all the sideshows of a hit series in the form of store openings, garden fetes, board games – there was even a plan to have the team record a full training programme for counter staff at retail outlets that would accompany literature and illustrations for stores and shops.

While Frank may have lost out on some dramatic work at the BBC due to Peacock's recognition, he had still been in demand elsewhere.

The initial success of *Me and My Girl* showed no signs of stopping and Frank's time in 1985 was almost entirely spent on the show, with no apparent hindrance when the BBC finally deigned to release the final series of *Are You Being Served?* more than a year after it was filmed.

In January of 1986, however, the first batch of principals left *Me and My Girl*, Lindsay and Thompson preparing for an opening on Broadway. Their replacements were the little-heard-of Enn Reitel and Su Pollard, riding the crest of a wave with her success as chalet cleaner Peggy in *Hi-de-hi!* The minimal box office that Reitel brought with him made it all the stranger that Frank remained third in the billing behind the two newcomers.

Frank remained with the production for a further three months, but changes were afoot that he didn't really approve of. He wrote to producer Richard Armitage urging him not to tinker with such a winning formula, particularly in a scene between Sir John and Sally that was in Frank's eyes being turned into an exchange too obviously contrived from *My Fair Lady*.

Frank decided that with the changes diminishing what he had enjoyed for so long, he would say farewell to the production in May of 1986 after five hundred and ninety-four consecutive performances, by far and away his most significant stage success.

He had decided to bring the curtain down on the run and set off on a holiday around the world with his beloved Beryl, starting with a flight to New York on Concorde and a bird-watching tour of Central Park under the guidance of a WWF representative. And of course, he could hardly be in Manhattan and not take in a show; where better to go than to the hottest musical in town – Robert Lindsay in *Me and My Girl*! Their tour of the States lasted five weeks before spending another month in Australia and then subsequently returning home.

The work Frank returned to wasn't quite as glamorous as a near-six-hundred-performance run in the West End. While *Me and My Girl* had brought him wonderful stage success, it seemed like television had forgotten him. A couple of villainous appearances in episodes of the children's television show *T Bag*, along with an appearance in *Great Expectations* as Mr Trabb, were pretty much all television had to offer for the remainder of the decade, so Frank was relying on theatre work to sustain him.

He had a fair amount of this offered to him. An appearance in *Harvey* opposite *The Golden Girls* star Rue McClanahan failed to repeat Frank's previous success.

The most novel of his offers was Robert Hardy's attempt at a musical based on Winston Churchill, jovially called *Winnie*, but it struggled to find an audience. Frank had a number of parts, including an apparently hilarious moment as General de Gaulle, but it's safe to say that of the two different Winnies that Frank appeared in, Hardy's curious attempt was the less successful one.

With no apparent banker stage roles in the offing, when old friend Derek Nimmo came calling with plans to take on the challenge of touring the Far East, Frank couldn't resist. However, the idea of being away from Beryl for a long overseas tour was not appealing; and so, for the first time in almost forty years, Beryl was persuaded out of acting retirement in order to join the tour.

Nimmo had assembled a cast for touring William Douglas Home's comedy *The Reluctant Debutante* and was kind enough to offer Beryl a three-line part that would allow her to be part of the company and share places she and Frank would never otherwise have seen.

Nimmo's schedule was a brutal one, with several weeks of rehearsal in the UK in August of 1989 before heading out to Hong Kong two weeks later. From there, the cast would take in Kuala Lumpur, Indonesia, Singapore, Thailand, Dubai, Bahrain, Oman and Egypt. As if that wasn't exhausting enough, they would finally touch down in England on the 12th of November before opening a month-long season at the Theatre Royal, Windsor just two days later.

Despite being the most aged of the cast after leading lady Moira Lister, who left the tour after the death of her husband Jacques de Gachassin-Lafite Vicomte d'Orthez, Frank embraced the challenging schedule and led from the front.

When the tour arrived at the Jakarta Hilton, before the first performance in Indonesia on the evening of 29th September, Frank and his castmates were summoned to assemble in full costume on the stage where they were confronted by a dozen or so gentlemen assembled along a green baize table, each armed with a large dossier. Together they represented a censorship committee.

The committee's seemingly sole English-speaking member translated to Frank their requirements. First up, he was instructed to introduce the full cast, including both their character name and their stage name, which immediately caused confusion as he had to explain how Beryl Evans was not Beryl Evans but actually Thornton, and why Jill Melford was actually Jill Lady Leon.

Not only was accuracy required to ensure that work permits were granted, but they were also expected to sign that they would not dance with hotel guests nor engage in any activity that might transgress the Indonesian moral code and lead to their having to present themselves for arrest by the authorities.

More challenging still was Frank's next task: to offer a summary of the play to ensure that Indonesian sensitivities were not offended by language, nudity or sexual innuendo. That last requirement was particularly tricky, given this was a British comedy being played to an audience almost entirely consisting of expatriates.

'I considered it wise to present the piece as if it were the most respectable, insipid and boring play ever to hit the West End,' Frank recalled, 'the mother's aversion to David Hoylake-Johnston being no more than objecting to him eating peas off his knife! My closing line to the scene – "Hope you're getting all you want" – was delivered with a boyish innocence redolent of Andy Pandy.'

Despite the hectic schedule, Frank and Beryl did manage some sight-seeing; but it was as ever grounded not in showbiz or publicity, but in quieter interests, Frank making a beeline for the Mai Po marshes while in Hong Kong, having been able to call on his membership of the World Wildlife Fund council to arrange a visit. He was rewarded with a sighting of the white-breasted kingfisher, an Asian variant of the colourful bird seen in England: 'It quite made my day. There it was giving us a fine display of fishing. The way I see it, you can go shopping anywhere, can't you?'

A decade later, when Nimmo appeared as a guest on Frank's *This is Your Life*, he recalled the challenging tour and Frank's unflappable support: 'As you can imagine, to take Frank and Beryl around the world: there can be no greater ambassadors for Britain than Mr and Mrs Thornton.'

While Frank was struggling to find work of any substance, something interesting was happening in the US that would ultimately lead to some-what of a rediscovery for him: *Are You Being Served?* was attracting an increasingly large following. In the pre-internet days, American television was based around the three major networks: ABC, CBS and NBC. There was no BBC equivalent to avoid commercials, but there was one way to watch British television, and that was via PBS, Public Broadcasting Service.

PBS didn't and still doesn't produce its own entertainment. Their offerings tend to be documentaries, antique shows and arts programmes. Anything in the entertainment sphere was imported. As such, it garnered a somewhat elitist reputation when compared with its rivals on the major networks.

Brandon Brock and Jeff Nunner are devoted fans of *Are You Being Served?* from across the Atlantic and have run a podcast for each and every episode of the show under the name of *That Does Suit Madam.* Having grown up watching the show, Brandon clarified how the staff of Grace Brothers began to have an impact:

> PBS is free, you don't have to have cable television, so back in the nineties, anyone with a TV set and an aerial could watch PBS. Everything on there has a slightly educational feel to it, like the high arts; yet out of nowhere here's this show from the seventies with a woman with pink hair and this guy with a moustache; it lacked that dripping-with-elitism feel like the Boston Symphony or the Metropolitan Opera. Everyone could see it.

Despite the rebellious reception by some in the British gay community to the somewhat over-the-top campness of Mr Humphries, when *Are You Being Served?* first appeared on PBS the equivalent community began embracing him Stateside. Jeff continued:

> The idea of Mr Humphries' character really spoke to queer teenagers. There was something about that campness that was like, 'Oh, this is a character that people are not laughing at, they're laughing with, and more often than not he's making the joke and leading the joke.'

Brandon concurred that *Are You Being Served?* reached an audience dynamic that nothing had really tapped into before:

> It was a different culture, a slice of life that proved that in my little, very conservative isolated little town where I was living as a kid in Arkansas, the world is much bigger than my back yard. I think that a lot of Americans who are Anglophiles would probably share that a little bit and I don't think there was any media that was anything like *Are You Being Served?* that I could have consumed at that age.

While Mr Humphries may have helped garner a community following, the increasing viewership were quick to recognise the importance of Peacock and the performance of Frank Thornton. As Brandon recognised:

> Comedy is based on conflict. The whole first half of the series is about the staff rebelling against their leadership – Captain Peacock, Mr Rumbold and to some degree Mr Grace. As it starts to near the routine senior salesman era, we see Captain Peacock start to become one of the gang and that is when Frank became able to play into that silly element.
>
> The fact that he's the straight man, the one with the tie and the carnation: for him to be so oblivious. He's saying about watching a programme on his colour television or something in his semi-detached house... even the fact that he calls himself Captain – he's always trying to make himself a bit better than any of the others. Jeff says in the podcasts, Frank Thornton isn't ever laughing, isn't ever smiling. It's like a higher craft of comedy to be hilarious but not give a clue to the audience that you know how funny you are. There's an episode where he does cross dressing as his wife and his wife dresses as him and the whole time, he is straight. He's still the floorwalker even though he's got panty tights and a garter belt!

PBS often ran fundraisers and the cast of *Are You Being Served?* were frequently flown out to assist, such was their appeal.

David Croft had promised the main cast of *Are You Being Served?* at their farewell dinner that he hoped to bring them back together again. True to his word, with the original show attracting such a cult following in America, Croft set about resurrecting the Grace Brothers staff. In the UK, the new show went out under the name of *Grace and Favour*, but in the States it was simply named *Are You Being Served Again?* and while the latter is rather obvious, Croft felt that had the British airing been given the same title, it might have garnered a stronger following.

The store setting had been exhausted, but the characters could still be utilised and so Croft created a show whose premise was that Young Mr Grace had died and, in his will, it was revealed that the company pension fund had been squandered almost out of existence. All that was left for the loyal staff was a run-down country hotel, Millstone Manor (quite what might have happened to the pensions of staff in the other departments was conveniently ignored!)

As the only potential recompense for their years at the firm, Mr Humphries, Mrs Slocombe, Miss Brahms and Captain Peacock were forced to try and run the place as a working hotel, with Mr Rumbold already in place and claiming management privileges.

To make the show work, new members were added to the cast. Dorset comedian Billy Burden played Morris Moulterd, with Fleur Bennett as his daughter Mavis. The pair were very much stereotypical country folks, as far away as possible from the other new character, Jessica Lovelock, played by Joanne Heywood. Lovelock was the person who had inadvertently killed Mr Grace by giving him a heart attack when her bikini top popped off when they were scuba diving!

The BBC seemed to be taking their new show a little more seriously than they had the final series of *Are You Being Served?*, with a double-page spread in *Radio Times* and plenty of press publicity. They went so far as to commission a second series before the first had even been aired.

Those of the cast that came back needed little to no persuading, the camaraderie was so strong. The only doubt was whether Wendy Richard could return, given that viewers were used to seeing her dour alter ego Pauline Fowler in *EastEnders*. Thankfully, the real Wendy Richard was considerably more glamorous than her *EastEnders* role and so it wasn't seen as a problem to have them both on screen at the same time.

It's hard to say whether the BBC were really as on board as they could have been. The two-page article in *Radio Times* wasn't nearly as enthusiastic as it might at first have appeared, once the reader had dug past the 'They're Free!' headline: 'It's safe to say that Millstone Manor country hotel and farm, setting for BBC1's *Grace and Favour*, is not for the ultra-sophisticated.' Hardly an introduction to sell the show. It continued, '*Grace and Favour* is wedged in the mid-seventies titter tradition as surely as if progressive comedy never happened.' The article didn't even get the start and finish years of the original run of *Are You Being Served?* correct.

The show would surely benefit from its new characters. Burden and Bennett were completely believable as they tried to acclimatise their new bosses to the ways of a working farm, as well as the insular machinations of village life.

As for the brazen Miss Lovelock, who had been promised the horses' quarters by Young Mr Grace, her voluptuousness and constant flirting with Captain Peacock and his reciprocal moustache twitching gave Frank a new facet of Peacock to explore, particularly welcome as Peacock's justification for superiority was now gone.

The merging of the new and old cast members worked well. 'I'd never met any of them before, so it was quite daunting initially,' recalled Heywood. 'They'd worked together so much; you knew you were coming into a family... but they were lovely. Molly was a real giggler, John was hilarious. Frank was just lovely – warm, funny, quick-witted – a true gent in the old-fashioned sense.'

The rapport between Heywood and Frank was clear and the dynamic between the two characters was all the better for it. Joanne remembered, 'In one scene I had to ride a motorbike, a 1000cc Kawasaki, and I could barely get my feet to the ground, but with Frank as pillion it was a bit more stable. The director had said, "Hold Joanna a bit higher up, I'll let you know if it's indecent." I said, "That's right across my boobs," and Frank said, "Don't worry darling, I can't feel a thing through all this leather." I said, "I can!"'

Despite the new cast and a slightly unexpected approach to Mr Humphries, who remained camp but was now sharing a bed with Mavis Moulterd, the press were unkind. It was almost as though they didn't want it to succeed as it was bringing back a show that, while popular, was still poorly regarded by critics at least. It even drifted into the business after the show had finished. Heywood was comparatively new to the industry and conceded, 'There was a snobbery, I felt, even in auditions. I would be asked what I'd done recently, and they'd go, "Oh, that."'

Filming fluffs were not unusual in any show, and *Grace and Favour* was no different. Billy Burden would often come in and say the wrong line and then, for the next take, come in and say exactly the same thing in exactly the same way. However, uncharacteristically Frank felt his own performances were lacking. He had recently been suffering from shingles, which he saw as the reason for what he deemed to be an increasingly low state of mental and physical energy and concentration during the studio recording sessions.

What had actually happened was more worrying. Frank had recently bought a new car, an Audi of which he was very proud. Because the car was somewhat lower in height than he was used to, when he went to pick something up from within the car he cracked the top of his head against the door frame. No bumps or bruises appeared, so Frank carried on as per normal; but his tiredness and a month or more of relentless headaches led him to get checked out.

It seemed that the damage was internal. On 3rd September 1992, two haematomas were discovered, and he was rushed to Charing Cross Hospital to have accumulated fluid drained off. The process involved shaving his head and drilling four holes.

It was a successful procedure and Frank took it in good humour, particularly now that he could find a reason for what he felt had been substandard performances. A look now at photos later in his career shows evidence of the wounds, with Frank carrying dents in his head – horns, as he sometimes referred to them. Ever the professional, though, Frank wrote to producer, writers and colleagues to apologise for his performances and explain, suggesting that maybe they do a version of *The King and I* instead while he waited for his hair to return.

Joanne Heywood remembered Frank struggling with some of his lines, without knowing the reason why; and his friend Nicholas Smith was quick to respond to Frank's apologetic mailshot. He joked:

> We won't now be able to use the phrase: 'I need that like a hole in the head' in your presence. As for the hair question I have this advice: do without it, it's nothing but trouble – join the exclusive group of those who have realised that hair is out of date, from an evolutionary point of view. Besides, IF we do *G&F* again, think what fun the make-up department may have, looking at photographs and recordings in order to work out Capt. P's precise hairline!

Unfortunately, the capitalised and underlined 'IF' in Nicholas Smith's letter turned out to be very shrewd. There were undercurrents that the BBC had quickly lost whatever enthusiasm they had for *Grace and Favour*. Normal procedure for a fledgling programme was to show a repeat run of the previous series in the hope that it picked up some traction for the new one. The BBC didn't do that, the first series getting no repeat.

It didn't escape Frank's notice either.

Towards the end of 1992, the BBC held a launch of their new season of programmes over a BAFTA lunch. The corporation's presentation included no reference to *Grace and Favour*, and the showreel that went out on television later that same week offered no indication that the show was part of the line-up of new programmes. Frank could not help but respond to the BBC on behalf of his colleagues:

> We all have a distinct feeling that the BBC is not proud of this product, though its reluctance to commit itself to a third series seems strange in face of the almost hysterical reaction to the show in the USA. Our fan mail from all over that large country praises the show to the skies and begs for more. Is this a market to be ignored?

The luncheon event was an uncomfortable one for the cast, given the apparent disapproving snub. Joanne Heywood was new and excited to be going to the BAFTAs, but she remembered finding it all a bit odd. The press would have been given a press pack, but she wondered why she was there, given that there wasn't even a clip:

> The reason I specifically remember it is because it was a lesson in how the press can twist things. Wendy Richard had expressed her dissatisfaction in no uncertain terms at the event; I was very young and wouldn't have dared say what I thought. I was working in theatre at Birmingham at the time, and I got on a train back to Birmingham. But when it was in the press it said, '… and Joanne Heywood had to be placated by BBC staff.' People didn't even know who I was and why I was there.

Frank took the snub one step further and he admitted in his letter to the BBC's publicity head that, 'I for one felt it might cause the BBC some embarrassment if I should meet the press after the apparent insult of being left out of the presentation, so I decided to forgo the luncheon and departed immediately the presentation finished.'

The note that Frank made of the American reception to the show was very true. Having not long been treated to the joys of Grace Brothers staff in the department store setting, to have more of their favourite characters so soon was very welcome. There was even talk about the show continuing with American funding despite the BBC opting to drop it after two series, but alas the finance couldn't be found to continue. Heywood confirmed, 'There was talk about BBC Worldwide making it rather than the BBC because it was so hugely popular in the States, and that's where I think they did miss a trick with it. They didn't give it its best chance, shall we say.'

Perhaps where *Grace and Favour* failed to capture a better reception lay in the new setting itself. One of the joys of *Are You Being Served?* at its peak was the almost class-like hierarchy: the incompetent boss above the snooty floorwalker above the established staff above the cheeky juniors. With the hierarchy gone, the conflict that the *That Does Suit Madam* podcast gents spoke so fondly of had gone. Brandon Brock believed that 'the *Grace and Favour* plot wasn't doing anything for these characters. The conflict was in the shop, the customers coming in and getting the drama and that gave a lot of oomph to the storyline, but at Millstone Manor there are no customers.'

Nunner agreed with his co-host: 'There's no one to interact with because even the hotel guests, we don't get to see them. There's not that interaction and I think that's why it wasn't as big a success as it could have been.'

Grace and Favour ended the story of the Grace Brothers staff, although murmurs did briefly resurface later in the 1990s about another possible return. Frank was reported to have discussed the possibility with John Inman, saying, 'I was worried that we would be too old or too dead. But John pointed out that the jokes were twenty years old when we first did them.' Perhaps understandably, the rumours of a further series never gained any more traction.

It was perhaps just as well for Frank, who was now firmly back in the public eye thanks to the two series in which his most famous character had been resurrected.

With Peacock's final screen appearance being a gentleman at an aged manor house, it was the perfect opportunity to cast him among the many who came calling at Crinkley Bottom, on-screen home to Mr Saturday Night, Noel Edmonds and his live light-entertainment tour de force, *Noel's House Party*.

Edmonds knew what Saturday-evening audiences wanted. Several decades before Ant and Dec were causing havoc with quiz elements, guest stars and celebrity pranks, Edmonds had already perfected the medium. He gave British audiences an hour of innocent escapism into a world where he owned the manor house in the village of Crinkley Bottom, and an array of guest stars would interrupt proceedings by ringing the bell at the manor's door in the guise of one of the villagers, most of whom poured scorn on Edmonds in the finest Not-In-My-Back-Yard style.

Noel was a big fan of Frank's from all his years on TV. He gleefully recalled:

> I was absolutely in awe of him when we had the chance to work together on *NHP*. Here was one of the great acting stalwarts happy to appear as the curmudgeonly next-door neighbour who despised absolutely everything the owner of the Great House attempted to do. His role, of course delivered to perfection, was to be the ultimate NIMBY. He couldn't wait for me to move and for Crinkley Bottom to return to its genteel madness.

Frank was perfect for the show. His *Grace and Favour* excursion had added to the character that was angrily arriving periodically at the door. But *Noel's House Party* ran a tight schedule, meticulously timed to the final seconds for its live airing. Noel acknowledged, 'It's fair to say that even the most experienced thespians found the live television aspect a little unnerving, but of course not Frank. Always word perfect and the master of comedic timing, Frank delivered his withering put-downs with forensic precision.'

Frank was even called upon to be the decoy when Noel was the victim of a 'Gotcha' prank on his own show. Throughout the rehearsals, Frank was the final person to ring the bell as the credits began to roll after Noel had started to sing 'You Don't Bring Me Flowers'. When the show went live, the bell didn't ring, and Edmonds was told that in fact they were staying on air until he sang the entire song.

What the studio audience saw, but viewers did not, was the aftermath as the whole cast of the programme assembled to enjoy Noel's reaction to being hung out to dry in front of millions of viewers. With his usual beaming smile, he noticed Frank enjoying the chaos he had helped create and pointed at him. 'You were supposed to ring the bell,' he proclaimed; and, as he held up his own 'Gotcha' award, he warned, 'You haven't had one of these yet.'

But of course, Noel loved having Frank on the show and Frank loved doing it. And as ever, Frank was the perfect gentleman throughout. Noel said, 'I do recall him on more than one occasion after the show, saying "You do realise, old boy, I'm only saying what's on the script; I love the show and you do it so well."'

They were not empty words, as Frank also wrote to producer Jon Beazley:

> I was weaned on live television, but these days most people are scared of it and/or couldn't cope anyway. For this reason, I must congratulate all the *NHP* team on the wonderfully efficient way you produce an accurately timed and very pacy show. I'm very happy to be part of it every so often, even if I haven't always lived up to the above-mentioned efficiency!

Now into his eighth decade, Frank's stock was very much on the rise again, somewhat appropriate for his next venture. After a guest-star role in ITV sitcom *The Upper Hand*, Frank received a call for an audition for a show whose host, Julian Clary, was trying to rebuild his career after a throwaway comment had sent it into a downward spiral. A risqué line at the 1993 British Comedy Awards about then Chancellor of the Exchequer Norman Lamont had been taken badly by seemingly every element of the media, but a few years later, producer Claudia Lloyd seemed determined to get Clary back onto screens.

Comedy writer David McGillivray received an approach from Lloyd about finding a comedy vehicle for Clary in 1995. The initial suggestion of a sitcom in which Clary would have been the governor of a prison was passed on, but what developed was a staged reality show that saw members of the public 'tried' for nonsensical crimes: *All Rise for Julian Clary*.

In early December, Julian went onto a few radio stations as they stepped up a search for potential punters to appear on the show. Only six calls came in off the back of those appearances, but plans proceeded anyway as a number of names were discussed for taking the role of Geoffrey Parker-Knoll, the clerk of the court expected to offer some gravitas to proceedings.

Of the potential candidates brought in for an audition, McGillivray noted in his diary, 'From the men, Peter Jones is my favourite. I think he's very funny, but Frank Thornton is hot favourite.'

Jones was an old chum of Frank's and was of course most recognisable for his role in *The Rag Trade* and for his many years on radio as the perfect antidote to Kenneth Williams's hysterical antics in *Just A Minute*.

As well as Peter Jones, Frank was vying for the role of the clerk with Peter Wear, but it soon became clear that a good audition would seal it for Frank. McGillivray noted of his choices that, 'Peter Jones was a disappointment. He has become very slow and his dithering over his lines was mostly genuine. Finally, another of my suggestions, Peter Wear, came in and Julian took an instant dislike to him because of his eyes and his clothes.' Clearly it was Frank's audition that made the biggest impact: 'When he read the proper stentorian tones, everybody loved him.'

Although McGillivray had been in the corner of Peter Jones until the audition, Julian Clary himself was in no doubt as to who was his preferred option. 'In my mind it was always Frank,' he remembered. 'He was just what I'd hoped: very unassuming, very pleased to be there and enjoyed it all. Always word perfect and understated and very funny. It's all about timing and he delivered his lines perfectly with that face.'

Somewhat inevitably, even though the BBC were prepared to take a gamble on Clary being back on television, they were constantly cautious about the content of the show. It was of course supposed to be an adult show aired after the watershed, but there was an undercurrent of fear at the BBC should their gamble rile the censors, and the need to question the script and break for rewrites seemed constant.

Rehearsals began in January of 1996. Frank turned seventy-five a few days before he went to the rehearsal rooms in North Acton. The constant writing and rewriting to appease the powers that be meant many delays, which saw the main contributors to the show disappear to other rooms to work on the material. There was little for Frank to do while these shenanigans were taking place except nap, which is exactly what he did.

It was in fact something Frank had made quite a habit of, delighting at recounting in his after-dinner speeches that snoozing almost on demand had become one of his specialities (although Peter Jones did recall in *This is Your Life* a few years later that Frank also had a talent for belching during performances, 'the second worst noise' one could make during a show!). Frank's own words recalling his snoozing talent describe it best:

If I gained a reputation for anything in the theatre it was for dropping to sleep. As a playgoer I have a fair working knowledge of a lot of second acts but only a sketchy grasp of Act One. My wife has threatened to buy an electric cattle prod. My narcoleptic tendency first showed itself when I was playing Lysander in *A Midsummer Night's Dream* in Donald Wolfit's company in 1941. It was then that I realised I couldn't *act* going to sleep, I could only go to sleep. When the two pairs of lovers are put to sleep by Puck I had arranged myself stage left, lying with my back to the audience and my head conveniently tucked out of sight behind a wing flat where a cooperative assistant stage manager slid a cushion under it. She then gave me a waking nudge when I was required to carry on with the acting.

Some time passed before I succumbed again. Fortunately, during my flying training in the Royal Air Force there was an infallible method of preventing sleep: it was known as air sickness.

Eventually the RAF decided to dispense with my services, so pocketing my princely gratuity of £47.15.6. I returned to trying to support my wife and baby daughter on the paltry pickings of weekly rep. And of course, if anything is designed to bring on immediate sleep, it is sitting down to learn your words.

But I managed until one day in 1965. Art with a capital A came my way in the shape of a play at the Royal Court Theatre. Roy Kinnear, Les Montague, Liz Frazer, Peter Collingwood and I all jumped at the chance because John Osborne was going to direct it – we had an eye on the future even though none of us had a clue what the play was about. We were all obviously getting so depressed that one evening John gave us an excellent dinner followed by a visit to the London Palladium for the Ken Dodd Show – and believe me, you don't sleep when he's on – that is provided he doesn't go on until three in the morning.

We opened to a negative press but soldiered on with very thin houses. In one scene, Peter and I were seated either side of a table upstage with nothing to say while Liz and the other two carried on a twenty-minute scene downstage – a perfect recipe for me to get a nice little nap. I propped a large book on my knee and acted absorbed reading until Peter kicked me under the table when my next cue came.

On several evenings we had noticed a rather persistent loud laugh, obviously emanating from just one man whom we eventually identified as an associate director at the Court, William Gaskill. After one performance, he descended on the dispirited Roy Kinnear in his dressing room to say, 'Oh it's so funny and you're all so marvellous.'

'Do us a favour, Bill,' said Roy, 'We can see them getting up and leaving as we do it!'

'Yes, but you should see the expression on their faces as they go!' [the jovial wisdom that Frank shared with a youthful Robin Askwith some years later]

Stratford's then Artistic Director, Trevor Nunn, cast me as Duncan [in *Macbeth*] and we started to rehearse in the large space that later became the Swan Theatre. Like so many modern directors, Trevor preferred talking to rehearsing, so I manufactured to place myself out of the way behind a flap until required to rehearse.

One morning, Trevor and all the eager young members of the cast were busily discussing his idea that Young Siward should be killed on stage instead of off as William Shakespeare had written it. While they were absorbed in working out who was available to do the deed, I could see Patricia Hayes's head nodding, while Nicol Williamson was stretched out on the floor apparently joining Patricia and me in a quiet nap. Happily, I had not slipped into unconsciousness when, in a pause in the discussion, I heard Nicol's voice: 'Trevor, why don't you play the part and bore him to death?' I could forgive him anything after that, even stealing Malvolio from me!

Later that morning I was roused from my slumber by the magic word 'coffee'. I stumbled towards the door and as I passed Trevor he said, 'Well, Frank, what do you think of the idea?' For once, God smiled and provided me with an answer. 'Well, Trevor, it needs a bit of digestion,' followed by a quick exit to the canteen to ask my colleague Ron Pember what the hell they had been discussing: 'Only whether you should play Duncan as a third man.' I did, but Mr Nunn never employed me again!

Shortly after, I went into *The Doctor's Dilemma* at the lovely old Mermaid Theatre. Playing Sir Patrick Cullen I was first on to congratulate Colenso Ridgeon on his knighthood. I then had to sit in my comfortable armchair while all the other medical gentlemen came on to deliver what George Bernard Shaw called their arias. The inevitable happened and one night a note from the stage manager appeared in my dressing room: 'Please continue to stay awake while on stage.' In my own defence I have to say I never missed a cue.

Back then to early 1996 and a snoozing Frank awaiting the results of the many rewrites. It wasn't until 19th February that the pilot went out and, despite reservations by many, Julian Clary was awarded a full series. His interaction with Frank was perfect, Frank delivering lines full of double meaning but delivered with such military precision and gravitas that it was the perfect foil for Julian, who recalled, 'It worked because of the incongruity of him being Frank Thornton and me being me – it was an unlikely pairing. It was a great marrying of the old-world comedy and the new wave comedy – the crossover worked really well.'

Frank, of course, couldn't resist imparting his years of wisdom to the producers. In a live recording of the pilot, Frank's outfit was more akin to a camp shipman of centuries ago than a clerk of the court, complete with ruffs, stockings and vast green bows on his shoes. Clary, as judge, was comparatively conventional in comparison.

Frank felt that his garish outfit wouldn't work correctly:

> As Geoffrey is meant to be the dry-as-dust legal expert who tries to keep Julian on the rails, it seems to me that he should be less, rather than more, fantastically dressed than the judge. I honestly think the comedy will come out more strongly if Geoffrey dresses in a more colourless, legal gear. You make your audience laugh by showing them something they recognise as real and then giving it a twist that they weren't expecting.

And being Frank, he immediately apologised for his suggestions: 'I do go on, don't I?'

But Frank was of course correct; and when the show went to series, he was dressed in more typical courtroom attire, standing out within an elaborately camp setting.

Claudia Lloyd, who had invested so much effort into the show, was thrilled with how the dynamic worked. She wrote to Frank after the conclusion of filming, gushing with praise: 'What can I say? We've all started the "Frank Thornton Appreciation Society". The show is editing beautifully and you're a constant delight to cut back to.'

And despite all the risqué lines that Frank was asked to perform, he still maintained his level of standards. McGillivray recalled that in one episode, one of the guests was a woman who was taking her boyfriend to Julian's court because he was obsessed with the 1940s. David suggested doing a black-and-white flashback segment, bringing the accused into Television Centre which would be redressed as a 1940s ballroom. Frank would dance past and be asked to say, 'I've just dropped a load over Dresden,' but it wasn't a line he felt comfortable with. When it came to rehearsal he asked if the line could be altered as he felt very bad about what had befallen Dresden and so on his request the line went out as Dusseldorf.

All Rise for Julian Clary had cemented Frank's place as that most overused of phrases, a national treasure (even though Frank didn't like the term) and he was now somewhat of a cult figure. The perfect blend of old-school gravitas and cutting-edge alternative comedy, meeting somewhere in the middle with the kind of innuendos to make Mrs Slocombe squirm, had worked perfectly.

But even as he approached his eighties, Frank was far from done. As Clary and company prepared for a second series, they found themselves hiring the wonderful June Whitfield to replace Frank as he was headed for further sitcom success, joining a pair of loveable old rogues in a comedy that had started way back when *Are You Being Served?* was just finding its feet.

9

Love, Truelove

AT SEVENTY-SIX YEARS OF AGE, MOST PEOPLE are considering retirement, if they're not already retired. In the acting profession, rarely is that the case. The DNA is programmed to keep working. Frank had always had this nagging doubt that the phone would stop ringing, and so the idea that he would voluntarily stop acting was never entertained.

Home life was perfect. He had no desire to head off to the countryside for a restful retirement, nor even get a second home away from London as so many do. Westmoreland Road was all he needed. A new conservatory on the back of the house meant that he and Beryl could enjoy their garden, something Beryl was very much in charge of. Frank was a very practical man, doing most of the DIY in the house. It's safe to say that Frank and Beryl's life was close to idyllic.

But then after the first series of *All Rise With Julian Clary* aired, agent David Daly brought news of an audition for what was intended to be a guest star role that ended up being the longest-running screen role of Frank's career.

Like *Are You Being Served?*, *Last of the Summer Wine* had begun life as a one-off *Comedy Playhouse* production. First aired on 4th January 1973, it had initially starred Michael Bates, Bill Owen and Peter Sallis as, as the *Radio Times* detailed, 'Blamire, Compo and Clegg... three opposites with one thing in common – determination to make each day as full as possible.'

The premise for the show had hardly inspired writer Roy Clarke initially; but when the BBC agreed to make the three pensioners at the centre of the stories, by accident or design, single, he took the opportunity to make mischief with these loveable rogues, determined not to drift into their twilight years without making the most of their lives. It was a simple show, gentle in humour and a loveable homage to the sights and sounds of life in the Yorkshire Peak District.

By 1997, *Last of the Summer Wine* had taken on a life of its own. With a strong ensemble cast it had survived a number of changes to its leading trio. While Sallis and Owen had remained a constant, the third man, as the character was often referred to, had altered several times. Bates had left the show due to ill health, to be replaced by Brian Wilde as Foggy Dewhurst; and Wilde himself dipped in and out on occasion, Michael Aldridge playing Seymour Utterthwaite during Wilde's first absence.

The trio of Wilde, Owen and Sallis had become the show's most recognisable and popular line-up, while the programme had found a very comfortable spot on the early-evening schedules of the BBC on Sundays. Christmas specials were a regular event for what had become a staple part of the BBC's light entertainment offering.

The news that Wilde was to leave the show once more, at least temporarily, left the writers and producers in a quandary. Their leading trio was to be split once again and, since the cast were now up to their eighteenth series, it seemed entirely possible that the BBC would decide to pull the plug.

Producer Alan J. W. Bell had been dining with Trevor Bannister when the idea of Frank Thornton appearing in *Last of the Summer Wine* had first occurred to him. Bell and Bannister had worked together, ironically with Wilde, in a one-series flop called *Wyatt's Watchdogs* about a self-appointed Neighbourhood Watch group.

Bannister had mentioned his long-time co-star and friend as a possibility, and so when Wilde contacted Bell to say that he was suffering from shingles and would not be available for the Christmas special to air in 1997, nor the early portion of the next series, Bell decided to see if Frank would be available to guest while Wilde recuperated.

In his book, *Last of the Summer Wine: From the Director's Chair*, Bell recalled:

> I arranged for Frank Thornton to come into the BBC to have lunch with me. I knew, of course, that Frank was a good actor, but I needed to be certain that he was fit enough to undertake the exhausting location filming in the uneven valleys and hills of Yorkshire. As I struggled to keep up with him on the long walk from the Television Centre reception area to the restaurant block, I could see that Frank Thornton was in very good physical condition indeed.

Health was indeed rarely an issue for Frank. He may have had his challenges with his various nasal operations and suffered with asthma, but aside from his bang on the head during *Grace and Favour*, he was rarely unwell. His fitness was excellent for a man of his age. Friend Madeline Smith had recalled from their years of friendship, 'Frank simply never did anything to excess.'

When quizzed for a 'My Kind of Day' feature in the *Radio Times*, he commented:

> I'm in pretty good shape for my age, which is probably because I've never done any unnecessary exercise. I do a few loosening exercises recommended by an osteopath – nothing vigorous – and a bit of breath control, filling and emptying the lungs one at a time. We eat and drink sensibly, but I don't do any of this calorie control nonsense. There's too much faddishness about food and I've always remembered the advice a doctor once gave to Wolfit: 'Eat whatever you like but not enough of it.'

With that initial unofficial physical assessment passed, what remained to be decided was just how to accommodate Frank into the shows, given that Wilde could potentially be returning to the programme midway through the next series.

Bell and Clarke's challenge began to fix itself. According to Bell, Wilde had mentioned that his location filming should be condensed in order that he was away from home less. It sent some warning signs to Bell; and then further communications with Wilde resulted in other demands being made, such as limits on the filming schedule, drivers not being permitted to speak to their passenger and various demands about dressing rooms. Eventually, and somewhat reluctantly, Bell decided that Wilde should be let go, making Frank the permanent number three if his debut went well. Clarke set about hastily rewriting the episodes that had been intended for Foggy, while Frank prepared for a new recurring sitcom role.

Robert Ross recalled meeting Frank in his early days on the show and discussing his previous thoughts of a potential guest appearance which would have blown fans' minds. 'Brian Wilde used to wear the same tie that Peacock had worn in *Are You Being Served?* and Frank thought it would be lovely if the BBC in their great wisdom would drop Peacock in as a guest character for a couple of episodes or a Christmas special.' It would indeed have been a remarkable crossover; but had it happened, it would have robbed Frank of the creation of his next most famous character after Peacock.

Frank was signed up to play Herbert Truelove, a retired policeman who constantly referred to himself as Truly of the Yard. He fitted perfectly as the new leader of the trio, constantly using his police background as a way to educate his two friends, and always drawing on his life experiences from being married for many years to 'the former Mrs Truelove', a character never seen but spoken of in abject horror by Truly.

Truly's first appearance came in the 1997 Christmas special, entitled 'There Goes the Groom'. Besides introducing Truly, the fifty-minute special was also used to give Foggy a send-off, albeit an ignominious one. We see a double's legs at various times as an alcohol-induced level of unconsciousness overcomes Foggy and he is whisked away by an overly amorous postal worker to spend the rest of his days under her watchful eye in Blackpool. Truly was first seen knocking back pints at great pace at the closing stages of a stag night, the groom and Foggy having safely drunk themselves under the table.

In this first episode we were already being treated to what would become trademark Truly characteristics. Like Captain Peacock, he was always dressed impeccably, a blue pin-striped three-piece suit, brown

mackintosh and hat, regaling tails of his past to both educate and enter-
tain those around him.

In this particular episode, his recollections of the horrors of marriage
are enough to scare the impending groom into a state of ice-cold feet and
cause a chase around the countryside to try and first recapture, then calm
the escaping husband-to-be.

The groom himself was played by Lloyd Peters, who remembered his
appearance with great affection, highlighting his sharing the screen with
such acting legends as Frank, Thora Hird and Stephen Lewis as one of
the proudest moments of his career.

However, he also noted that Frank was graciously wary of his being
the new face on a show that by now had been running for twenty-four
years. 'The cast were all kind and supportive, especially Frank,' Peters
recalled. 'Perhaps he empathised with my "newbie" status. I did not know
that it was his debut episode which might explain why I detected a slight
reticence in suggesting notes or comments.'

Peters and Frank were both well aware that rocking the boat in any
way on such an established programme would do them no favours. Even
the younger members of the cast, albeit only by comparison to their more
senior colleagues, began to call Frank 'Baby Frank' in honour of his
freshness to the series.

Frank took on the physical challenges with gusto. Bell recalled Frank
wanting to run into a lake himself, but as was often the case with the aged
cast, the stunt double was called upon at the behest of the producers.
Frank still insisted on dunking himself to mirror his double; but while he
was earning plaudits and affection by enjoying throwing himself into his
role wholeheartedly in the true spirit of the *Summer Wine* ethos, Owen
and Sallis were tiring of such antics.

Peters remembered:

Bill and Peter had no hesitation in letting it be known that the schedule (and
some of the widescreen shots where they had to walk long distances) were
rather gruelling for men of their age. In fact, because of their urgings, I had
the blabbermouth temerity to inform the director as such, presumably
because I was seen as dispensable. Suffice to say these 'observations' didn't
go down too well with Alan J. W. Bell.

What Peters mentioned regarding widescreen was among many *Last of the Summer Wine* firsts: it was the first comedy to be filmed in widescreen, just as it had been the first for stereo sound and high-definition filming. Not bad for a programme that so often seemed to be mocked for its old-fashioned nature.

Frank took to his role like a duck to water, and the cast and crew took to him. While many people will remember the Compo, Clegg and Foggy trio as their favourite, Frank very quickly brought Truly into the fans' hearts. He did so in a quiet manner, which endeared him to those around him. Bill Owen had clashed with Wilde, and indeed Bates, over political stances, and at times there had been an uncomfortable atmosphere. While Frank was not averse to political opinion, he came to *Last of the Summer Wine* with an eagerness to make a success of the role but also to make as few waves as possible.

Morris Bright MBE, who, with Robert Ross, spent much of Frank's first series on location with the team for book research, recalled how discreetly effective Frank became. 'He was very keen to ensure that while he brought a new character to it, he didn't in any way try and usurp,' Bright recalled. 'It felt like a very happy time and from the people I spoke to probably the happiest times they'd had were with Frank as the third man. By the time Frank had got there they were all a bit older and chilled out and Frank just fitted in. Everybody loved him. He was a gentle man – not just a gentleman, but a gentle man.'

Recognising his joy at establishing himself in such a series at seventy-six years of age, Frank told Bright and Ross, 'One thing I shall always remember is that after I had been filming for a couple of weeks and still thinking, "Where am I?" Peter Sallis came over and quietly said, "You know you've got it, don't you?" He meant that I'd got the character. It was very heartening to have my colleague say that.'

At the same time as Frank's first full series in *Last of the Summer Wine* was being aired, the BBC ended years of neglect for *Are You Being Served?* and for the first time began repeating it on Saturday evenings. It had been treated harshly enough by the corporation when it was in production; end of season cast gatherings always went ahead with a degree of uncertainty as to whether they were going to return, and the final series had been in the can many months before the powers that be deigned to screen it.

Finally getting its reruns, *Are You Being Served?* found a new audience. Adults took a trip down memory lane while new viewers who had never seen the show before were exposed to Mrs Slocombe's pussy… Now they knew what their parents had been laughing at for the previous twenty-five years!

Frank was not surprised by the success of the repeats, achieving around eight million viewers in the Saturday teatime slot, but he knew exactly why he thought *Are You Being Served?* had been kept away.

'It has taken twelve years for this to happen,' he was quoted as saying. 'We have been victims of the dreaded disease; political correctness has stepped in with its humourless tread.'

So, in the late 1990s, Frank was to be seen starring in two of the BBC's most successful sitcoms of all time, one on Saturday evening, the other on Sunday evening. Quite the achievement for somebody who always felt he would forever be the jobbing actor playing behind other more established stars. But for comedy fans, Frank *was* a star. Robert Ross rightly concluded that, 'To us, they sort of are because every week they came into our living room and made us laugh. I said to Frank that what he did was so important, but I guess that's the humbleness of the jobbing actor.'

The success of *Last of the Summer Wine* didn't signal an end to Frank's stage career. In 1996, while he was filming his *Summer Wine* debut, he was still to be found in the West End in the production of *Cash on Delivery*, a farce directed by Michael Cooney, son of renowned farce director Ray Cooney. It was an interesting match of generations, Frank on the bill with another sitcom legend and future 'Wino' Brian Murphy, with up-and-coming comic Bradley Walsh in the starring role.

Reviews were somewhat scathing, but it didn't escape the reviewers' attention that the legends that were lost lower down the billing were those who came from a history of stage performances that could have saved the production from its mauling. Sheridan Morley in *The Spectator* noted:

The tradition of great British farce going back to the Aldwych company of the 1920s, and then moving forward through Brian Rix to Cooney, has always depended on a team of lightning-quick comedians knowing the genre as intimately as members of the RSC once knew their Shakespeare. Unfortunately, we no longer breed such people, nor outside the Whitehall is there any real work for them: the legacy of Robertson Hare and Tom Walls and Ralph Lynn effectively stops at Thornton and Murphy in comparatively minor roles, while the principals chase each other around the set wondering how on earth plays like this were ever made to stand up at more than the now-requisite thirty television minutes.

In Walsh's defence, he would acknowledge that this early in his own career, 'It was fantastic to work with living legends like Frank Thornton and Brian Murphy, but they soon realised I was like this sheet metal worker adrift in their world.'

Notwithstanding the comparative failure of *Cash On Delivery*, Frank was still in demand on stage. In 1999 he was asked about appearing in Nick Hytner's world premiere of *Cressida* for the Almeida Theatre Company, in which Frank would have played Jhon, a dresser in a seventeenth-century acting company run by an actor-manager played by Michael Gambon.

Frank was intrigued, but not enamoured. Heading towards his seventy-ninth birthday, and with his role in *Last of the Summer Wine* proving such a success, he was reluctant to take the part. Beryl was very keen, suggesting, 'It's the Almeida, Hytner and Gambon. You should do it even if it's a poor play and runs for one night.' Frank was less keen, conceding that with the success of *Last of the Summer Wine* and his age and financial situation, he didn't need to do it, so he passed.

Having seemingly struck gold with Frank to prolong *Last of the Summer Wine*, Bell and Clarke had to deal with the loss of Bill Owen shortly into Frank's run. Morris Bright was on set on Owen's final day of filming. He recalled:

It was a scene from the Millennium Special. That was on the Friday, and they literally took him from there to the hospital and he never came out of hospital again. Peter said to me he went to visit him, and he said, 'I've still got so much more I want to do.' But Bill had always said, 'I got this job when I was fifty-eight when a lot of actors were thinking about stepping back.'

The BBC had a problem. Frank had proven to them that losing one of the main trio of characters was surmountable, but the show had rotated that third man several times over the years. One of the reasons the programme had continued to survive those cast changes was because of Compo's permanency and his appeal to the child in all of us. Losing Compo was a completely different challenge. Frank remembered:

> With so much invested, the BBC could not just cancel the series; and, if we carried on, Compo could not just disappear. And so, in great haste Roy Clarke wrote three episodes covering the death and funeral of Compo. With the death of the actor behind the character, there was great poignancy in these episodes, but they were also very funny. This was great writing and the actors responded accordingly – great comedy is firmly based in real life.

When answering some fan mail a few years later, Frank would cite a story Wilfrid Brambell shared with him from his time working on *Steptoe and Son* as evidence of the importance of reality for good comedy. Frank was actually the most frequent actor in *Steptoe* after Brambell and Harry H. Corbett and he recalled an episode where Harold was, not for the first time, threatening to leave home, causing Albert to fake a heart attack in order to keep his son from fleeing the nest. Albert would of course make a miraculous recovery once Harold had abandoned his plans for freedom.

Frank recalled Brambell's story:

> Wilfrid Brambell said to Galton and Simpson, 'Albert is going to have a real heart attack because my mother (in real life) always had something similar whenever I really displeased her or threatened departure, recovering when this crisis had passed. It was real, not feigned.' Galton and Simpson were rather disturbed by this, saying, 'This is sitcom, not drama. You can't do that.' And Wilfrid said to them, 'You don't know how good you are! The depth of your writing will take it and I'm going to do it!'
>
> The proof that indeed it did work came a few days later when the episode was transmitted. On that evening a friend called to take my wife and myself out to dinner. We had no recording machine in those days and told him we must watch *Steptoe and Son* before going out. All three of us sat riveted to it as Albert had his heart attack. This was sitcom and one of the principals was near to death! Unprecedented. So much comedy is one-dimensional – real comedy is firmly rooted in real, recognisable life.

Those extra three episodes of *Last of the Summer Wine* were indeed hugely poignant. Looking back at them now, there is a warmth running through all three. A huge part of that is that the majority of the comedy lines come from Truly, not Clegg. Clegg is lost without his chum, and Frank's delivery of comedy and sincerity in appropriate measure ensures that the emotional farewell to Compo, and indeed Owen, never falls into despair but always maintains the light touch of comedy drama that the situation needed.

Despite reservations by some of the cast, who fully expected the show to end, the writers found a way to keep *Last of the Summer Wine* going by writing in Compo's previously unknown of son, played by Bill Owen's son Tom. The unlikely story worked well enough to persuade the BBC to continue to commission a further series.

Now into his eighties, Frank was more than happy to throw himself into his new role, some saying that his arrival gave other cast members a new lease of life. However, for all of his energies in the programme, his desire to perform on the stage seemed to be waning.

He had already turned down the role in *Cressida*; and it started to become a theme that, while producers were keen to employ him, Frank felt his age precluded him from taking the roles offered. He also turned down a potential role in *Sherlock's Veiled Secret*, suggesting that they needed somebody in their fifties; and when he was approached to play Arthur in Terrence Rattigan's *Harlequinade*, he again turned it down, suggesting that, if he were to take the role, they would need to engage a couple of centurions to play other characters in the play!

For Frank, it was time to start picking and choosing what work he took. His financial security meant that he could afford to do this, but he still believed that he had something to offer on stage. Robert Ross recalled a conversation during a recording of audience reactions for *Last of the Summer Wine*:

> We were sat backstage, and he was trying to think of a play he could tour in that was funny but was a really good part for an older actor. We were wracking our brains and I thought I had the best one: *The Man Who Came to Dinner*. You always knew when you had impressed Frank because he looked me right in the eyes, gripped my shoulder in his vice-like grip and

said, 'That's a brilliant idea because not only is it a brilliant play, but I can spend the entire play sitting in a wheelchair.'

The role would have been a fine one for Frank, who was aware of the immense popularity he and Captain Peacock still had in North America and Australia. The part of Sheridan Whiteside, a radio comic who becomes wheelchair-bound through an injury sustained when arriving for a dinner party and remains at the hosts' home for a month of recovery, would have suited him perfectly. Being co-written by George S. Kaufman, who had written for the Marx Brothers, would have added to the appeal. An admiring Ross recalled:

> He would have been brilliant at that because he had that wonderful authoritative way of delivering a line, but you also liked him as well. That Frank still wanted to schlep around Australia or America at that age in a tour: brave is too strong a word, but these people were in terms of just getting on with it. He seemed so in love with the business and so grateful to still be in it.

Truly was bringing him a good wage, unlike most of his previous successes; and, while still very fit for his age, filming in Yorkshire meant Frank was spending more time apart from his beloved Beryl, so anything that added to his time away from home had less appeal if she couldn't accompany him.

He still loved his poetry and, as he wrote home from Yorkshire, he titled the below ditty, written at 5.45am, 'Huddles in a Humdrum Huddersfield Hotel':

> Allit'rative lim'ricks are lousy;
> Laborious, leaden and lousy,
> To invent vivid verse
> In terms trenchant and terse
> Can't be done, darling. Dammit, I'm drowsy!

> The title is literally true, love

> Love,
> Truelove

Frank didn't give up on theatre entirely once his *Last of the Summer Wine* stint became more established. In 1999 he became involved in *The Jermyn Street Revue* under the direction of Sheridan Morley and, at the age of seventy-eight, he was still getting fine reviews in a production that was given an otherwise lukewarm reception. The theatrical press was still acknowledging his enthusiasm as he threw himself into a performance as a music-hall comedian at the bottom of the bill singing 'Small Time'.

For some time now, Frank had seen very little work in the cinema. However, one of his more well-known movie appearances came in 2001 in the most unlikely of forms, with a brief role in Robert Altman's Oscar-winning *Gosford Park*, unlikely both for the unexpected nature of it and because his role – consisting merely of butler, Mr Burkett, enquiring if his aristocratic employer is ready before accompanying her to her waiting car holding an umbrella, getting soaked himself while ensuring 'M'lady' stays dry – was such a minor one that it is somewhat puzzling why Frank became so recognised for it. Maybe it was because he had not been seen on the silver screen for some time, or because the generation watching Academy Award-nominated movies were not likely to be regular followers of Truly, Clegg and company on a Sunday evening. Either way, Frank was equally baffled.

Upon receipt of a certificate from the Screen Actors Guild honouring 'the outstanding performance by the cast', he felt compelled to write to producer David Levy:

> Since I probably had the smallest part in the picture, you can imagine my surprise at being included. It has been a rule of what I laughingly call my career that the bigger the part I have, the lousier the picture. It reached its peak when I played the valet to tyrannosaurus Rex in *A Flea in Her Ear*. So often have I done my bit and gone on my way, another job of work completed with precious little to remember. *Gosford Park* was quite different. Never have I had so little to do but felt so involved, so much 'part of the family'.

Perhaps Frank's bemusement at being so acknowledged for such a brief role was best summed up by an item of fan mail that amused him greatly, coming from a fan in South Carolina, who wrote: 'I nearly spilled my popcorn and drink at the showing of *Gosford Park* when, lo and behold, Captain Peacock was escorting a lady to her Rolls in the first frames of the movie.'

When watching that opening scene as Burkett waits patiently on his own until the departing car has left sight, there is a brief moment of poignancy on reflection. Although Frank made a couple of 'blink and you miss it' cameos in his final few years, *Gosford Park* was Frank's last movie role to speak of. As the opening scene sees him looking dutifully through the rain until the demands of his position allow him to move inside, the last big-screen glimpse of this particular dignified English gentleman tugs surprisingly hard at the heartstrings.

10

A True Gentleman

THE BBC VULTURES WERE ALWAYS CIRCLING IN THE later years of *Last of the Summer Wine*. As had been the case with *Are You Being Served?* the cast and crew never knew if the series they had most recently finished would be the last. It remained a record-breaking run and the writers and producers had done a remarkable job in keeping the cast as fresh as it could be without losing the core message: that it was okay to age disgracefully and live life's later years with an element of mischief.

By its final series the show had shifted focus, so while Peter Sallis and Frank were still in the programme, the leading trio element was now taken up primarily by Burt Kwouk, Russ Abbott and Brian Murphy.

Eventually, after conceding to allow one more series in 2010, the axe finally fell on the loveable retirement home that was *Last of the Summer Wine*, once described by its creator Roy Clarke as 'Just William in long trousers'.

Despite being a who's who of the acting generations of yesteryear, and still getting good viewing figures for a comparatively small budget, the BBC just couldn't resist axing the programme. Writing of the show's demise in the *Sunday Telegraph*, William Langley lamented, 'The old boys in Holmfirth have had their day. But it has been a good one, and many may feel that it is now time for the chaps who killed them off to grow up.'

For the final few series, Frank and Peter had been restricted to interior shots for insurance purposes. Seemingly gentlemen in their late eighties strolling across the stunning Yorkshire countryside and wandering the windy streets around Holmfirth were not something insurance companies were too keen to cover.

Frank's agent, David Daly, recalled, 'He relished playing Truly in *Last of the Summer Wine*, but I had a call from Alan J. W. Bell that year [2010] and he said, "This is the last year we can use him, for insurance purposes." Nobody would insure Frank at the age of ninety, so that was really the end anyway.'

It would seem then that, even had the show been given a reprieve, Frank may well not have been able to appear; so as much as it was sad that there was no opportunity to give the Yorkshire favourites a send-off, the show having only been cancelled after filming had ended, a *Last of the Summer Wine* with no Frank and potentially no Peter Sallis would have been a tricky move to pull off.

In those later years, Frank and Beryl remained a partnership, spending a lot of time going to the theatre, although it's notable that Beryl had a greater interest than Frank did. By now, of course, his own theatre career had ended; but he was back to the original love he'd had as a child, when he was to be seen skipping his way home from the Capitol Cinema through the fog doing his Stan and Ollie impressions.

The cinema had held a lifelong fascination for him, but it had always been the medium he had felt he would be least likely to achieve success with. It meant he had even more admiration for those who could make people laugh on the big screen:

> I have such tremendous admiration for, for instance, directors like Billy Wilder and actors like Jack Lemmon and Tony Curtis, who can make a film like *Some Like It Hot* which was brilliantly funny, and yet it was all shot cold in the studio with no audience to tell you what they think is funny.

His relationship with the theatre had also become more complicated in later years. For all the joy it had brought him, he disliked the way things had moved away from the actor-director era of Wolfit and Gielgud. He had no issues with performers: quite the reverse. He was always a staunch supporter of the jobbing actor, even though he did feel that repertory companies offered new talent a far better training ground than any university could.

But he hated the fact that where it would once have been Gielgud's *Macbeth* or Wolfit's *Hamlet*, the names were now of the director over the acting talent. It was understandable that he would bemoan such a change in focus, given that more often than not people were attending the theatre to see the play itself or the star name at the top of the bill, not the production company or director.

Frank harked back to his experience of Rex Harrison's 'star' demands. He pondered that it was once a difficult balancing act to judge whether the advantages of an egomaniac outweighed the disadvantages. With *My Fair Lady* they clearly did, but not so with *A Flea in Her Ear*. But as the new approach to director kudos took over, he pondered, 'I wonder if it is a good thing or not that such a problem has almost no chance of presenting itself in today's set-up, the director's theatre... the soil is not conducive to the growth of the star actor.'

He recalled his experience at the RSC in *Macbeth*: 'The leading part was played by actor number thirty-seven in the alphabetical billing, three below me, Nicol Williamson.'

Frank was also able to continue engaging in battle by post as he often did. He liked things to be accurate and could be remarkably enthusiastic about correcting what he perceived to be errors. He wrote to correct Anne Robinson's pronunciation on *The Weakest Link*, as well as Jeremy Paxman's on *University Challenge*, but he always did so with an air of humility and something of self-mockery for having done such a thing.

He once gave an interview to Forces Radio at the height of the success of *Me and My Girl*. When the host mistakenly referred to Gilbert O'Sullivan as opposed to Gilbert and Sullivan, Frank quickly corrected him, but spent more time apologising and admonishing himself for having the audacity to point it out. 'I do beg your pardon,' he politely said. 'I'm so sorry, I shouldn't have corrected you.'

With his ninetieth birthday looming, it would have been reasonable to assume that with the end of Truly, Frank would be retiring. In effect his age did that for him, but he continued to work when opportunity permitted. He could be seen in 2010 as one of the judges in a semi-final of *Masterchef* amongst a host of fellow comedy greats for a themed set of judges. And amazingly, in 2012 at the age of ninety-one he made a very brief non-speaking cameo, as much of the British comedy roster did, in the brutally dismissed Ray Cooney farce *Run For Your Wife*, a film version starring Danny Dyer and Neil Morrissey. It was a token entry on many great British comics' CVs that was the most palatable element of an otherwise woefully badly received movie.

'*Run For Your Wife* was just Ray getting all of his old pals to sit on a bus,' remembered Jane Thornton. 'I think they panned it because of the era. We were moving into today's era and old-fashioned comedy was becoming a no-no. Unfortunately, his timing was wrong. When you look at it, it's just like an old-fashioned *Carry On...* film.'

Certainly, Cooney was gathering all of his old mates... a look at IMDb will see the vast array of British classic comedians and actors that made a fleeting cameo. Cooney was always aware of how dependable Frank was and it was a nice way to acknowledge him in his last sighting on the cinema screen: 'Frank worked on quite a few of my productions and he was one of the most reliable actors and a delight to direct and produce. I must have had Frank in about twenty of my productions over the last thirty years! An absolute professional.'

As he entered his tenth decade, Frank was definitely tiring. He turned ninety-two in January of 2013, but by now there were a limited number of people he was interested in seeing. Agent David Daly, the Shepherds, Michael Noakes and the Bannisters were largely the only people he made a point of trying to see with any regularity.

Anya Noakes remembered inviting Frank and Beryl for supper at her flat in early spring of 2013. 'I'd invited someone called Charles Lewson who used to write about Edward Lear and I thought it would be quite a nice mix. Beryl rang in the morning and left me several messages and she said she was terribly sorry but Frank was not feeling very well.' Beryl was very keen to attend, so she said she would arrange for a driver; but, to Anya's surprise, when she arrived Frank came along as well. 'The first half of the evening he was quite animated but then he was clearly just very, very tired. He did actually die a few days later so I was very glad that they did come.'

Frank Thornton passed away in his sleep at the age of ninety-two on 16th March 2013. His career had lasted more than seventy years; and, whether by design or not, his belief that it was better to be lower on the bill than the star performer had served him well.

Apart from brief spells in his early post-war years where he had to supplement his acting income with other employment, he had chalked up an astonishing body of work. And yet despite his protestations to the contrary, he really was a star performer. *Are You Being Served?* would not have worked without him: he was the glue that held the warring factions together. *Last of the Summer Wine* could easily have faltered had he not so seamlessly stepped in to complement Peter Sallis, Bill Owen and the later cast members. Those two series alone made him a star, but the staggering amount of stage, screen and radio work he had amassed by the time of his death shows that he really was one of the most in-demand performers of his generation.

'It struck me, despite his lugubriousness, that he was very content with the way his career went,' recalled Anya Noakes. 'Certainly, he was contented in those later years with what he had achieved.'

Frank had told Richard Bentine towards the end of his career, 'It's a wonderful business, you know. Where else can you get a three-year contract at eighty-seven years old?'

As contented as he was, one cannot help but feel that for all the good feeling there was towards Frank, his lack of star behaviour led to a certain missed opportunity for public acclaim. Seeking recognition for either his contribution to his chosen profession or for his charity work was most definitely not in his nature. However, he performed a multitude of functions in the charity world. He left gifts to the David Shepherd Foundation in his will and did regular fundraising work for the Friends of Barnes Hospital, while always donating to other worthy causes close to his heart including the Royal Theatrical Fund and the Kidney Research Aid Fund, as well as many wildlife and animal charities. He was also a member of the World Wildlife Fund council, president of his local RSPCA branch, and along with Beryl an active fundraiser for, and member of, the RSPB.

Frank and Beryl's involvement with the Friends of Barnes Hospital was of particular note. The pair were regularly helping out in some form or other almost from the moment they arrived at Westmoreland Road, supporting an array of events and meeting the patients who were mostly suffering from Alzheimer's or dementia. On these visits, typecasting worked. Patients who would not necessarily recall the actor Frank Thornton could still recognise Captain Peacock from years before. Frank would happily oblige them with his time and conversation, and they would excitedly send photos back to friends and family of their shot with a star. Friends trustee Mary McNulty confirmed, 'He was at home with them; he wasn't visibly put off or startled by patients who might be a bit wandering. And really, there was nothing in it for Frank. He wasn't going to get big headlines; it was really just done out of generosity.'

That generosity was of goods, money and time. The events thrown by the Friends would invariably have Frank and Beryl's support, but they didn't just meet obligations. If there was a concert for Christmas, the pair would understand the other elements in the show and carefully select poems that would fit the occasion, tailoring their participation accordingly.

For Beryl, that meant calling ahead to see what colour schemes any flowers would follow in order that she might dress appropriately. And her involvement didn't stop at coordinating her sartorial elegance. Friends chairman Kathy Sheldon recalled, 'We would have Christmas sales and Beryl often brought her clothes, beautifully wrapped in tissue paper and boxes... and if they couldn't help you, Frank would always apologise in handwritten notes. They always made you feel that you were important.'

All of this giving back was what Frank and Beryl *wanted* to do, rather than what they felt obliged to do. And yet despite all of their contributions, upon his and Beryl's being granted Honorary Membership of the Friends of Barnes Hospital, Frank still felt compelled to acknowledge that their delight was accompanied by not feeling they deserved it. They excelled at simply being part of the community, far and away from photo opportunities and self-gratification. Frank was extremely quiet about his charity involvement, but others felt he should be recognised for his efforts, as well as for his long career.

Frank's humility in terms of recognising his achievements even went so far as for him to reject such an acknowledgement at one point. He was nominated for *Debrett's Distinguished People of Today* in 1989, a variant of the popular *Who's Who* books of the time, but Frank declined the invitation. Of the unnamed person who nominated Frank, he simply commented:

> It was a kind gesture of my distinguished friend to put my name forward for your publication and I had not the heart to tell him that I felt distinctly unsuited for it. I can claim no more than to have managed to make a living as an actor for nearly fifty years and to have reached the rank of Flying Officer in the RAFVR during the war while training as a navigator. At the age of sixty-eight I am delighted to be able to carry on with my chosen career and support my wife, but the title 'distinguished' would, I fear, look like miscasting.

Not long before he died, Vivienne Noakes set about trying to right the wrong of the lack of acknowledgement. Without Frank or Beryl's knowledge, she enlisted David Shepherd and farceur Brian Rix to encourage them to put pen to paper in an attempt to have Frank recognised in the Queen's Honours List. Rix signed off his letter to the appropriate bodies by saying, 'Frank Thornton has never sought stardom and has always felt unwilling to seek public approbation... I am certain he deserves a public acknowledgement of his remarkable contribution to the theatrical profession and to the happiness of mankind.'

The current definition of the criteria for nominating somebody for an honour is for them to have made achievements in public life and/or committed themselves to serving and helping Britain. Frank Thornton achieved both. He was seen worldwide as the quintessential English gentleman within his chosen profession, and his achievements in public life went far beyond his acting career.

One cannot but feel that Frank's lugubriousness stretched to his charity work. Recognition was not in keeping with the act of charity, so he sought none. At birthdays and anniversaries, he and Beryl would urge friends to resist sending gifts, instead making sizeable donations to such things as the Royal Theatrical Fund, the Cats Protection League, Perennial (the Gardeners' Royal Benevolent Society) and David Shepherd's efforts in supporting anti-poaching operations to protect elephants in Zambia.

Alas, the efforts to bestow Frank with an honour came too late for him to be recognised, but as thrilled as he would have been with some letters after his name, he would undoubtably have considered himself not worthy of such a thing; he was a jobbing actor, in his eyes. For him, honours and public acclaim were not the priority. He had achieved his aim of earning a good living from doing something he enjoyed, making a lot of people happy along the way.

Frank's friends and family got to say goodbye to him in a memorial service on 12th July 2013, held at St Paul's in Covent Garden. Michael Noakes read the lesson, Sir Donald Sinden read from Act II, Scene V of *Twelfth Night*, while June Whitfield read from Kahlil Gibran's *The Prophet*. Gyles Brandreth gave a eulogy which included quoting 'A Word to Husbands' by Ogden Nash:

To keep your marriage brimming
With love in the loving cup
Whenever you're wrong, admit it;
Whenever you're right, shut up.

It was fitting that the farewell offered that extra nod to Beryl, for while a family lost their father and grandfather, and the public lost one of its most adored actors, the double act that had been joined at the hip for almost seventy years, Frank and Beryl, had lost its Frank.

As we have seen, in the early days of his career Frank had tried his hand with a solo spot interpretation of Artemus Ward, so it is perhaps apt that the tribute to Ward creator Charles Browne paid by his executor, T. W. Robertson, in 1868 reads as though it could have been written for Frank: '...beloved and regretted by all who knew him... and when he drew his last breath there passed away the spirit of a true gentleman.'

Epilogue
People Like You

ON SEVERAL OCCASIONS, FRANK THORNTON'S FAMILY had been approached to gain their approval and cooperation to entrap Frank for an episode of *This is Your Life*. He wouldn't have been the first of his castmates from *Are You Being Served?* to be treated to the tribute: John Inman and Mollie Sugden were both honoured in the mid-1970s when the show was at its most popular. Frank, however, was far less enamoured with the idea. He would have happily been a guest on *Desert Island Discs*, although rather surprisingly he was never given that option, but he felt *This is Your Life* offered too much opportunity for backslapping and self-congratulatory reflection. He was too modest for all of that and wasn't the least bit 'showbiz'.

Frank knew how to behave and understood the relevance of billing to the professional actor, but he maintained a modesty throughout his career. During the run of *When We Are Married* in 1970 he was lunching with his trusted agent at the time, Max Kester, at the Savage Club where they were chatting to J. B. Boothroyd of *Punch* magazine fame. Max did his appropriate selling routine, telling Boothroyd that Frank was appearing in *When We Are Married*, to which Boothroyd enquired as to whether Frank was playing Ormonroyd. 'No,' replied Frank. 'Fred Emney is playing him.'

'There,' said Boothroyd, 'speaks the first modest actor I've ever met.' Asked to explain, he expanded on his comment to say that nine out of ten actors, when asked the same question, would have replied, 'No, I'm playing so-and-so,' ensuring the focus remained on them over the production.

Not long after joining the cast of *Last of the Summer Wine*, the researchers of *This is Your Life* came calling again. It was Donald Sinden who persuaded Beryl that this time she should say yes. Frank was now in his late seventies and more than twenty years had passed since Mollie and John had been honoured with the Big Red Book. Since then, Frank had returned to being a regular face on television and was now a comforting presence in British homes on a Sunday evening. The timing seemed right and so Beryl acquiesced.

The surprise reveal for Frank was scheduled to take place not on location or in the studio but at a special event marking twenty-five years of *Last of the Summer Wine* in October 1998.

As the actors in the show became older it had become increasingly difficult to perform the interiors in front of a live audience, so they would shoot the exteriors and then hire a film studio for the interiors. The two would be edited together and then played to a live audience and members of the cast would attend. It was a routine that worked exceptionally well for the last fifteen years of the programme.

To celebrate the twenty-fifth anniversary of the show, the plan was to capitalise on the fact that in this particular series, Pinewood had been chosen to host the interior scenes and audience recordings. Filming would finish on the first Friday in October and then, before the celebration event on the Sunday, the sets would be left up for attendees to browse. To the side of Pinewood Mansion House, a marquee had been set up to accommodate four hundred people keen to enjoy the tribute to one of the BBC's best-loved comedies.

Only a handful of people knew that the occasion wasn't going to end as they might have expected. As one of that select group, Morris Bright MBE carried the responsibility of trying to organise an event with one of the hottest tickets in town while also trying to engineer the surprise for Frank without giving the game away.

The event was to include a charity auction and the unveiling of a comedy plaque in honour of *Last of the Summer Wine.* Hosting the auction was Jeffrey Archer, who had to be included in the deception as he had originally planned to leave upon conclusion of the auction. Certainly, with cameras present, it would do his running for Mayor of London no harm at all, so it was that argument that persuaded him to remain a little longer than scheduled. Those who like to think Archer looked put out that he wasn't the recipient of the book when Michael Aspel appeared will be sadly disappointed to discover that he knew full well who the recipient was.

As we have already heard, when Frank joined the cast of *Last of the Summer Wine,* he was very keen to not ruffle feathers. He discreetly slipped into the role with ease, endearing himself to all in the production, but his humility prevented him from taking much credit. This likeable approach almost broke the plans for *This is Your Life.*

All seemed to be going well until Bright was given a message at the end of the Friday's interior filming: Frank Thornton wished for him to come and see him as there was something he wanted to discuss ahead of the weekend's celebrations.

Still decked in his Truly pin-stripe suit and mackintosh, Frank met Bright at the studio. He had something on his mind. Here was a big celebration, everybody who was anybody in the television business wanted to be in attendance; but, of the twenty-five years being marked, Frank had only been in one series and a Christmas special. Bright recalled the conversation that followed: 'I'll never forget this – he said, "It's a big event Sunday, twenty-five years of the show. They'll all be there – Peter, Bill – it's their event, please don't make a fuss of me."'

Bright had no choice but to lie through his teeth in response to the magnanimous gesture from the veteran actor: 'No, of course not, I totally understand Frank. I will not make a fuss of you at all. I look forward to seeing you both, I can't wait.'

Sunday came and Frank tried his best to keep out of the limelight that he felt belonged to Peter Sallis and Bill Owen in particular. Bright was in his element. The trio of stars were seated on the same table, and Owen was reunited with Betty Box with whom he had worked in the 1950s.

The stars sat through a lengthy auction which raised a huge amount for a cancer charity, including one recently bereaved lady who paid £14,000 for a day on the set and a walk-on part in an episode. Next up, Frank, Bill and Peter arrived on the platform to receive framed pictures of the plaque they had earlier unveiled. It seemed the most efficient way to get them on stage together ahead of the surprise to come.

Beryl looked on nervously, at which point Betty Box questioned why she looked so anxious. 'Something is about to happen,' she conceded as a ripple of murmurs began to spread around the marquee.

Michael Aspel had appeared out of hiding and sidled up to the stage. Archer was in on it; Owen and Sallis had already been given the honour. Frank looked somewhat nonplussed by the situation, not believing that he could be the target. But shortly the words, 'Frank Thornton, This is Your Life,' were aimed in his direction. He looked immediately to Beryl: 'I've been betrayed,' he jokingly uttered.

They were whisked off to a waiting studio where Frank's friends and family would gather to mark his life and career. Frank had time to speak to Morris Bright before they left. 'I hear you were involved in this,' he said. Bright apologised for having broken his promise of no fuss in the most spectacular of fashions. Of course, Frank was gracious as ever, nodding at his friend and saying, 'Hmm… I shall forgive you on this occasion.'

Frank, as Sinden had predicted, genuinely loved his *This is Your Life* tribute. Friends from his stage days under Donald Wolfit were there; Michael Bentine's son Richard was there to represent his late father, the most influential comedy figure in Frank's career; Sinden was, of course, present to take the blame for the subterfuge. Cast members from *Are You Being Served?* and *Last of the Summer Wine* were present, as were non-showbiz friends like the Shepherds and Noakeses. There was even room for a cuddly Eeyore, originally made for Frank by daughter Jane to keep him company in his dressing room when appearing in *Winnie the Pooh*, and Frank couldn't help but try a side-by-side impersonation of his lugubrious alter ego. It was the perfect evening of celebration for a man to whom self-congratulation didn't come easily.

Frank's perception of success was at odds with the industry. Despite having a side to his character that became agitated by insignificant things, he was a largely vulnerable man, even shy at times.

Interviews were fairly uncommon; like Ronnie Barker, being himself in front of a camera wasn't something he particularly enjoyed. And when reflecting on his career he considered himself to have achieved his aim, namely, to be employed in the acting business for the duration of his life. But he had all of the acting talents necessary to have been a leading man and perhaps should have been.

As we have learned, he found the 'star' antics of Rex Harrison somewhat irritating but wondered where he would have got had he employed such tactics. He also undervalued his contribution to the profession. In *Last of the Summer Wine* and *Are You Being Served?* he already achieved more than most actors, many of whom would have claimed to be stars. Robert Ross acknowledged this when recalling the success of Captain Peacock: 'I always saw Peacock as similar to Kenneth Horne in *Round the Horne*. He does have funny lines, but he's like the solid totem pole that all the crazy dance around. John Inman's Mr Humphries is only so brilliantly funny because you've got that wonderful hundred-per-cent granite reaction of Frank.'

Add the vast stage career and his remarkable work with every comedian of his time and you realise the value that he brought to his industry. But self-validation simply didn't interest him. He seemed somewhat bemused when recalling his *This is Your Life* night: 'There were all my friends, ones on the programme, others sitting in the audience. So, it gives you a very comfy feeling, a very nice feeling – people like you.'

Frank's agent David Daly remembered of his client and friend, 'He was a very unselfish actor. I think that's probably why people loved working with him, because he was so generous to other people.'

When Donald Sinden appeared on Frank's *This is Your Life*, he offered a quote from writer and poet Hilaire Belloc: 'There's nothing worth the wear of winning, but laughter and the love of friends.' It was apt as Frank enjoyed his evening of 'massaging the ego', as he described it. But in the end, it was an appropriate way to describe Frank and Beryl's life, because that is what he, or perhaps they, delivered for all: laughter from a vast career, punctuated by the finest comedy British television, stage and radio had to offer, and devoted friendship that transcended the acting profession.

To paraphrase the character of Young Mr Grace, he did very well!

Appendix
List of Performances

WHAT FOLLOWS IS A COMPREHENSIVE LISTING of the perform-ances of Frank Thornton. While every effort has been made to ensure accuracy, any omission is purely accidental.

Stage appearances

French Without Tears, 1940, Brian Curtis (Yorke-Clopet Company)
The Sport of Kings, 1940, Panama Pete (Yorke-Clopet Company)
The Outsider, 1940, Mr Vincent Helmore FRCS (Yorke-Clopet Company)
White Cargo, 1940, The Skipper and Worthing (Yorke-Clopet Company)
Smilin' Through, 1940, Charles (Bedales)
Arms and the Man, 1940, Major Paul Petkoff (Witney Repertory Theatre)
The Scarlet Pimpernel, 1941, Lord Anthony Dewhurst (Dundee Repertory Theatre)
The Merry Wives of Windsor, 1941, Fenton and Bardolph (Donald Wolfit Shakespeare Company)
Smilin' Through, 1941, Willie Ainsley (Harry Hanson Company)

The Scarlet Pimpernel, 1941, Lord Anthony Dewhurst (Donald Wolfit
    Shakespeare Company)

The Family Upstairs, 1941, Charles Grant (Sheffield Repertory
    Company, Little Theatre, Southport)

The Farmer's Wife, 1941, Richard Coaker (Sheffield Repertory
    Company, Little Theatre, Southport)

Hamlet, 1941, Laertes (Donald Wolfit Shakespeare Company tour)

Richard III, 1941, Sir William Catesby (Donald Wolfit Shakespeare
    Company tour)

The Merchant of Venice, 1941, Bassanio (Donald Wolfit Shakespeare
    Company tour)

A Midsummer Night's Dream, 1942, Lysander (Donald Wolfit
    Shakespeare Company, Strand Theatre)

Volpone, 1942, Mosca (Donald Wolfit Shakespeare Company,
    St James's Theatre)

Macbeth, 1942, Old Angus (tour and Piccadilly Theatre)

Rebecca, 1942, Robert, a footman (Lyric Theatre)

Housemaster, 1942, Philip de Pourville (Richmond Theatre)

Flare Path, Understudy, 1942/3 appearing as Sergeant Dusty Miller, Fl.
    Lt. Teddy Graham, Percy and Corp. Wiggy Jones (Apollo Theatre)

Thirty-One, 1943, cast (Station Theatre)

*The Years Between/Lady from Edinburgh/Grand National Night/The
    Gleam/Fools Rush In/Is Your Honeymoon Really Necessary?/Private
    Lives/While the Sun Shines/The Two Miss Carrolls/Lovers' Leap/Love
    in a Mist*, 1947, various (South Parade Pier, Southsea)

The Dancing Years, 1947, Franzel (tour)

One Wild Oat, 1949, Fred Gilbey (understudy) (Garrick Theatre)

The Ghost Train, 1950, Herbert Price (Regent Theatre, Hayes)

The Dominant Sex, 1950, Mr Webster (Regent Theatre, Hayes)

Present Laughter, 1950, Garry Essendine (Spa Theatre, Bridlington)

Green Pack, 1950, Mark Eliot (Regent Theatre, Hayes)

*Rope/Double Door/Peace Comes to Peckham/The Happiest Days of Your
    Life/Top Secret/French Without Tears/I Have Been Here Before/
    Pickled Salts/Isle of the Umbrellas/The Paragon*, 1950, various (Spa
    Theatre, Bridlington)

*A Hundred Years Old/One Wild Oat/Murder at the Vicarage/Dr
   Angelus/The Chiltern Hundreds*, 1951, various (Spa Theatre,
   Bridlington)
The King's Rhapsody, 1951, Prime Minister (tour)
Wild Horses, 1952, PC Osborne/Louis Beile/Trumper Norton (tour)
Artemus Ward, 1953, solo routine (The Players)
The Distant Hill, 1953, Harry Forsyth (tour)
Liberty Bill, 1954, PC Carp (tour) (renamed to *The Party Spirit*)
The Party Spirit, 1954, PC Carp/Leonard Bilker MP (Piccadilly Theatre)
The Party Spirit, 1956, Leonard Bilker MP (tour)
Green Room Rag, 1956 (Adelphi)
On the Englishman Abroad, 1956, solo routine (The Players)
A Crimean Album, 1956, company (The Players)
Strange Request, 1956, Det Insp Grant (tour)
The Empty Chair, 1956, Mouche (tour)
Private Lives, 1956, Elyot Chase (tour)
Ring for Catty, 1957, John Rhoses (Windsor Theatre)
The Whole Truth, 1957, Lewis Paulton (tour)
The Hidden King, 1957, The Paduan (tour)
*The Queen and the Welshman/The Hollow/Sabrina Fair/The House by
   the Lake*, 1958, various (Queen's Theatre, Hornchurch)
Tour of Cyprus, 1958
Speaking of Murder, 1959 (tour)
The Golden Touch, 1960, Bishop Zog of Nixos (Piccadilly Theatre)
Don't Shoot, We're English, 1960, revue
Hassan, 1960, Caliph (tour)
Naked, 1960, Ludovico Nota (tour)
Robinson Crusoe, 1960, Will Atkins
Five Players in Four Plays, 1962, Hangman/Baga, the Prime Minister
   (Aldeburgh Festival)
The Shapes, 1962, Jumbo Smith
A Juan by Degrees, 1965, Don Rodriguez Campeador
Meals on Wheels, 1965, Edward (Royal Court Theatre)
The Little Hut, 1965, Sir Philip Ashlow (Grand Theatre, Leeds & tour)
Alibi for a Judge, 1966, Thomas Empton QC (Savoy)

Smithson's Ark, 1967, Les (Comedy Theatre)

Prose and Poetry, 1968 (Purcell Room of Comedy)

The Young Visiters, 1968, Procurio and Minnit (Piccadilly)

Staircase, 1969, Charlie Dyer (Richmond Theatre)

When We Are Married, 1970, Albert Parker (Yvonne Arnaud Theatre, Guildford, tour and Strand Theatre)

Winnie the Pooh, 1971, Eeyore (Phoenix Theatre)

The Andy Pandy Roundabout Black and White Variety Knockout Show, 1972 (Birmingham Repertory Theatre)

Winnie the Pooh, 1972, Eeyore (Phoenix Theatre)

I Must Become a Father, Madam, 1973, Eusebius (Devonshire Park, Eastbourne)

French Without Tears, 1974, Lt. Commander Rogers (Royal Lyceum Theatre, Edinburgh)

Twelfth Night, 1974, Sir Andrew Aguecheek (RSC, Stratford-upon-Avon)

Macbeth, 1974, Duncan (RSC, Stratford-upon-Avon)

The Doctor's Dilemma, 1975, Sir Patrick Cullen (Mermaid Theatre)

Play by Play, 1975, Actor One (King's Head, Islington)

Are You Being Served?, 1976, Captain Stephen Peacock (Winter Gardens, Blackpool)

Roger's Last Stand, 1977, Roger (Preston and Scunthorpe)

Shut Your Eyes and Think of England, 1977, Sir Justin Holbrook (Apollo Theatre)

Bedroom Farce, 1979, Ernest (Haymarket, Leicester, then Windsor)

I Wonder What Happened to Him, 1979 (London Palladium)

Jumpers, 1979, George (Leatherhead)

We're Strangers Here, 1980 (Theatre Royal)

The Chairs, 1980 (Royal Exchange, Manchester)

Habeas Corpus, 1980, Dr Arthur Wicksteed (Australian tour)

The Heiress, 1981 (Yvonne Arnaud Theatre, Guildford)

Twelfth Night, 1982, Malvolio (Watermill Theatre, Newbury)

HMS Pinafore, 1982, Sir Joseph Porter (Queen Elizabeth Hall)

Dial M for Murder, 1982, Chief Inspector Hubbard (tour)

Habeas Corpus, 1983, Dr Arthur Wicksteed (Australian tour)

Last of the Red Hot Lovers, 1983 (The Mill at Sonning)

Son et Lumière, 1984 (Hampton Court Palace)

Me and My Girl, 1984, Sir John Tremayne (Haymarket, Leicester then Adelphi Theatre, Strand)

Royal Variety Performance, 1984 (Victoria Palace)

Sting in the Tale, 1986 (Leatherhead)

The Cabinet Minister, 1987, Sir Julian Twombley (Royal Exchange, Manchester)

The Pirates of Penzance, 1987, Major General Stanley (Plymouth)

Winnie, 1988, Godfrey Lloyd Allingham (Victoria Palace)

Peter Pan, 1988, Captain Hook and Mr Darling (Connaught Theatre, Worthing)

The Tutor, 1988 (The Old Vic)

Ivanov, 1989, Count Shabyelsky (Yvonne Arnaud Theatre, Guildford)

Much Ado About Nothing, 1989, Leonato (Strand Theatre)

The Reluctant Debutante, 1989, Jimmy Broadbent(Far East Tour, then Theatre Royal, Windsor)

The Pirates of Penzance, 1990, Major General Stanley (London Palladium)

The Best of Friends, 1991, George Bernard Shaw

Spread a Little Happiness, 1991 (King's Head)

It Runs in the Family, 1993, Sir Willoughby Drake (Playhouse)

A Celebration of Wolfit, 1993 (Palace Theatre)

Discover the Lost Musicals, 1994 (Barbican Theatre)

Harvey, 1995, Dr William Chumley (Shaftesbury Theatre)

A Patriot for Me, 1995, General Von Hotzendorf (Barbican Theatre)

Cash on Delivery, 1996, DSS Inspector (Whitehall Theatre)

Hobson's Choice, 1996, Hobson (Lyric Theatre, Chichester)

Spread a Little Happiness, 1996 (Adelphi Theatre, Strand)

Jubilee, 1999 (Her Majesty's Theatre, Haymarket)

The Jermyn Street Revue, 2000 (Jermyn Street Theatre)

Carousel, 2002, Dr Sheldon and the Starkeeper (International Festival of Music Theatre, Cardiff)

Television roles

The Centre Show, 1950, Compère (BBC)
The Secret Sharer, 1950, Sailor (BBC)
Juvenile Court, 1951, Solicitor (BBC)
The Passing Show, 1951 (BBC)
The Empty Street, 1951, First Ambulance Man (BBC)
My Dear Petitioner, 1952, Miguel Esteban d'Alvarez (BBC)
Children's Television: John Hewer, 1953, Bad-Tempered Customer (BBC)
Bits and Pieces, 1953, Major Blower (voice) (BBC)
Nine Days Wonders, 1955, Gentleman & Secretary (BBC)
The Granville Melodramas: The Silver King, 1955, Geoffrey Ware
    (Associated Rediffusion)
The Calculating Boy, 1955, Gentleman (BBC)
The Human Radar, 1955, Secretary (BBC)
Big City, 1956, Hotel Manager (Associated Rediffusion)
I Killed The Count, 1956, Martin (Granada)
Assignment Foreign Legion, 1956, Foreign Legion Doctor (Bartley
    Productions/Intel films)
Henry Hall's Guest Night, 1956, Men's Fashion Sketch (BBC)
Children's Television: Monday Magazine, 1957 (BBC)
Children's Television: Charlie Quick, 1957 (BBC)
Call Back Yesterday, 1957, Sleazy Pianist (British Lion Film Corp)
Murder Bag, 1957, Det Insp (Associated Rediffusion)
Dixon of Dock Green, 1957, PC Cox (BBC)
Children's Television: Charlie Quick, 1957, Sergeant (BBC)
Closed Circuit, 1958, DIY Expert (BBC)
The Adventures of William Tell, 1958, Heinburgher/Tax Collector/
    Assistant (ITC)
You Are There: The Trial of Captain Dreyfus, 1958, Maitre Demange (BBC)
You Are There: The Fall of Robespierre, 1958, Collot (BBC)
You Are There: The Conspiracy against Gustavas III of Sweden, 1958,
    Captain Anckarstrom (BBC)
The Four Just Men, 1959, various (ITC)
The Verdict is Yours, 1959, unknown (Granada)

Men from Room 13, 1959, Warder (BBC)

Billy Bunter, 1960, Hubert Tankerton/Lerouge (BBC)

It's A Square World, 1960-1963, company (BBC)

The Friday Show, 1960 (BBC)

Life of Bliss, 1961, Policeman/Theodore Marling (BBC)

Hancock, 1961, Donor (BBC)

The Avengers, 1961, Sir William Bonner (ABC)

Armchair Theatre: His Polyvinyl Girl, 1961, Mr Leslie (ABC)

The Man in the Bed, 1961, Hobkins (BBC – unaired)

Our House, 1961, Insurance Man (ABC)

The Rag Trade, 1961, Mr Davis (BBC)

Show Train, 1961 (BBC)

Citizen James, 1961, Ministry Agent (BBC)

Comedy Playhouse: Clicquot et Fils, 1961, unknown (BBC)

Comedy Playhouse: The Channel Swimmer, 1962, Official (BBC)

Steptoe and Son, 1962, The Seller (BBC)

Suspense, 1962, Det Insp Gwilliam (BBC)

The Odd Man, 1962, Senior Undersecretary (Granada)

Hugh and I, 1962, company (BBC)

Armchair Theatre: Always Something Hot, 1962, Frank (ABC)

The Bulldog Breed, 1962, Head Waiter (Granada)

The Benny Hill Show, 1962, Frindyke and Great Korsikoff (BBC)

Time and the Conways, 1962, Gerald Thornton (Granada)

Steptoe and Son, 1963, Barman (BBC)

Comedy Playhouse: Our Man in Moscow, 1963, First Secretary
    Mortimer (BBC)

This is Your Life (Michael Bentine), 1963, guest (BBC)

The Benny Hill Show, 1963, Mr Kenwood (BBC)

The Sentimental Agent, 1963, Tailor (ATV)

For King and Country: Tunnel Trench, 1963, Brigadier Gen Lloyd
    (Granada)

Vicky and the Sultan, 1963, Richard Acton Hicks (Anglia)

Christmas Night with the Stars, 1963 (BBC)

Foreign Affairs, 1964, Foreign Office official (Granada)

A Touch of the Norman Vaughans, 1964 (Granada)

The Dickie Henderson Show, 1964 (Rediffusion)

Steptoe and Son, 1964, Butler (BBC)

Good Luck Sir, You've Got a Lucky Face, 1964, Jessop (BBC)

The Villains, 1964, Fowler (Granada)

HMS Paradise, 1964, Commander Fairweather (Rediffusion)

The Frankie Howerd Show, 1964 (BBC)

Hugh and I, 1965 (BBC)

Emergency Ward 10, 1965, John Ross (ATV)

The Man in Room 17, 1965, Chief Inspector Bascombe (Granada)

Six Shades of Black, 1965, Mr Inchcape-Lewis (Granada)

A World of Comedy, 1965, Catesby (Rediffusion)

Call It What You Like, 1965 (BBC)

Here's Harry, 1965, Richard Mullery/Doctor (BBC)

Steptoe and Son, 1965, The Frenchman (BBC)

Three Rousing Tinkles, 1966, Albert (BBC)

The Liars, 1966, Aldogrando (Granada)

Coronation Street, 1966, Hospital Patient (Granada)

Rikki, 1966, Benchley (STV)

Armchair Theatre: Daughter of the House, 1966, Station Sergeant (ABC)

Danny the Dragon, 1967, Sergeant Bull (Children's Film Foundation)

The Harry Worth Programme, 1967 (BBC)

The Champions, 1968, Clerk (Filmakers Ltd)

Architruc, 1967, Baga, the Prime Minister

City '68, 1968, Douglas Quinn (Granada)

The World of Beachcomber, 1968 (BBC)

If There Weren't Any Blacks You'd Have to Invent Them, 1968, The Undertaker (LWT)

Inside George Webley, 1968, Maitre d' (Yorkshire)

B and B: Baby Talk, 1968, Benjamin Burton (BBC)

Life With Cooper, 1969 (Thames)

Thicker Than Water, 1969, Ted Rumbold (BBC)

The Incredible Adventures of Professor Branestawm, 1969, King Kong (Thames)

September Song, 1969 (LWT)

Frost on Saturday, 1969 (LWT)

From a Bird's Eye View, 1970, Spink (ATV)

Not in Front of the Children, 1970, Mr Wilkinson (BBC)

Mr Digby Darling, 1970, Mr Skidmore (Yorkshire)

Here Come the Double Deckers, 1970, Mr Parsons (Century Film Productions)

UFO, 1970, Insurance Man (Century 21 Pictures)

The Morecambe and Wise Show, 1970, Waiter (BBC)

Comedy Playhouse: Who's Your Friend?, 1970, Mr Walters (BBC)

Two D's and a Dog, 1970, Hawkins (Thames)

As Good Cooks Go, 1970, Pangbourne (BBC)

A Cuckoo in the Nest, 1970, Claude Hickett MP (BBC)

Plunder, 1970, Simon Veal (BBC)

The Troubleshooters, 1970, TV Interviewer (BBC)

She Follows Me About, 1970, Meevors (BBC)

Afternoon Theatre: Fawcett! Fawcett!,1970, Corner (BBC)

The Other Reg Varney, 1970 (LWT)

Scott On... 1970 (BBC)

Some Matters of Little Consequence, 1971 (BBC)

The Val Doonican Show, 1971 (ATV)

And Mother Makes Three, 1971, Shop Assistant (Thames)

Misleading Cases, 1971, Mr Ladle (BBC)

Bachelor Father, 1971, Vicar (BBC)

The Goodies, 1971, Restaurateur (BBC)

A Variety of Reg Varney, 1971 (LWT)

Sykes, 1972, Dr Taplow (BBC)

The Double Deckers, 1972, TV Producer (BBC)

Saturday Variety, 1972 (ATV)

Are You Being Served?, 1972-1985, Captain Stephen Peacock (BBC)

By Jeorge, Mr Gorridge, 1972 (Thames)

Love Thy Neighbour, 1972, Barman (Thames)

The Reg Varney Comedy Hour, 1972 (LWT)

It's Lulu, Not to Mention, Dudley Moore, 1972 (BBC)

Michael Bentine Time, 1972 (BBC)

The Reg Varney Revue, 1972 (LWT)

Comedy Playhouse: The Birthday, 1973 (BBC)

The Gordon Peters Show, 1973 (BBC)

The Tommy Cooper Hour, 1973 (Thames)

Thirty Minutes Worth, 1973 (Thames)

Armchair Theatre: That Sinking Feeling, 1973, Arthur (Thames)

The Village Concert, 1973 (Thames)

Steptoe and Son, 1973, Travel Agent (BBC)

Crown Court, 1974, Prof. McIver (Granada)

Holiday with Strings, 1974, Travel Agent (BBC)

Fall of Eagles, 1974, Prince Albert (BBC)

The Tommy Cooper Show, 1974 (Thames)

Sez Les, 1974, Travel Agent/Waiter (Yorkshire)

This is Your Life (Mollie Sugden), 1975 (Thames)

Eleventh Hour: The Boundary, 1975, Bunyans (BBC)

Whodunnit, 1975, John Harvey (Thames)

Shades of Greene, 1975, Rev Simon Milan (Thames)

The Molly Wopsy, 1976, Chief Constable (Thames)

Husband of the Year, 1976 (Yorkshire)

The New Avengers, 1976, Roland (ITV)

Ken Dodd's World of Laughter, 1976 (BBC)

Seaside Special, 1976 (BBC)

The Dick Emery Show, 1976 (BBC)

Your Move, 1977, Travel Agent (BBC)

Bruce Forsyth's Generation Game, 1976 (BBC)

Jackanory Playhouse: Princess Griselda's Birthday Gift, 1977, King
    Balthazar (BBC)

The Goodies, 1977, Punk Toast Master (BBC)

This is Your Life (Arthur English), 1978 (Thames)

Authorship, 1978 (Thames)

Larry Grayson's Generation Game, 1978 (BBC)

Kelly Monteith, 1979, Bank Manager (BBC)

Word for Word, 1979, Jogran (BBC)

Money-Go-Round, 1979 (Thames)

The Taming of the Shrew, 1980, Gremio (BBC)

The Dick Emery Show, 1980 (Thames)

3-2-1, 1981 (Yorkshire)

The Gentle Touch, 1981, Leo (LWT)

The Kenny Everett Television Show, 1983 (Thames)

The Sooty Show, 1983 (Thames)

Let's Parlez Franglais, 1984 (North West Television)

Jane in the Desert, 1984, Commander L (BBC)

Jackanory Playhouse: The Knighties, 1984, Sir Torrence (BBC)

Blankety Blank, 1984 (BBC)

The Kenny Everett Show, 1985 (BBC)

This is Your Life (Sheila Mercier), 1985 (Thames)

The Sooty Show, 1985, Dr Hugh/Mr Wolfe (Thames)

T-Bag Strikes Again, 1986 (Thames)

Jimmy Cricket Show, 1987 (Central)

T-Bag Bounces Back, 1987, Count Boris (Thames)

Great Expectations, 1988, Mr Trabb (Primetime Television)

Five to Eleven, 1988 (Forge Productions)

The Return of the Musketeers, 1988, The High Baliff/The Cavalier
    (Burrill Productions)

Mr Majeika, 1989, Headmaster (TVS)

T-Bag and the Revenge of the T-Set, 1989, Bill Wagadagger (Thames)

The Krankies, 1990 (BBC)

Wogan, 1990 (BBC)

Grace and Favour (*Are you Being Served Again?* in US), 1990, Captain
    Stephen Peacock (BBC)

Children's Royal Variety Performance, 1991 (BBC)

Haunts of the Olde Country, 1992, Tour Guide (Davis and Zimmerman)

Noel's House Party, 1992 (BBC)

The Main Event, 1993 (Grundy TV)

The Paul McKenna Show, 1994 (Celador Productions)

The Old Curiosity Shop, 1994, Mr Witherden (Curiosity Productions)

Who Framed Charles Dickens?, 1994, Ghost of Charles Dickens (BBC)

This is Your Life (Gretchen Franklin), 1995 (BBC)

This is Your Life (June Whitfield), 1995 (BBC)

Telly Addicts, 1995 (BBC)

The Upper Hand, 1995, Reverend Hale (Central)

All Rise for Julian Clary, 1996, Geoffrey Parker-Knoll (BBC)

Call My Bluff, 1997 (BBC)

Tellystack, 1997 (Zenith Productions)

This is Your Life (Trevor Bannister), 1997 (Thames)

Last of the Summer Wine, 1997-2010, Herbert 'Truly' Truelove (BBC)

Heroes of Comedy: Tony Hancock, 1998 (Thames)

Celebrity Ready Steady Cook, 1998 (BBC)

In the Presence of Julian Clary, 1998 (LWT)

Lily Savage's Blankety Blank, 2000 (Pearson Television)

This is Your Life (Julian Clary), 2001 (BBC)

Casualty, 2001, Edward Gutheridge (BBC)

This is Your Life (Bill Oddie) 2002 (BBC)

Holby City, 2004, Douglas Archer (BBC)

Children in Need, 2007, Restaurant Manager (BBC)

Masterchef, 2012 (Judge) (BBC)

Radio appearances

London Calling Europe, 1942

Double Bedlam, 1946

Hello Children (Children's Hour), 1949

The Great Fire of London, 1949

By and Large, 1956

English by Radio, 1958

Home at Seven, 1958

The Wind in the Willows, 1958

We're in Business, 1959

Midweek, 1962

Benny Hill Time, 1963

Round the Horne, 1965

The Embassy Lark, 1965

The Navy Lark, 1966

Scientifically Speaking, 1966

Dinner With the Family, 1968, Butler (BBC)

The Big Business Lark, 1969

Brothers in Law, 1970

Dad's Army, 1973
No Name, 1973
Alice's Adventures in Wonderland, 1973
The Affairs of Uncle Albert, 1974
Theatre Call, 1975
Albert and Me, 1976
Open House, 1977
Ernest Fontwell versus The Experts, 1977
Share and Share Alike, 1978
My Sainted Aunt, 1978
Oh Mother, 1980
Know Your Place, 1980
Sounds Natural, 1980
Dusk, 1980
Men of Property, 1981
Morning Star, 1981
The Late Show: Round Midnight, 1982
The John Dunn Show, 1982
Christmas Pantomime: Dick Whittington and His Cat, 1982
A Pillar of the Society, 1983
The Sleeping Beauty, 1983
Nature Quiz, 1984
Give Us a Conch, 1985
The Afternoon Play: A Pillar of Society, 1985
Hoax, 1986
Mind Your Own Business, 1991
Hoax, 1991
Level 3, 1993
Bodyguard of Lies, 1994
Loose Ends, 1994
The Comedy Quiz, 1997
Monsieur Gavioli's Wonderful Contraption, 1998
After the Funeral, 1999
Cole Porter: Jubilee, 1999
Take it From There – June Whitfield at 80, 2005

Film appearances

Neutral Port, 1940, Esperanto Soldier (cut)

Radio Cab Murder, 1954, Inspector Finch

Scotland Yard: The Silent Witness, 1954, George the Barman (uncredited)

Stock Car, 1955, Doctor

Portrait of Alison, 1955, Jack

Johnny, You're Wanted, 1955, Det Insp Wilson

Cloak Without Dagger, 1956, Mr Markley

My Wife's Family, 1957, uncredited

Battle of the V-1, 1958, Scientist

Danger Man, 1959, Police Captain

Tarnished Heroes, 1960, Trench Officer

The Cheaters, 1960, Long

The Tell-Tale Heart, 1960, Barman

Operation Stogie, 1960, uncredited

Victim, 1961, George

The Impersonator, 1961, Police Sergeant

Hair of the Dog, 1961, uncredited

The Dock Brief, 1962, Photographer

It's Trad, Dad, 1962, TV Producer

The Comedy Man, 1962, Producer

Doomsday at Eleven, 1962, BBC Announcer

A Hard Day's Night, 1964, Chauffeur (deleted scene)

The Wild Affair, 1965, Manager

The Big Job, 1965, Bank Manager

The Murder Game, 1965, Radio Announcer

The Early Bird, 1965, Drunken Doctor

Gonks Go Beat, 1965, Mr A & R

A Funny Thing Happened on the Way to the Forum, 1965, Brutal
    Slave Driver

Carry On Screaming, 1966, Mr Jones

Ride of the Valkyrie, 1966, Car Chauffeur

Lucy in London, 1966, Passport Officer

30 is a Dangerous Age, Cynthia, 1968, Registrar

A Flea in Her Ear, 1968, Charles the Butler
The Bliss of Mrs Blossom, 1968, Factory Manager/The Scientist
Monsieur Lecoq, 1967/8 (unreleased), CID Inspector Hawkins
Till Death Us Do Part, 1968, Council Officer
The Bed Sitting Room, 1969, The BBC
The Assassination Bureau, 1969, Count von Kissen
Crooks and Coronets, 1969, Cyril
The Magic Christian, 1969, Police Inspector
Some Will, Some Won't, 1969, Purvis
The Rise and Rise of Michael Rimmer, 1970, Tom Stoddart
The Private Life of Sherlock Holmes, 1970, Porter
All the Way Up, 1970, Mr Driver
Up the Chastity Belt, 1971, The 2nd Major Domo
Siddhartha, 1972 (uncredited voiceover)
Our Miss Fred, 1972, British Colonel
That's Your Funeral, 1972, Town Clerk
Digby, The Biggest Dog in the World, 1972, Estate Agent
Bless This House, 1972, Fizzo Drinks Manager
Steptoe and Son Ride Again, 1973, Insurance Agent
No Sex, Please…We're British, 1973, Glass Shop Manager
Vampirella, 1973, Mr King
Keep it Up, Jack, 1974, Mr Clarke
The Bawdy Adventures of Tom Jones, 1976, Whitlow
Tomb of Ligeia, 1975, Peperel
Side by Side, 1975, Inspector Crumb
Spanish Fly, 1975, Dr Johnson
Are You Being Served?, 1977, Captain Stephen Peacock
The BFG, 1989, Mr Tibbs (voice)
Out of the Black, 2001, Philip Hart
Gosford Park, 2001, Mr Burkett
Back in Business, 2007, Gardener
Run For Your Wife, 2012, Man on Bus

Commercials and voiceovers

Lifebuoy; Vim; Bird's Eye Peas; Devil's Bait; Marabou; Cross & Blackwell Soup; Ridgeways Tea; Kiwi; Sporting Life; Trumans Beer; Ryvita; Callard and Bowser's Juicy Jellies; Oat Krunchies; The People; MacDonald's Crispbread; Gillette; Mars; Spillers; The Tea Set; McVities; Walls Ice Cream; Silexine Stone Paint; Huntley and Palmers; Proctor & Gamble; Harvey's Bristol Cream; Blue Riband; Camay; Harp Lager; Crawfords Shortbread; Cadbury's Milk Tray; Chivers Jelly; Trebor Mints; Gallaher Cigars; Benson & Hedges; Ambassador Cigarettes; Triumph 1500 (unreleased); Kodak; British Rail; Road Safety; Horror Bags/Fangs; Egg Marketing Board; Slumberland Beds; Ontario Pork Producers Marketing Board; Castella; Post Office; Asda; Jif Lemon Juice; Whitmont Shirts; Liquid Gold; British Airways; National Coal Board; Son et Lumiere (as Horatio Nelson for use on HMS *Victory*); Scottish Gas Board; Mind Your Heart (BBC Further Education on obesity); Another Funny Thing About Pain (medical supplies promotional film with Geoffrey Palmer); Cadbury's Double Decker; Standard Life Assurance; Schweppes; Lemtea; British Wool Marketing Board; Vauxhall; Cooper's Furniture; Haze; Lymeswold Cheese; Currys; Kentucky Fried Chicken; Today; Debenhams; Mr Sheen

Bibliography

Bell, A. J. W., *Last of the Summer Wine: From the Director's Chair* (Tomahawk Press, 2012)

Bentine, M., *The Reluctant Jester* (Bantam Press, 1992)

Bright, M. and Ross, R., *Last of the Summer Wine: The Finest Vintage* (BBC Books, 2000)

Croall, J., *Gielgud: a Theatrical Life* (Methuen Publishing, 2000)

Croft, D., *You Have Been Watching: the Autobiography of David Croft* (BBC Books, 2004)

Dunn, C., *Permission to Speak: An Autobiography* (Century, 1986)

English, A., *Through the Mill and Beyond* (Mildmay, 1986)

Harwood, R., *Sir Donald Wolfit: His Life and Work in the Unfashionable Theatre* (Secker and Warburg, 1971)

Lindsay, R., *Letting Go* (Thorogood Publishing, 2009)

Lloyd, J., *Listen Very Carefully, I Shall Say This Only Once: An Autobiography* (Ebury Publishing, 1993)

Marx, G., *Groucho and Me* (Victor Gollancz, 1959)

Reader, R., *Ralph Reader Remembers* (Bailey Brothers, 1974)

Sallis, P., *Fading into the Limelight*, (Orion Publishing, 2006)

Webber, R., *50 Years of Hancock's Half Hour* (Century, 2004)

Webber, R., *I'm Free!: The Complete Guide to Are You Being Served?*
      (Orion Publishing, 1999)
Wright, A., *A Tanner's Worth of Tune: Rediscovering the Post-War
      British Musical* (Boydell Press, 2010)